The
UNIVERSITY of GLASGOW
LIBRARY

Friendly Shelves

The
UNIVERSITY of GLASGOW
LIBRARY

Friendly Shelves

THE FRIENDS OF GLASGOW UNIVERSITY LIBRARY

in association with the University Library

Published by The Friends of Glasgow University Library in association with the University Library.

Celebrating the history and progress of the Library and marking the 40th Anniversary of the Friends of Glasgow University Library, a charitable society formed to help develop, support and promote it.

Membership of the society is open to all, as are its events.

www.gla.ac.uk/fgul   www.friendsofgul.org

ISBN 9780993518508 (hardback)
ISBN 9780993518515 (softback)
ISBN 9780993518522 (e-book)

First published in 2016.
Designed and typeset by Shirley Lochhead.
Printed in Glasgow by Bell & Bain Ltd.
All publication rights reserved.

Editorial Team

Dr Peter V. Davies
General Editor
Hon Secretary, The Friends of Glasgow University Library

Susan Ashworth
University Librarian

Helen Durndell
Emeritus University Librarian

Peter Hoare
Consultant Editor

Lesley Richmond
Deputy Director Library and University Archivist

Graeme Smith
Chairman, The Friends of Glasgow University Library

View of Glasgow Green and a Passing Storm, oil by John Knox, around 1820, also showing the University Tower in the High Street to the immediate right of Nelson's obelisk. Courtesy of the National Trust for Scotland.

Contents

Foreword from Chancellor Sir Kenneth Calman   6

Foreword from Principal and Vice-Chancellor Anton Muscatelli   7

Introduction 8

1   Renaissance and Reformation *From Foundation to 1700*   14

2   Enlightenment Emerges *The 18th century*   46

3   Industrial Expansion and Migration *The 19th century*   72

4   War, Peace and Opportunities *The 20th century*   98

5   New Horizons *The 21st century*   138

6   Illustrated Books in the Library Holdings *More than just words can say ...*   148

7   Unique and Distinctive Collections   168

8   The Friends of Glasgow University Library   262

Afterword   268

List of Librarians across the centuries   270

Contributors and Acknowledgements   272

Bibliography   274

Index   280

Frontispiece illustration: The University of Glasgow from Kelvingrove, water-colour by Robert Eadie, RSW, from *The Face of Glasgow*, 1938. Courtesy of the Eadie family.

Foreword

Chancellor
Sir Kenneth Calman

For hundreds of years the process of writing, in whatever language or style, has provided a method of communicating ideas and thoughts. These writings, collected into books, preserved these thoughts for future generations to consider, and allowed them to be reviewed and revised. Some books used the imagination of the author to tell stories and showed ways in which we can see the world at a different time and place. As the numbers of books and writings increased, the collections formed provided a place for examining areas of knowledge. The books and libraries became the focus for learning and research, and for innovation.

These great collections summarise human history and point to the future.

Books have changed over the years, from parchment scrolls, to bound leaves as books and into the present digital storage solutions. Glasgow University Library has them all while maintaining the same functions as a resource for learning and research. These books also allow us to acknowledge the basis of our society, culture and the arts, together with developments in science and technology. Such an investment becomes even more important as we look to the future.

All collections and libraries need staff, curators, and specialists to maintain the quality of the material and to interact with library users. The library shelves are not just inanimate constructions, but become living with the material and the interaction between staff and the readers. They are 'friendly shelves' able to provide help and ensure that the reader has access not just to the range of books, but the specialist knowledge and experience of the curatorial staff at the service of those who need help. On a personal note, as my own interests have changed from science to medicine, to the arts and to literature, the Library and its staff have responded to my needs in so many ways.

Libraries also need friends to support the staff and to encourage and enhance the library in many different ways, and we are fortunate that the University and the Library have such a group. On behalf of the University and readers, I should like to thank them, for their help and the production of this magnificent volume.

Foreword

Principal and Vice-Chancellor
Anton Muscatelli

This is a fascinating book not least because it reminds us of the centrality of the Library to the life and learning of the University. In a very real sense when books were the only media to store and acquire knowledge, the Library was the information hub of the University. Now knowledge is available to us 24/7 and in many respects it doesn't have to be physically housed anywhere – many of our books are digital, our access to them via the web and the cloud. This may be true. But as with any great institution – and Glasgow University Library is certainly that – the Library has never stood still but has sought to both shape and respond to the environment it finds itself in. And so it has embraced every medium for the transfer of knowledge and has been alert to the changing patterns of learning. Where reading in solitary silence might have been the standard approach in times past, now the Library sees itself at the centre of a vibrant learning community, embracing the multiple approaches we have to learning which can be solitary and social, individual and communal, silent and interactive.

But critically if, as recently, the Library has been re-clad and it changes its outer skin, or transforms its spaces within, its heart and soul remain the same! It has remained true to its core mission to hold, share, make accessible and collaborate in facilitating the availability of information to support research, scholarship, teaching and learning. The Library remains the keeper, custodian, and promoter of humankind's great intellectual heritage, working to bring that heritage closer to succeeding generations of scholars and students. It's clear today, and as this book underlines, that in spite of all the doomsday scenarios over the future of libraries, the University Library is a success story, an immensely popular place for all who are drawn to the spaces it provides to learn, to meet, to be part of a community of learning at the heart of our campus.

The Library's success would not be possible without the commitment of its staff, and the support of the many friends of the Library. *Friendly Shelves* is a welcome testament to their enduring commitment, and a fitting tribute to a great Library, at the centre of a great University.

Introduction

Top: The University seen from the Boyd Orr building on University Avenue with the Library on the horizon (left) and the Gilbert Scott Building with its tower (right). Photographic Unit.
Bottom: An interior view of the Library. Photographic Unit.

This illustrated overview of the University of Glasgow Library involves the collaboration of past and present librarians, archivists, academics, interested members of the general public and one postgraduate student, all of us united in our commitment to a key University institution that serves not only the local campus but also Greater Glasgow and the worldwide community of learning. Charting the evolution of the Library from its late medieval origins to the present day, our volume also outlines its extensive and often unique holdings and indicates possible future developments, thereby updating its invaluable predecessor, William P. Dickson's 1888 study, *The Glasgow University Library: Notes on Its History, Arrangements, and Aims*. We conclude with a short account of our motley association of local bibliophiles, the Friends of Glasgow University Library (FGUL), whose fortieth anniversary our publication celebrates.

For readers as yet unfamiliar with the cultural and social history of Glasgow or the numerous publications on the City's first university, some contextual background may be helpful.

Origins

As Britain's fourth oldest university founded by papal bull in west central Scotland (doubtless to complement its eastern counterpart created forty years earlier in St Andrews), Glasgow University by its origins in 1451 invites a broad European perspective. Unlike the wealthy and established colleges of Oxbridge, until 1574 when developments began leading to its re-foundation or *Nova Erectio* three years later, Glasgow was a single-college institution teaching Arts, Law and some Divinity. It operated as part of a European network of universities until the Reformation crisis of 1560 led to near-total collapse. It was, however, saved through the efforts of its French-educated Protestant Principal Andrew Melville (1545-1622), whose revitalisation of the curriculum along humanist lines attracted European interest and boosted student numbers.

Glasgow had already drawn a leading European independently-minded intellectual, the prolific Scottish philosopher, Ockhamist logician, political theorist and historian John Mair, aka Major (1467-1550), to serve as Principal from 1518 to 1523. Written and published during his Glasgow years, his famous *History of Greater Britain, England and Scotland (Historia majoris Britanniae, tam Angliae quam Scotiae*, Paris, 1521) sought to sift fact from myth insofar as his limited documentation allowed, supplying details overlooked by previous historiographers.

Diversity, Trade and Class

During the seventeenth century the College expanded greatly so as to feature the largest university buildings in Scotland, reflecting the continuing growth of the mercantile city and the creative tolerance which imbued its urban development and civic administration. Political corruption and royal bickering notwithstanding, in the ostensibly ordered neo-Palladian world of Hanoverian Britain, the liberalism and tolerance of the Scottish Enlightenment so admired by Voltaire contributed to increased social mobility, free thinking, satire and (sometimes disastrous) financial speculation, which drove colonial expansion.

This economic development was important for Glasgow, which was ideally placed on the west coast for trade with Caribbean sugar plantations and the American tobacco colonies, based on slave labour. The two Glasgow refineries founded by 1669 began distilling rum two decades later, while the first cargo of tobacco arrived in 1674 to be followed soon by cotton, and a dynamic Glasgow business community developed to seize the golden trading opportunity. Already sizeable by the later 1690s, its growth accelerated after the 1707 Treaty of Union, ensuring that by the 1730s the city would have Scotland's first millionaires and after 1772 would be dubbed 'Emporium of the World' following the dredging of the Clyde that enabled large ships to dock in the city centre.

Yet transatlantic trade and the Industrial Revolution with its international dimensions accentuated social and ethnic divisions, evident in Annan's photographs of Glasgow's inner-city slums in the late 1860s that eloquently qualify Victorian Glasgow's proud claim to be the 'second city of the British Empire'. The resulting class consciousness still characterises Britain today.

Philanthropy and Libraries

Fortunately for their fellow-citizens, despite the loss of the American colonies after 1783, from the mid-eighteenth century onwards diversification enabled a number of affluent Glaswegians (tobacco lords, cotton and sugar importers and other industrialists), eventually joined by the emigrant Scottish American billionaire industrialist Andrew Carnegie, to use their wealth to set up libraries for adult education, although for many years most users were required to pay a subscription which restricted membership. Like alumni today, Glasgow students likewise paid for Library privileges.

In 1753 pioneering bookseller John Smith Snr established the first Glasgow circulating library, based in the Trongate. At its peak it stocked 7,000 volumes, and charged ten shillings [10/-] a year for membership or smaller sums for shorter periods down to one penny per night. A rival bookseller in the High Street, Archibald Coubrough, started his own circulating library in 1778 with 4,500 volumes. Smith's library was replaced in 1827 by his namesake grandson's well-stocked reading room strategically sited near the City Post Office. Other local subscription or specialist libraries included: Glasgow Public Library, from 1804; the Royal Faculty of Procurators in Glasgow Library, from 1817; the Council Chambers library established in 1844 by Provost William Hector; the library of the Glasgow Athenaeum (founded 1847), now part of the Whittaker Library of the RSAMD-Royal Conservatoire of Scotland; the library and museum of the Andersonian University (founded as the Andersonian Institute in 1796), and the predecessor of today's University of Strathclyde Library, open to the public for a guinea entrance fee (£1.05) and a half-guinea annual subscription; the library of the Institution of Engineers and Shipbuilders, founded in 1857 by Glasgow University's eminent Regius Professor of Civil Engineering and Mechanics, William J. M. Rankine (1820-1872); and the Campbell Library and reading room, founded in 1882 on Main Street (now Shawbridge Street), Pollokshaws, thanks to local businessman Robert Campbell.

Nevertheless, in 1791 the first free public library in Scotland, the Stirling Library (now part of the Mitchell Library), was founded in Glasgow following textile printer Walter Stirling's bequest of £1,000, his house in Miller Street and his collection of books for local public benefit as stated in his will. In 1823 a group of Dawsholm papermakers established another free public library in Maryhill, financed by charges for lectures and by donations from local gentry.

Though the ground-breaking Public Libraries Act in 1850 (England) and 1853 (Scotland) gave local burghs the power to establish free public libraries funded by a locally imposed tax of one penny in the pound, take-up was often slow (as in Glasgow) because it required at least two-thirds of local ratepayers to vote in favour before the burgh could finance the initiative. Manchester led the way in 1852 as its Mayor, Sir John Potter, supported by the local Chetham Society, campaigned so energetically to establish Manchester Free Library at Campfield that only forty of 4,002 eligible voters opposed the proposal. In 1860 the free William Brown Library and Museum (now Liverpool Central Library and World Museum) was completed, the Museum section predating the Library by three years. Whereupon, stoutly defending his city libraries' extensive holdings, the piqued Glaswegian columnist 'Senex' tacitly conceded that few books in Glasgow were freely available to the public, including those of the University.

In 1863 the Paisley-born lawyer George Baillie (1784-1873) invested venture capital for twenty-one years hoping to found an educational establishment (Baillie's Institution) with its own free public library. By 1884, however, the

Tolbooth and Tron Steeple, water-colour by Robert Eadie, RSW, from *The Face of Glasgow*, 1938. Courtesy of the Eadie family.

accrued sum was merely sufficient to support the library, which opened to the public in 1887. Until financial pressures forced its closure in 1981 Baillie's Library compiled an impressive array of material, mostly of Scottish – especially Glaswegian – interest, thanks to bequests and local societies' donated collections. The large Mitchell Library (founded while Baillie's capital was accruing) now holds its stock and continues to draw on the generous support of the Trustees and Governors of Baillie's Institution.

The Mitchell opened in 1877, housed on two floors of a warehouse at the corner of Ingram Street and Albion Street and funded by almost £70,000 left in 1874 by another benefactor, tobacco manufacturer Stephen

The Transylvania in Dry Dock, water-colour by Robert Eadie, RSW, from *The Face of Glasgow*, 1938. Courtesy of the Eadie family.

Mitchell (1789-1874). Despite setbacks such as the crash of the City of Glasgow Bank in 1878, the initial stock of 14,000 volumes, acquired through small donations and the purchase of three large collections, quadrupled in just seven years, prompting the library's inclusion in a major – though not comprehensive – survey in 1885 of Glasgow libraries by the librarian Thomas Mason. In 1891 it moved from its first

home to Miller Street, but soon these premises also proved inadequate and potentially unsafe following a fire in a neighbouring warehouse. This awkward situation remained unresolved until the final move to its present site in North Street in October 1911.

Although the Glasgow Libraries Committee included strong supporters of free libraries (e.g. yarn merchant Councillor William Smith, 1817-1893, who proposed a special Libraries Act for the city using Corporation funding), in 1890 Andrew C. Bradley, Glasgow's Regius Professor of English Language and Literature, roundly condemned the Council's delay in agreeing to form a Free Library funded by local ratepayers. Eventually, after further foot-dragging, the Glasgow Corporation (Tramways, Libraries, etc.) Act, 1899, provided a public library service supported from the rates.

Glasgow City of Culture

Library provision in Glasgow now went from strength to strength, with sixteen new public district libraries opening by 1916 thanks largely to Andrew Carnegie's generosity. Despite a slowdown in the Depression of the inter-war years, the number of public libraries in the city reached thirty-seven by 1965 as new housing areas opened up within the greatly expanded boundaries of the city. Today there are thirty-three public libraries despite the near halving of the city population. Following the nationwide expansion of higher education advocated by the 1963 Robbins Report, new central academic libraries attached to such institutions as Glasgow Caledonian University and the City of Glasgow College in its campuses of Riverside and Cathedral Street have joined the more established Glasgow School of Art Library, currently under reconstruction after a traumatic fire.

The year 1968, when the University's new library opened, marked a watershed in the post-war reconstruction of the city and the start of the motorway system. Greater Glasgow has moved from traditional heavy industry to a new information technology economy owing to changes in national prioritisation. The city's reinvention since the 1970s has been reflected in a huge stone-cleaning programme, the broadening of library services including the Mitchell's diversifications from 1980, numerous festivals and other high-profile, award-winning cultural developments, most significantly the opening in 1983 of the Burrell Collection, gathered by ship-owner Sir William Burrell. Many of these still attract international visitors, and Glasgow City libraries and the University of Glasgow Library play supporting roles in, for example, the 'Aye Write!' creative writing festival and Glasgow Film Festival, both launched in 2005.

But all great things start from small beginnings. So too the Library of the University of Glasgow, which first moved from a library room (*libraria*) in the Cathedral to premises in the High Street nearer to Glasgow Cross and eventually to Gilmorehill, has helped lead new developments in education, philosophy, science, medicine, and many more areas of human curiosity and ingenuity.

Across many centuries young sons of families in and around Glasgow were educated just off the High Street. Daughters had to wait until the 1890s before being able to graduate at the University, now at Gilmorehill, but have since more than caught up.

The authors and Friends hope you enjoy reading the book.

| **Peter V. Davies and Graeme Smith**

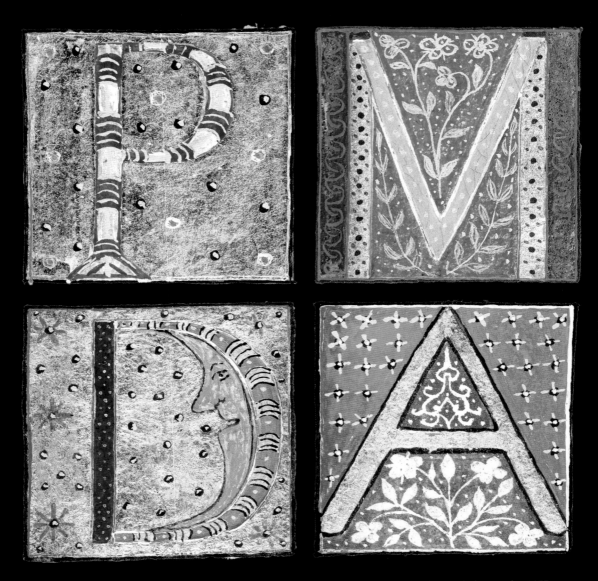

Four illuminated Initials P M D A, from *Scriptores historiae Augustae*, Milan: Philippus de Lavagnia, 1475. Archives & Special Collections [Hunterian Ds.2.6-7, detail from vol. 1, E6v, L8v; vol. 2 D5v, H6r].

Part 1: Origins to 1633

Steven J. Reid
University of Glasgow

If it is true that great things start from small beginnings, then the Library of the University of Glasgow (founded in 1451) must be great indeed. As with the libraries of Scotland's other two medieval universities – the University of St Andrews (founded in successive stages between 1410 and 1413), and King's College Aberdeen (founded 1495) – there is no definitive moment when the Glasgow Library was created, only a slender trail of evidence that points to its gradual evolution. All three universities were established by papal bull with the right to confer degrees, and they taught theology, canon (ecclesiastical) and civil law, and the liberal arts (with medicine also briefly provided at Aberdeen), while their constitutions and curricula were modelled on those of Paris, Orléans, Padua and Bologna. Papally sanctioned and deeply Catholic, all three institutions had close links with the local ecclesiastical community and had access to the libraries of their respective cathedrals and local monasteries, which probably negated the immediate need for their own collections. Glasgow, for example, is known to have had a library room (*libraria*) in the local cathedral

Bologna University, founded in 1088, as it is today. Its democratic teaching model was adopted by Glasgow.

and further books in the local chapter of the Blackfriars, just off the High Street (Higgitt, 2006: xxxix; Reid, 2011: chapter 1).

That said, the purchase of books was a priority from the outset at St Andrews, where on 17th January 1416 the Faculty of Arts assigned five pounds sterling to buying 'books of the text of Aristotle, and commentaries on logic and physics' ('libros textus Aristotelicis et commentaria de logica et physica'). The money was diverted in the following May to commission a mace for the faculty, showing that even then the need to promote a corporate identity was seen as a priority by university

Old College, High Street entrance. Thomas Annan, *Memorials of the Old College of Glasgow*, 1871. Archives & Special Collections [Photo B16].

management (Dunlop, 1964: 6). A faculty library was established in 1456, when the acta record on 13th August the ordering of a wooden lectern-desk ('una ambo') to which books could be chained for consultation by staff and students. Each of the colleges (St Salvator's, founded 1450, St Leonard's, 1513, and St Mary's, 1552) also had some form of college library, or at least a collection of books that the students had access to, though how well these were maintained is questionable – John Mair, who moved to the principalship of St Salvator's College in 1523 after five years at Glasgow, was ordered to repair the college library at St Salvator's in 1534 owing to the disarrayed state that it was in, and to re-catalogue the books. However, if the post-Reformation inventory of books for each of the colleges, featuring 262 books for St Leonard's, around 130 for St Mary's, and 57 for St Salvator's, is anything to go by, these 'public' or common libraries must have been sizeable by the time of the Protestant Reformation of 1560 (Dunlop, 1964: 6; Higgitt, 2006: xlii-lvi, lists S3-4, 13-15, 21-30).

Although King's College was founded in 1495, it took its founder, the stellar Glasgow alumnus and burgess Bishop William Elphinstone, almost a decade to staff and equip the University. Elphinstone hired its first Principal, the historian and philosopher Hector Boece, from Paris in 1497, and teaching commenced at the University in 1505 (Royan, 2004). In his final years Elphinstone supplied the college with a core library of books donated from his personal collection, chiefly relating to theology, civil and canon law, arts and medicine. The group of staff assembled by him at Aberdeen was the single largest group of humanists

Glasgow University as it is today. Photographic Unit [GUPU 14-215 (27)].

anywhere in Scotland, and they too supplied the library with books (Pickard, 1987: I, 100 ff.). The college used a dedicated library room in the south-east tower of the college (known as the *vetus bibliotheca* or 'old library') until a new library was built in the decade after 1532 along the south side of the university chapel, by Bishop William Stewart (Higgitt, 2006: xlix; McLaren, 1995: 1-2; Pickard, 1987: I, 7). A 1542 Aberdeen inventory of goods and furnishings does not give any details of books held in the library but notes some forty-five liturgical books in the college chapel, which were looked after separately by the college Sacrist (Higgitt, 2006: xlvi). Most of these had illuminated capitals, and only two were printed. King's is also the only one of the three pre-Reformation universities in Scotland to have a borrowing register. Compiled on two sheets of vellum and with its final entry dated 26th April 1557, the register shows one hundred and thirty-two loans to twenty-six different borrowers, including staff and students, but also 'outside' members including the bishop, members of the local Franciscan order, and even monks from as far afield as the Cistercian abbey at Kinloss (Pickard, 1987: I, 11).

By contrast, the establishment of the Library at Glasgow appears to have taken much longer after its foundation than that of its counterparts, and to have been much more modest when it did finally happen. The earliest surviving record relating to the Library dates to 1475, when two donations of manuscripts were recorded by John Laing, Bishop of Glasgow and thus *ex officio* Chancellor of the University from 1474 until his death in 1483, and Duncan Bunch, one of the first regents at the University (Innes and Robertson, 1854: III, 403-405). Although Laing's donation is presented in the minute of the gift as coming first, it is likely that the earlier donation was made by Bunch, who had studied at St Andrews and Cologne and was Principal from 1460 until his death in 1474, and Rector in 1468-1469. Bunch was also probably responsible for the construction of the Principal's House on the High Street, which freed up the space in the old quadrangle on Glasgow's High Street for the University Library (Brown and Moss, 2001: 5; Durkan, 1977: 104; Durkan and Kirk, 1977: 77-79). For the first century and a half of its existence (until it was replaced by new premises circa 1659 as part of an extensive University rebuilding programme) it occupied a small room in the south-west wing.

Laing's and Bunch's gifts were followed some eight years later by a further donation from another Principal, John Brown (d. 1483; Innes and Robertson, 1854: III, 405-406). Brown hailed from Irvine, and received his licence in Arts in 1473 from the University; he was the first person from the west of Scotland to hold the post of Principal, and held the office from 1480 until 1482 and that of Rector in 1482–1483 (Durkan and Kirk, 1977: 140-42). All three donations consisted chiefly of manuscript volumes with transcriptions of various texts by Aristotle (in Latin, not the original Greek) and commentaries and *quaestiones* thereon, though the collection gifted by Bunch also included works by Porphyry, Jean Buridan, Boethius and John Athilmer (also known as Elmer), as well as 'a Bible on parchment in a small volume fully written out in the best characters' (*una biblia in pergamino in parvo volumine litera optima complete scripta*). Brown's donation included works by Sacrobosco, Peter of Spain, Thomas Aquinas and Duns Scotus, as well as several other 'authors of natural and moral philosophy' (*auctores philosophie naturalis et moralis*).

The medieval universities had the singular fortune of being 'the only library-owning ecclesiastical institutions to survive the Reformation' (Higgitt, 2006: xxxii), but not without cost to their collections. At Aberdeen the rich collection of books kept by the Sacrist were scattered and never recovered; at St Andrews the library at St Salvator's College, along with the rest of its goods, were briefly removed at the Reformation, although there is evidence that it was reconstituted by 1588 when a new list of books was drawn up; and in 1560 James Beaton, Archbishop of Glasgow and Chancellor of the University from 1551, fled to the Continent at the onset of the Reformation with an unknown quantity of Glasgow's papers and valuables (and presumably at least some of its books), most of which were lost to the fires of the French Revolution (Brown and Moss, 2001: 7). The Reformation also caused massive disruption to teaching at Glasgow, leaving just the beleaguered figure of John Davidson, the Protestant university Principal (1556-1574), to teach single-handedly (Durkan and Kirk, 1977: 232-34). The University benefited from a number of small gifts in the immediate post-Reformation period which helped it retain solvency, including a grant from Queen Mary in 1563 of thirteen acres of land formerly owned by the Dominicans near the University, together with its rents, to support five poor bursars, and a subsequent award from the Town Council in 1573 conferring upon the University the rights of all the ecclesiastical lands the town controlled within the burgh (ibid.: 247). We are thus met with stony silence regarding the Library's development until 1578, when the dynamic university Rector, Andrew Hay, made a gift of books, including notably a copy of Sébastien Châteillon's Protestant Latin Bible, and sixteen further books were gifted by none other than George Buchanan, arguably the most famous neo-Latin poet in Europe (Innes and Robertson, 1854: III, 407).

With the coming of the Reformation there were also major changes to the university system in Scotland, with two new foundations – Edinburgh University (founded 1582 and inaugurated 1583) and Marischal College in New Aberdeen (1593) – joining the three 'ancient' universities. Attempts were made, under the aegis of the church and university reformer Andrew Melville, to replace the medieval and Catholic constitutions of Glasgow, St Andrews and King's College with new Protestant and humanist charters of foundation, and although these failed fully to take root at Aberdeen and St Andrews, Glasgow was successfully re-founded between 1574 and 1580 under Melville's principalship. This process was formally enshrined in the *Nova Erectio* approved by

Andrew Melville, scholar, theologian and religious reformer. Principal of the University of Glasgow, 1574-80.

George Buchanan, 'the most profound intellectual sixteenth century Scotland produced'. © The Hunterian, University of Glasgow 2016 [GLAHA44169].

parliament in 1577, a document which retained a central constitutional importance at Glasgow until the Universities (Scotland) Act of 1858. This was a new Protestant age, and the defining features of the new 'Melvillian' programme were the teaching of Greek and other biblical languages alongside Latin, together with a broad range of Greco-Roman authors, humanist subjects such as history and sacred chronology, and 'controversial' authors such as the anti-scholastic French logician Petrus Ramus. Although recent research has shown that the continuation of the medieval Aristotelian and scholastic curriculum at the universities was far more extensive than has previously been appreciated, a new focus on humanist teachings emerged at Glasgow in particular, where Melville had virtually *carte blanche* to reform teaching as he saw fit. However, despite differences over the best way to teach, a key aim of the university curriculum throughout Scotland was to secure a good harvest of well-trained graduates for the ministry (Reid, 2011: *passim*).

The Prospect of ye Town of Glasgow from ye North East, c. 1693, showing the cathedral, from *Theatrum Scotiae* by John Slezer, 1719. Archives & Special Collections [Hunterian Ce.2.12].

Gifts to the University during Melville's ascendancy and in the decades afterwards reflect these two strands. Buchanan's 1578 grant endowed the Library with an impressive range of early printed Classical editions and commentaries, including the works of Plutarch, Plato, Aristophanes and Euclid, all of which were in Greek. In 1581 there was also a large bequest from James Boyd, the titular Protestant Archbishop of Glasgow and University Chancellor, though a number of the books in this gift had originally belonged to the absconding Catholic Archbishop James Beaton, and can be identified by the stamp featuring his coat of arms on their cover (Durkan, 1977:

107). Boyd had provided considerable support and help to Melville in securing the annexation of the revenues of the parish of Govan to the College and a range of other small annual rents and incomes. Like a series of small gifts given by Peter Blackburn in 1582, the Rector Archibald Crawford in 1586, and Mark Jameson, the minister of Kilspindy, in 1590, Boyd's collection was mainly of Patristic authors or of Protestant interpretations and commentaries on the Bible. However, Jameson also donated six medical works, and books bought for the University via its common funds in this period included *The Hail Actes of Parliament* and a Bible for shared use in the parish of Govan (where the Principal also served as minister under the terms of the parish's annexation to the University), alongside large editions of the works of Augustine, Cicero and Aristotle (Reid, 2011: 81-84; Innes and Robertson, 1854: III, 408-10).

The early seventeenth century was an age of civic benefaction and civic development for the Scottish universities, where local burgesses and ex-alumni started to invest in earnest in the educational provision available in their towns (naturally with a clause attached to any gift that it should benefit their family members first,

should they undertake a degree). A bequest by the lawyer Clement Little to the Town Council of Edinburgh formed the core of a theological library for the town in 1580, which was handed over to the University on its inauguration in 1583; and Marischal College lacked a library until the bequest of books given by the mathematician Duncan Liddell in 1613, which was followed by a similar large grant of books from James VI and I's Latin secretary, Thomas Reid, in 1624 and from the town council in 1632 (McLaren, 1995: 2-3; Finlayson, 1980: *passim*; Kirk, 1982; Reid, 2007). Glasgow

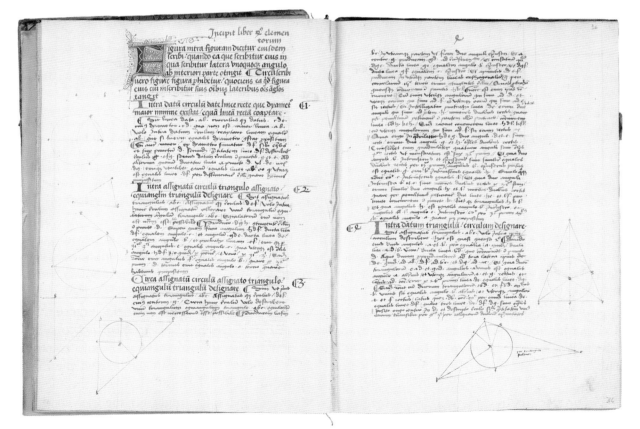

Euclid's Elementa, 1480, mainly on geometry, probably one of the earliest surviving textbooks. Archives & Special Collections [MS Gen 1115 folios 35v & 36r]

Medical book donated in 1590, the *Practica Ioannis Michaelis Sauonarole*, Venice, 1497 edition. Archives & Special Collections [Bm6-d.12, folio a2r].

University, more than either of the other two ancient foundations, was influenced by this wave of civic benefaction, with twelve separate gifts (including purchases made with student donations) recorded between 1590 and 1627 that added almost three hundred separate works to the library collection. Almost half of this total came as a single bequest in 1619 from John Howieson, the radical Presbyterian minister of Cambuslang, whose staggering gift of a hundred and twenty-four volumes (chiefly relating to Reformed theology, including the first known copies of the works of Calvin to be deposited in the Library), warranted the creation of its own 'taffill buird and ane pres' to house them (Innes and Robertson, 1854: III, 413-16, 567; Durkan, 1977: 111). However, substantial gifts were also provided by three other key benefactors: the Regent Alexander Boyd, who gave some sixty volumes similar in nature and content to those of Howieson in the same year; the Edinburgh minister (formerly of Glasgow Cathedral) William Struthers, who donated fifty volumes to Glasgow and Edinburgh apiece before his death in 1633; and James Law, Archbishop of Glasgow from 1615 to 1632, whose 1627 gift in particular provided the Library with an impressive range of editions of Patristic authors (Durkan, 1977: 110-113; Innes and Robertson, 1854: III, 416-21).

Intellectually, the early seventeenth century also saw a resurgence of scholastic approaches to philosophy (particularly used by Calvinist theologians to develop their own systematic theological frameworks in response to the well-established canon of Catholic teachings) and, among Protestant circles in particular, a re-engagement with the branch of speculative philosophy known as metaphysics, which Melville had completely outlawed in his teaching just a few short decades before (Reid, 2011: chapters 7 and 8). There is evidence of a clear shift in the bequests to accommodate these ideas, with a focus on 'new' and systematised forms of logic such as those by Bartholomew Keckermann, Antonio Rubio, Jacopo Zabarella, Pedro de Fonseca, the Coimbra school, and Clemens Timpler, among others. It is probably no coincidence too that at the outset of the brief

Europa from Mercator's Greater Atlas, the *Atlas sive cosmographicae meditationes de fabrica mundi et fabricati figura. De movo multis in locis amendatus novisque tabulis auctus studio Judoci Hondii*, 1642. Archives & Special Collections [Sp Coll q540].

principalship of Robert Boyd of Trochrague (1615-1622), who had taught to great acclaim in the reformed academies of Saumur and Montauban before being called home by James VI and I to Glasgow, a purchase was made using student donations that included a fascinating range of geographical, scientific and comparative religious texts, such as Mercator's *Greater Atlas*, Camden's *Britannia*, a copy of the Koran (*Mahometis Alcoranum*), and a set of mechanical globes, 'one of the heavens, the other of the earth', valued at £25 for the pair (*Globi Duo Cosmographici / cum suis fulcris / caelestis unus / alter terrestris … Empti 25 lib.*; Innes and Robertson, 1854: III, 411-12; Durkan, 1977: 110-11; Reid, 2012: 17).

Part 2: 1633 to 1700

Miles Kerr-Peterson
University of Glasgow

Reflecting the general fortunes of the University as a whole, after its inauspicious development in the fifteenth and early sixteenth centuries the University Library went through a period of rapid institutional maturity between 1633 and 1700. Remarkably, it achieved this against the backdrop of political turmoil, civil wars, famine and plague, as these were the years of the Wars of the Three Kingdoms (1639-1651), the Cromwellian Regime (1651-1660), the Restoration (1660), and the Glorious Revolution (1688). Haynes suggests that 'The state of the library appears to have been one of the main factors driving the redevelopment of the University's High Street site from the 1630s' (Haynes, 2013: 18). A visitor in 1636, the much-travelled writer and politician Sir William Brereton, described the University and cramped Library premises as follows:

> *There [at Glasgow] is a good handsome foundation propounded and set out, to add a good fair and college-like structure to be built quadrangular; one side is already built, and there hath been collections throughout Scotland towards the building of this college, and much more money is collected than is needful to the building hereof. Here the library is a very little room, not twice so large as my old closet: that part of it which is now standing is old, strong, plain building.*
> **(Hume Brown, 1891: 152-53)**

Extracts from the Minutes of the Burgh of Glasgow

'TO MAK ANE LIBRARIE'

25th September 1630: College Library:

'The quhilk day, the provost, baillies, and counsell of the said brught, upoun petitioun maid to thame be the principal [Principal Strang] and regentis of the college of Glasgow, for help and supplie to the building of ane new wark within the said college, have condescendit and aggreit to give to the building of the said wark, ane thousand merkis money quhen the wark is in building, and as the samyn gois on; and ane uthir thousand merkis money to buy buikis to the librarie, quhen ever they by their buikis, to mak ane librarie to the said college, be advys of the provost and bailleis of the said burgth for the tyme.'

'LOVE AND RESPECT TO THE FLOURISCHING ESTAIT'

28th July 1655:

'The said day, notwithstanding the towne payed of befoir to the Colledge twa thousand merks for the help of the fabric thairof, yett, for the love and respect they have to the flourisching estait of the samyne, It is aggreit and condiscendit to be thame to bestow farder therin sax hundredthe pundis, and ordains John Andersoune to deburse the samyne out of the first end of the moneys he receaves from the collectors of the mylnes.'

'TO HELPE TO PUT ON THE ROOF'

23rd October 1660:

'The same day, by pluralitie of vots, its agried unto and condischendit, that ane thousand punds Scots be given to the Colledge, to helpe to put on the roof on the foir wark they are building – Theis who wer appoyntit to treat with them anent the Bibliothecar having first receavit satisfactioune theranent.'

By 1660 the buildings of the Old College had been completed, collectively ranking among the finest architectural achievements in early modern Scotland. They were a far cry from the humble beginnings of the University when it lodged awkwardly within the cathedral and friaries. Bookended by the royal provision of a fund to improve the Library and fabric of the University generally in 1633 (which, in a great twist of irony, was ultimately only provided by Cromwell) and a few years after the creation of the first full library inventory in 1691, this period saw many crucial developments in the organisation and operation of what became the common library.

A Plan of Glasgow inset in Charles Ross's map of Lanarkshire, 1773. Archives & Special Collections [Mu60-a.26].

Glasgow was notably absent from participating in a major intellectual trend in the dissemination of research and the showcasing of academic excellence that appeared at the Scottish universities in the first half of the seventeenth century. This was the production of printed theses for the annual MA graduation ceremony, where the graduating class would each take a thesis from the printed list and defend it in front of friends, family and patrons. The earliest record of a printed set of theses for arts is that produced by the Regent George Robertson at Edinburgh in 1596, closely followed by sets at St Andrews from 1600 (though theses in Physics and Divinity were produced for defence by individual students there from the mid-1590s), at Marischal College from 1616 and King's College from 1622 (Reid, 2011: 256-57). Glasgow only started printing its own theses in 1643 when, as Regent, James Dalrymple (who in later life, as Viscount Stair, would exercise such a massive influence on Scottish legal and enlightened culture) produced the first set, and it seems clear from discussion by Robert Baillie in his 'Overtures' for reform of the University in 1640 that the practice of printing theses had as yet not been adopted at Glasgow.

James Dalrymple Viscount Stair, oil by John Baptist de Medina. Courtesy of National Trust for Scotland.

In other respects, however, Glasgow developed substantial advantages over the other universities in this period, and especially in terms of architecture. In 1630 Principal John Strang set about an ambitious programme of building works, which would be completed almost thirty years later under Principal Patrick Gillespie and which, according to Haynes, appears to have been largely prompted by the deficiencies of the University Library by comparison with its counterparts at St Andrews and Edinburgh (Haynes, 2013: 18). The University's finances were in a relatively healthy state and the problems and poverty of the pre-Melvillian era were long gone, thanks to a range of bequests flooding in from many sources to help with the new building programme. Work was interrupted from about 1639 and continued at a slow or non-existent pace until the mid-1650s, when the political turmoil of civil wars had subsided. For all members of Scottish society this was of course a difficult period, compounded by famine and plague, the latter of which forced the University to relocate temporarily out of Glasgow to the fairer coastal climes of Irvine in 1645 and 1648 (Mackie, 1954: 95-118). The Library itself was enlarged as part of the general rebuilding in 1651 and an additional chamber was added in 1691. 'Accounts from the 1650s indicate that the new library was housed in the east range of the Inner Close, probably on the ground floor to the south of the central entrance' (Haynes, 2013: 19). In 1687 we gain a glimpse of the library interior, with mentions of green serge and red leather book cases – although after 1689 green and red paint had to suffice when an extension was added (Durkan, 1977: 117, 122). As such, the Library was probably the best in Scotland in terms of accommodation at the time. Its only real rival was Edinburgh, which had built a new library between 1642 and 1646 (Morgan, 1937: 130; Fraser, 1989: 34). St Andrews was

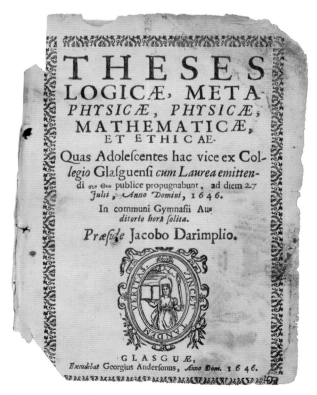

The title page of the first printed Glasgow graduation theses before 1646. Archives & Special Collections [Sp Coll 623 (item 3), title page].

still using the common library set up in 1612, which was only renovated in 1642 thanks to a £1,000 bequest from Alexander Henderson, the Covenanting minister of Leuchars, while King's College's library operated from a low lean-to erected onto the side of the chapel (Cant, 2002: 69; Stevenson, 1990: 120-21). Marischal College's library, housed in part of the old Greyfriars, almost burnt down in 1639, but aside from some opportunistic theft during the chaos caused as the town rushed out to quench the flames, the building and books survived (Anderson, 1889: 232).

As in the post-Reformation period, the University of Glasgow Library was helped along by civic benefaction and the generous donations of books from private individuals. In July 1633 King Charles granted the University £200 sterling for the building maintenance and the 'advancement of the Librarie' (Innes and Robertson, 1854: III, 422), a gift which was ultimately only fully realised when the regime of Oliver Cromwell seized power in Scotland. In 1637 Zachary Boyd, minister of the Barony Kirk of Glasgow, declared that when he died he would leave his books to the Library, a gift which specifically named fourteen volumes but included many more besides, and which can still be identified either by Boyd's signature or by 'Z.B.' being stamped on the covers (Innes and Robertson, 1854: III, 424; Durkan, 1977: 114-15). Other substantial donations included some thirty-nine books given by Robert Meldrum in 1639, twenty-two from the widow of James Forsyth in 1646, and thirty-two from the widow of Dr Robert Mayne in 1649. The University occasionally had to go to some expense to retrieve donated volumes: in

the mid-1650s, for example, a number of books were bequeathed by Patrick Maxwell, which had to be collected all the way from France at considerable expense (Durkan, 1977: 114-17). A notable donation to the Library came from Ayrshire-born John Snell, an alumnus of the University and founder of the 'Snell exhibition' which still sends Glasgow students to Oxford today. While also donating to Balliol College, Oxford (nearer his new Warwickshire home), he actively donated a number of volumes to Glasgow in the 1670s. In the covering letter to his donation of a six-volume Bible in the 'Orientall languages', he stated that 'I do conceive that it is a book very worthy [of] so famous an University as Glasgowe, for it is justly esteemed by all learned men to bee the best in that kinde that ever was yett extant'.

Zachary Boyd, minister of the Barony Church of Glasgow and Rector and benefactor of the University of Glasgow, oil, attributed to George Jameson, 1640s. © The Hunterian, University of Glasgow 2016 [GLAHA 44156].

Student Life

Life in the new buildings changed slowly. In the mid 1600s the 150 or so students, most of them boys in their early teens, assembled at 6 a.m. on weekdays, 7 a.m. on Sundays, attended prayers twice a day and the kirk on Sunday. The regents were responsible for their spiritual welfare and every student was required to have his own Bible and read it. They must wear red gowns inside and outside the College and speak only in Latin. In 1642 'lawful games such as gouffe, archarie and lyke sports' were held to be licit but carding, dicing, billiards, 'and the indecent exercise of bathing' were forbidden. These at least were the rules.

The most flagrant offences were those of wearing swords, of robbing the College orchards, and of 'being found drinking in an ale house with some touns people at 11 of the clock at night'.

Classes were summoned by a bell and began with prayer followed by the reading of the 'catalogue', the register. The Arts curriculum was nominally the same – Greek, some Latin, Logic and the elements of Arithmetic in the first two years; Ethics, Metaphysics, Arithmetic and Geometry in the third; Natural Philosophy in the fourth – but the content of classes changed to reflect a revived but Protestant scholasticism.

Snell also sent other volumes to his *alma mater*, primarily on theological matters (Innes and Robertson, 1854: III, 434-35; Durkan, 1977: 120).

What marks this period out most from the preceding age, however, is the fact that as well as taking these various donations, the Library was increasingly able to fend and purchase for itself, with money dedicated specifically for just that purpose. Like Edinburgh two years before it and St Andrews five years later, in June 1637 Glasgow also formalised the system whereby students were to contribute money towards the Library before their final examinations in the Arts faculty, with fees set at forty-eight shillings for the sons of noblemen, thirty-six shillings for the sons of lairds and twenty-four shillings for the rest, excluding those deemed 'destitute of meannes to susteine themselves'. This system was extended to the Theology students in 1655 (Innes and Robertson, 1854: II, 325; III, 423; Anderson, Lynch and Phillipson, 2003: 38; Cant, 2002: 24). In the 1630s the University employed a cousin of the Regent, later Principal Robert Baillie, William Spang, graduate of Glasgow, to act as its agent for purchasing books. He was the minister to the Scots congregation at Veere in Holland, the staple port of trade between Scotland and Holland. The University also commissioned Patrick Bell to do the same in London (Durkan, 1977: 113, 116). On 28th May 1641 Margaret Graham, the widow of John Boyd of Kirkdyke near Kilmarnock, left a bequest of 2,500 merks which was dedicated by her advisors, David Dickson, the Professor of Divinity at Glasgow and John Stewart, former Provost of Ayr, for the use of the University Library. (A merk was 13s. 4d. Scots, two-thirds of a Scots pound, or 13½ English pence, making the Graham donation worth £1,666 Scots, or £138 15s. sterling.) Specifically a thousand merks of this sum was to be used to purchase 'the choysest books which the Colledge had not before' on theological matters, the covers of which were to be stamped with Margaret's name and the covering page to have a note of her bequest. Another thousand merks was to be given to a student of Theology to record 'the rarest passages of

Gods providence fallen forth in the memorie of famous persons living and witnessed bee them' to be kept in volumes among the University's collections. In the age of the Covenant this donation reflected the increasing predominance of the teaching of Theology over Philosophy and other liberal arts at the University, a trend that can be seen in University curricular changes and staff appointments as well (Innes and Robertson, 1854: III, 426-28; Mackie, 1954: 98-101). The effort put in to endowing the Library with a semi-regular income stream, through the graduation fees and the Graham bequest, alongside the on-going

one-off payments of generous individual civic benefaction, all handsomely bore fruit in 1666 when the Library was able to purchase 340 books from the collection of the former principal Robert Baillie (Durkan, 1977: 119). Glasgow really stands out from the other universities in this period in terms of how well-developed and substantial its regular library income and expenditure were; there is no trace of a similarly developed system in Edinburgh, for example, which relied only on fines, one-off monetary bequests and graduation fees (Finlayson and Simpson, 1982: 43-53; Anderson, Lynch and Phillipson, 2003: 38-39).

The College of Glasgow in the High Street, c. 1693, from *Theatrum Scotiae* by John Slezer, 1719. Archives & Special Collections [Hunter Ce.2.12].

Alongside the obvious growth of its collection, it is as an institution that the Library made significant advances. Some institutional reforms were small, others large. In 1656 large and small library stamps were purchased – a tiny gesture, but a sure mark of increasing institutional sophistication (Innes and Robertson, 1854: III, 545). Of the larger and more fundamental reforms, on 13th May 1641 Thomas Hutcheson of Lambhill – who also founded Hutchesons' Grammar School and whose brother established Hutchesons' Hospital – left 2,000 merks to found 'the office of ane Bibliothecare', the University's first library keeper as the post was generally known before the nineteenth century. This Librarian was to be a qualified Master of Arts and, if possible, the son of a burgess of the town, preferably with the surname Hutcheson or Herbertson. The candidate was to be presented by Hutcheson in his lifetime, and thereafter by the Town Council. The Librarian was to keep the Library in order, working at least from 10 a.m. to noon, then 2 p.m. to 4 p.m. each day, although he was to open up at other times should the University staff require access to the books (Innes and Robertson, 1854: I, 373-75; II, 320-21; III, 424-26; Hoare, 1991: 27-28). Glasgow was the fourth Scottish university to establish a librarian: Marischal College was the

Thomas Hutcheson of Lambhill, founder of the post of Bibliothecare. From W H Hill, *History of the Hospital and School in Glasgow founded by George and Thomas Hutcheson of Lambhill, A.D. 1639-41*, 1881. Archives & Special Collections [Sp Coll Bh11-y.10].

Extracts from the Minutes of the Burgh of Glasgow

'TO CONFERRE ANENT THE BIBLIOTHECAR'

18th February 1660:

'To conferre with (the Colledge) anent what is best to be done for rectifeing of the present debait betwixt the towne and Mr Gillespie anent the Bibliothecar, and to report theranent the nixt meiting.'

'NIXT TURNS'

28th September 1732:

'Which date etc, ...agree to the proposal given in by the Masters of the University, that instead of changing the Library Keeper every four years, to make the office *ad vitam aut culpam*, ... and a contract to be extended, and the present *Liberarius* to be the Colleges turn, and the Town to have the nixt turn.'

first, establishing a post with the bequest of Thomas Reid in 1624 (see part 1 above), and with the first dedicated appointment made in 1632. King's College, Aberdeen seems to have followed suit by 1635, although this role was usually performed by a serving regent alongside his existing responsibilities (Anderson, 1889: 194-204; Anderson, 1893: 89; Stevenson, 1990: 78). The Principal of Edinburgh also served as Librarian until 1635, when the University authorities established the office as a dedicated position (Anderson, Lynch and Phillipson, 2003: 38). Glasgow was ahead of St Andrews, where the University did not appoint its own Librarian until 1642 (Salmond and Bushnell, 1942: 46-48).

The first appointee to Glasgow was Andrew Snype, who graduated that same year 1641 and served until 1645, when he became a minister, and four years later was ordained in Rotterdam before becoming minister of the Scots kirk in Campvere, Veere. Snype was succeeded as librarian by James Hutcheson, the only individual to benefit from the founder's stipulation in favour of his kinsmen. He in turn was replaced by Patrick Young in 1647, who also served as a regent from 1651, and this plurality of responsibilities reflects the difficulties in recruitment caused by the general crisis of the times (Durkan, 1977: 115, 117; Mackie, 1954: 103; Hoare, 1991: 40-41). In the same year the Hutcheson bursary was supplemented with an additional hundred merks a year by the University, but with the condition that presentation to the position should now be exercised alternately by the University as well as the Town Council (Innes and Robertson, 1854: II, 320-21). This arrangement was formalised in 1656 in a contract between the Town Council and University (when the Librarian was also given an enhanced status, being allowed to dine on the second table below the masters). This was prompted by a dispute which had arisen over the presentation by the Town Council in 1655 of Robert Hoggisyard, a tanner's son, whose appointment was soon declared void, the decision having been made without a full quorum. He was replaced by Robert Baillie, the son of Professor Robert Baillie (later Principal). As a way to justify his unashamed nepotism Professor Baillie described the position (perhaps overly dismissively) as 'but ane honararie attendance, without more charge; the benefite of it is the dyet with the regents, a good chamber, and some twelve pieces a year'. In justifying the removal of Hoggisyard, Baillie stated that the position 'was not like those of Profesours and Regents, which required much abilitie of gifts, nor yet of our bursars whose foundation required povertie; but that was of a third nature' (Hoare, 1991: 29-30). Baillie's view should not be taken as the definitive description of the library keeper, although it does indicate the relatively humble status and function. In 1660 a further agreement, prompted by the council funding a substantial roof repair in the college buildings, stated that the college, when it was their turn to present, should ensure that the post was given to a qualified son of a burgess (Innes and Robertson, 1854: I, 373-75; Hoare, 1991: 29). Glasgow was not alone in its disputes with its Town Council: a similar clash over who possessed the right of presentation

Extracts from the Minutes of the Burgh of Glasgow

'ANE POOR BOY GOEING TO THE COLLEGE'

18th October 1662:

'The same day ordaines the Mr. of Work to buy and provyd for .... Abercrumbie, ane poor boy goeing to the College, being a burges sone, ane clouk goune, and ane hatt of the qualitie as the Magistratis sall appoint him.'

'GREAT WRONGS AND ABUSES'

4th March 1665:

'The same day appoints the Provost and Baillies to speik with the Principall and Regents of the College, anent the great wrongs and abuses done by the Collegianes to the Gramer Shoole.'

Campvere (Veere), Zeeland, the staple port for trade between Scotland and the Low Countries, c. 1600.

to the librarianship happened at Marischal College in Aberdeen, first between the Town Council and the successor of the College's founder, the Earl Marischal, and then between the council and the College itself. The College eventually triumphed after arbitration by the Court of Session (Innes, 1854: 339; Anderson, 1889: 204). At Glasgow seventeen individuals held the librarianship between 1641 and 1700, usually for four year terms. Most served without much incident worthy of remark, save for James Young, who served from 1679 to 1687 and was fined 1,200 merks for being complicit in the theft and sale of several dozen books by Patrick Wilson, who served three months in gaol for the crime (Hoare, 1991: 30, 40-41). The incumbent in 1700, Robert Wodrow, son of the Professor of Divinity, is the first to note

being overworked in the office, especially in cataloguing, and he even suggested the need to re-found the Library for its better organisation. However, these plans were ultimately shelved before he moved on in 1703 (Durkan, 1977: 122; Hoare, 1991: 31).

In July 1643 the first laws of the Library were formally set down. These were an exact copy of the rules of the Library of Edinburgh University of 1636 and prohibited unsupervised access, improper removal of books, writing in the books, reading near an open flame, making noise above a whisper or taking books already being borrowed by others. Importantly the library was not just for the use of the staff and students, but for anyone who had taken the library oath, meaning that it could be used by townsmen (Innes and Robertson, 1854: III, 428-29; Durkan, 1977: 115; Morgan, 1937: 213-15). These rules were supplemented in the following year with rules regarding borrowing outside of the area of the burgh (Innes and Robertson, 1854: III, 429-30). In 1659, in order 'for the remedie and preventing of the many abuses relateing to the Publict Library', further statutes were ordained. These included the stipulation that only authorised persons be allowed to purchase books for the Library with University funds (the Quaestor and senior staff, but not the Librarian); that the purchasing of books should not exceed the available budget; that the various Library catalogues should be available to consult in the main hall; that these catalogues should be properly updated once a year, rather than *ad hoc*; and that all new books should be properly stamped and a record made on each indicating from which bursary or fund the book was purchased. It was also noted that a fine was now in place for overdue books, for anyone who exceeded the limit of sixty days and had to pay the cost of replacement (Innes and Robertson, 1854: III, 430-32).

By the time the University's famous lion and unicorn staircase was installed in the outer quadrangle in 1690, the University Library had thus progressed from a mere room containing a patchy collection of hand-me-down books to a living institution with a Librarian, a formalised system of rules and regulations and a revenue stream specifically for the purchase of new books (although this was, at times in the period to follow, little more than a trickle). Underfunding would, however, slow the potential development of these advances across the next two centuries. Thus, while the

University acquired a growing international reputation, the Library played an equivocal role in this transformation.

The 1691 Shelf Catalogue – A Snapshot of an Academic Library at the End of the Seventeenth Century*

Stephen Rawles
University of Glasgow

The 1691 Catalogue of Glasgow University is not a catalogue in the sense commonly understood now. Rather the *Catalogus librorum bibliothecae Universitatis Glasguensis anno 1691* (Catalogue of the Books in Glasgow University Library, 1691) is a press catalogue or shelf list. Other than by browsing, one would search in vain by author or title. Neither is the catalogue to be precisely dated to 1691: the initial series of entries was clearly added over several years, with further additions being made well into the eighteenth century. What emerges is a developing library, at a moment when a decision was reached to establish an accurate listing of the stock. There is no knowing whether an author catalogue existed alongside the shelf listing.

Although the Library was first mentioned in 1475, and despite the existence of lists of donations, the 1691 catalogue is the earliest surviving formal attempt to list the holdings systematically, even if earlier documents imply the existence of an earlier catalogue or catalogues. Indeed, what amounts to an acquisitions register from 1578 is called the *Catalogus librorum communis Bibliothecae Collegii Glasguensis* (Catalogue of Books in the Common Library of Glasgow College: Innes and Robertson, 1854: III, 497 ff.). Again, in what must have been an attempt to marry up acquisitions with a proper public

Fig. 1: *Catalogus librorum bibliothecae Universitatis Glasguensis anno 1691*. Archives & Special Collections [MS Gen 1312, p. 1]. Considerably reduced.

record, the Library regulations of 1659, rules IV and V, mention a public catalogue:

> IV: That the subscribed Catalogue of the bookes of the Publict Librarie be not henceforth in the Bibliothecarius custodie, but that it lay with other publick records of the house.

> V. That no bookes be writtin in the Publict Catalogues by the Bibliothecarius or any maister of the house, but that once in the yeir

at the makeing of the Questores Accompts the Catalogue be made wp conforme to the Accompts, and the additional bookes be subscrived in the Catalogue. (Innes and Robertson, 1854: III, 431).

The 1691 Catalogue itself is actually two catalogues, one being a more or less fair copy of the other. This study deals exclusively with the copy taken to be the original – the volume now known as MS Gen 1312 (Fig.1). This is a manuscript written on paper, rebound in the mid-twentieth century. There are 296 numbered pages, followed by 208 unnumbered pages. The basic text is in a fairly typical and quite readable seventeenth-century hand, with various additions in various other hands, some of them difficult to decipher. Unusually, the pressmarks on the surviving volumes from this point in the Library's history have not been erased, and so it is normally easy to be certain which copies from the period are under examination. A number of different ownership marks were used on books from this period: provenances from the Buchanan, Struthers and Law donations, for example, are given in some detail; other works are marked with the signature of the Principal: many works are so marked with the signature of William Dunlop, who was Principal from 1690 to 1700, and who presided over the exercise of establishing this catalogue; the practice of marking ownership with the Principal's signature was apparently established earlier. However, most works are only identifiable from their typical Glasgow pressmarks, in the format: AT f4 n23, indicating section AT, shelf ('forulus') 4, book N° 23 (Fig.2).

In 1691, as now, the library stock was classified: the books were arranged on the shelves with

other books deemed by a Librarian or Librarians to 'belong' together. The 1691 order of the books is actually very similar to that of other libraries of the period: what is now the Bibliothèque de

Fig. 2: *Aurifondina scientiarum et artium a drexelio* on 12mo, Edit: Antwerp: 1641. Archives & Special Collections [Bh8-I.13 title page]. Enlarged.

Genève for one, Trinity College Cambridge for another. (See, for example, Ganoczy, 1969, and Gaskell, 1980: 112-13.)

A	Biblia	AL-AM	Philol. Prof.	
B-C	Philologi sacri	AN	Juridici	
D	Patres Graeci	AO	Medici	
E	Patres Latini			
F	Concilia et Decret	AP	Ex dono Jo. Snell	
G	Bibliothecae Pat. et Ritual.	AQ-AR	Theol. Pract.	
H-K	Scholastici	AS-AZ	Miscellanei	
L-M	Comment. Reformati			
N-O	Comment. Pontificii	BA-BB	Philologi	
P	Theologi didactici	BC	Polemici	
QX	Polemici	BD-BE	[Misc. Theol.]	
Y-Z	Hist. Eccles.	BF-BM	[Misc.]	
AA-AC	Hist. Civil	BO	Philologi	
AD	Politici	BP	Juridici	
AE	Geographia	BQ	Medici	
AF	Mathem	BR	Historici	
AG-AI	Philosophici	BS	Philos & Math	
AK	Poetae			

The prioritisation of categories in this arrangement clearly reflects the continuing primary role of the reformed University as a college for churchmen at this period much as in the pre-Reformation era (Brown and Moss, 2001: 9). Indeed, the most immediate feature of the Library is the vast preponderance of Theology and allied disciplines: in sections A-AW, 191 pages are devoted to Theology alone, and only 156 pages to all the rest.

The Glasgow classification uses the usual 23-letter alphabet of the period, excluding J, U, and W, although, in transcription, W often does duty as V or U. The Bible comes first, followed by Biblical criticism. The Greek and Latin Fathers follow, and then the Councils of the Church. Then back to more patristics, and ritual. Then scholastics, then Reformed, followed by Roman Catholic biblical commentary. Then 'didactic' theology, perhaps equivalent to practical theology. Then much 'polemic' of various hues, and then Church History. This accounts for the first alphabetical sequence. Non-theological subjects follow, with sizeable amounts of non-Church history and Philosophy, and even more of 'Miscellaneous' items, with books donated by John Snell kept together (AP),[1] and finally more practical theology. It is the author's view that the sequence labelled BA-BS was added later, probably in the first decade of the eighteenth century, and this sequence is not considered here. While the BA-BS section has not been examined in detail, it is certainly true that many more eighteenth-century books are found there, and, perhaps more tellingly, that many shelves begin with books dated from 1701 or later.[2]

In sections A-AW, 4,222 volumes are recorded. Among the miscellaneous items the shelves in sections AY-AZ, like sections BA-BS mentioned above, appear to have been filled later. The bulk of the work appears have been done as a single exercise, with a degree of correction being carried out shortly after the main job was finished. Otherwise, and unsurprisingly, shelves in all sections were filled with works dating from both earlier and later than 1691: this was a working and developing library, and newly acquired books would be added in appropriate places, and existing volumes moved. For example, AM:3:25: 'Adami Litletoun Ling: Lat: Dictionarius Liber Quadripartitus in 4to Edit: Lond: 1678', has a note added to the entry: 'These stands [sic] now in BB: f.4.n.1 & 18'. Unusually full details of the purchase of this work survive (see below, p. 41).

This study necessarily allows for some flexibility of dating: it is not the Library of 1691 which is under scrutiny, but the Library of the 1690s and at the turn of the eighteenth century. This dynamic situation is illustrated by section AI, shelf 6: there are entries in five hands for twenty-two books dating from 1565 to 1704, with eleven dating from 1691 or later. This shelf had probably been left empty to allow for expansion, with books added, probably at five different times, corresponding to the different hands. Additions were made to the catalogue until well into the eighteenth century. In sections A-AW almost 4% of the stock listed dates from 1690-1720.[3]

As a working hypothesis, the assumption is that each of the lettered sections (A, B, C, etc., through to AZ) corresponds to a vertical tier of shelving, which means that there were at first forty-six tiers with another eighteen being added (or at least filled) somewhat later, in sections BA-BS.

Within each of these tiers the books were arranged by size, in up to seven shelves. It is clear that the shelves were numbered from the bottom, since the larger books are in the lowest numbered shelves. In section AT the bottom shelf was at least 36 centimetres high, and the total shelf height for the seven shelves in the tier was at least 142 centimetres; allowing for clearances and the thickness of the shelves, we must assume that the tiers were about two metres high (not so very different from those in the Library now). At least some shelves in the Library were considerably longer than modern library shelves, however: in Section AT they must have been at least 115 centimetres wide (the modern standard is 90 centimetres). This length implies very strong shelves, and high cost.

A typical catalogue entry is provided by S:5:5 (Fig.3):

> Peiter De Moulein's buckler of faith Gall: Printed at Charmtoun 1619 in 8vo.
>
> It: Peiter De Moulein's Examen against Arnout's the Jeſuit: Ibid.

Here we see several typical features:

a) The cataloguers as a general rule avoid any language other than Latin or Scots; thus here, while the entry is in Scots, we have an indication that the book itself is in French – 'Gall.'.

b) The cataloguers do not attempt to provide a transcript of the title – instead they say what the book is in a short descriptive phrase.

c) A place of publication is also usually provided; in this case the 1691 scribe was flummoxed by the French place name Charenton, east of Paris.

d) A date of publication is usually given.

e) An indication of size is nearly always provided by a statement of the format.

The illustration of the title (Fig.4) includes the 1691 pressmark, which, as stated above, is of the utmost value when ascertaining whether a book in the hand now was the book on the shelf at the end of the seventeenth century.

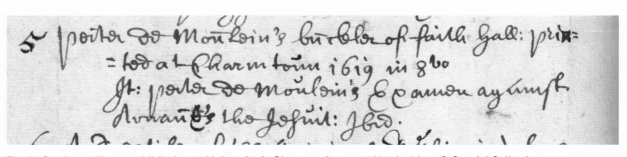

Fig. 3: *Catalogus librorum bibliothecae Universitatis Glasguensis anno 1691*. Archives & Special Collections [MS Gen 1312, detail from p.106].

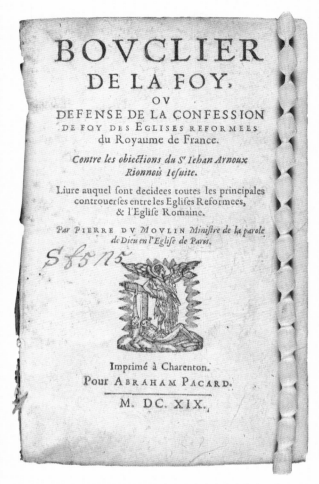

Fig. 4: Pierre du Moulin, *Le Bouclier de la foy* (Charenton: Abraham Pacard, 1619). Archives & Special Collections [Bk8-i-12 title page]. Reduced.

The catalogue, here as in many cases, lists the various works contained within a single volume; these details were frequently added later, in different hands. This degree of detail was of course helpful for the user, but can now make it difficult to ascertain whether more than one publication (or 'bibliographical unit') is involved.[4] Of course, the ultimate source of information would be an examination of all the volumes in question, but this has not been possible here.[5] This aspect of the catalogue constitutes one of the chief analytical problems that it poses. In terms of measurement and the physical formation of the Library, it is the volumes which count; in terms of intellectual content, it is the 'bibliographical units' or individual publications which require analysis. In Section A ('Biblia') there are seventy-four volumes, accounting for sixty-four bibliographical units; in section AT (part of 'Miscellanei') there are 179 volumes, accounting for 264 bibliographic units. This is not surprising given the nature and size of the publications involved. The first shelf of the Biblical section contains only the monumental folio polyglot Bibles of Walton, and of Plantin, in six and five volumes respectively, occupying 890 mm of shelf length, and accounting for only two bibliographical units (See Fig.1). The fifth shelf of AT (part of 'Miscellanei') contains twenty-nine volumes, accounting for sixty-two bibliographical units, occupying 990 mm of shelf, in which one volume alone (AT:5:9) contains nineteen different pamphlets. It is therefore important to distinguish between the number of volumes as listed, and the number of publications that they contain. Henceforward, proportions are expressed as percentages of the best possible estimate of the numbers of bibliographical units involved.[6]

Multi-volume works, ranging from two to fourteen volumes, account for 717 volumes in 253 bibliographical units, and 245 volumes contain more than one bibliographical unit, in the range of two to twenty-seven per volume.

Country of origin

This table indicates the percentages of printed books from various countries of origin:

England	30.18
Germany	18.53
France	17.74
North Netherlands	12.87
Switzerland	10.83
South Netherlands	3.50
Scotland	2.59
Italy	2.47
Poland	0.46
Spain	0.26
Ireland	0.22
USA	0.12
Others	0.24

Perhaps the most striking aspect of this table, apart from the paucity of Scottish publications, and the unsurprising preponderance of English works, is the strong showing of French books, as the third most frequent, when all the other areas in the top five were fundamentally Protestant.[7] Within France, Protestant centres such as La Rochelle are represented, but the vast majority of the French material is from the two main centres of printing: Paris (roughly 60% of the French material), and Lyon (roughly 22%).

The Scottish works listed comprise about 150 publications, spread between Aberdeen, Edinburgh, and Glasgow, with about 73% of the total emanating from Edinburgh, 20% from Glasgow, and about 6.5% from Aberdeen.

Towns of origin

	Percent
London	29.08
Paris	11.70
Basel	5.14
Cologne	5.09
Geneva	5.02
Leiden	4.89
Frankfurt	4.68
Amsterdam	4.41
Lyon	4.24
Antwerp	3.42

No towns are mentioned in the entries for about 240 volumes. Ten centres (London, Paris, Basel, Cologne, Geneva, Leiden, Frankfurt am Main, Amsterdam, Lyon and Antwerp) account for more than 75% of the items in the 1690s library. London accounts for by far the greatest number of bibliographic units (almost a third), a preponderance attributable to a large number of pamphlets from the 1640s. Parisian books account for a further 12%.

Date

The following chart depicts percentages of dated records for publications from the various decades of the sixteenth and seventeenth centuries. The publication dates of items listed show a remarkable peak in the mid-seventeenth century, the summit in the 1610s being particularly noticeable.

Obviously, dates of publication give no indication of the dates of acquisition in the Library. They do, however, indicate dates before which the acquisition could not have taken place.

Dates of Publication

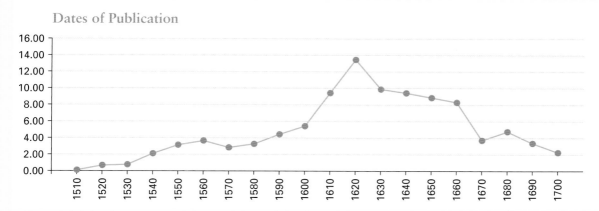

Graph detailing the percentage of works listed in the 1691 catalogue by decade of publication.

Acquisition

Some indication of acquisition dates is available in the published archives (Innes and Robertson, 1854: III, 403-64). These records largely chronicle significant donations, from such notables as George Buchanan (1578), James Boyd, Archbishop of Glasgow (10th June 1581), William Struthers, Minister of St Giles in Edinburgh (died 1633, his books being acquired by the Library in 1634), and James Law, Archbishop of Glasgow, who listed bequests in his will of 21st June 1627 and died on 12th November 1632. Few acquisitions by purchase are mentioned. An early example appears, however, in a note of 1577, listing six works under the rubric 'Empti sunt per Quaestorem 1577' (Bought by the Quaestor: Innes and Robertson, 1854: III, 409),[8] including a 1539 two-volume edition of Cicero from the Estienne press in Paris.[9] A number of volumes acquired in the 1690s carry both Principal Dunlop's inscription and the note 'Empt: propriis Academiae sumptibus' (Bought with the Academy's own funds).

The fact remains that acquisition by donation was clearly important.

Among the patchy surviving financial records of the University for book purchase, which have not yet been fully investigated, is the following entry for 1678-1689:

Item the 31 March 1680 to William Colvane to give to John Rae for Littletounes Dictionary: £10-16s-0d.[10]

This clearly relates to the entry at AM:3:25, which was mentioned above in connection with the dictionary's later re-location (p. 37):

Adami Litletoun Ling: Lat: Dictionarius Liber Quadripartitus in 4to Edit: Lond: 1678.

There is strong evidence of systematic acquisition of certain sets of publications. One such is the set of quarto classical texts 'in usum Delphini' (for the use of the Dauphin). Commissioned by Charles de Sainte-Maure, duc de Montpensier,

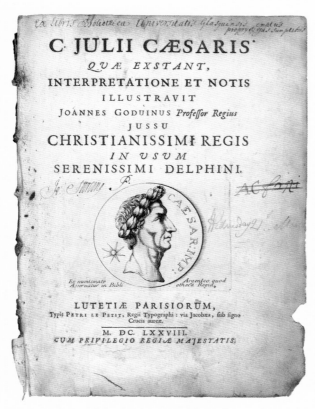

Fig 5: *Julii Caeſaris Opera in uſum Delphini* in fol: (sic)
Edit: Paris: 1678. Archives & Special Collections
[Sp Coll Bm6-f.18 title page]. Reduced.

the governor of the Dauphin, and partly edited by the learned scholar and book collector Pierre-Daniel Huet, the collection comprised textual commentary, summaries, and simplified paraphrases, maintaining the traditional all-Latin format, requiring the reader/student to operate without the vernacular. The texts were to a degree bowdlerised: the pejorative use of the tag 'in usum Delphini' developed with this sense in some traditions as a result of these publications. However, the editorial format was presumably well suited to the Glasgow University environment, providing good texts with interpretative help.[11] The Library appears to have owned fifty volumes from the series, all in Latin despite Greek texts also having been published. In 'AC – Hist Civil' we find Caesar,[12] Livy, Tacitus, Justinus and others, occupying the whole of shelf 2 and the beginning of shelf 3. At AF:2:11 we find Manilius's *Astronomicon*, an influential first-century astrological work rediscovered in the Renaissance. Pliny occupies AH:3:1-5 in 'Philosophici'. The whole of AK:3 in the 'Poetae' section is taken up with Latin poets, although Ovid and Horace are not found. Section AM – 'Philol. Prof.' Cicero accounts for six volumes (AM:3:4-9), alongside, for example, Terence (AM:3:11), and Aulus Gellius (AM:3:13).[13] Of works from the collection, the Caesar volume at AC:2:1 (Fig.5), the Tacitus volumes (AC:2:8-11) and the Quintus Curtius (AC:3:1), at least, indicate that they were acquired by purchase, since their titles bear the Library inscription: 'Ex Libris Bibliotheca Universitatis Glasguensis emptus proprii ejus sumptibus' (From the books of Glasgow University Library, purchased from its own funds) – or analogous wordings. All three works also carry the signature of John Stirling (Principal from 1701 to 1727), but it is unlikely that the works were acquired during his principalship. Certainly the entries for AC:2 were made to the catalogue in the first stages of its compilation, in the earliest hand found, and with no later additions. Here, as elsewhere, the Principal's signature as a mark of ownership was added retrospectively, in this case with the note of purchase from Library funds.

The question of the tradition of using the signature of the Principal as a means of identifying the Library's ownership of books also arises in the case of another series, of geographical texts on individual countries published by Elzevier in Leiden in the 1620s and 1630s. At least twenty-nine volumes from the series were shelved in 'Hist. Civil' at AA:6:2-19 and AB:6:5-16, and all bound in a uniform vellum, possibly by the printer/publisher. The countries covered, with some ambiguities arising from changing names and frontiers, include Savoy, Poland, Persia, the German states, England, the Venetian republic, Switzerland, the Turkish empire, Hannover, Luxemburg, Lithuania, Livonia, the Netherlands, Liège, Muscovy, Hungary, Bohemia, Southern Austria, The Balkans, Scandinavia, Japan, China, Rome, the Hanseatic states, and Greece. Practically all the volumes are signed by Robert Baillie (Professor of Divinity from 1642; Principal 1661-1662). Baillie donated several works to the Library; the late John Durkan was of the view that Baillie's donations usually carried his personal inscription, including the Greek motto 'τὸ μελλον ἀορατον' ('the future cannot be foretold').[14] Since none of the copies of the Elzevier series signed by Baillie includes the motto, we should probably conclude that these works were acquired by purchase at about the time of Baillie's Principalship, therefore in the early 1660s; it is of course possible that the series was acquired by gift, but nonetheless signed by Baillie. A volume, clearly from the same series, Peter Van der Kun's *De Republica Hebraeorum* (The Hebrew Republic), 1632, was added in 1691, by purchase, and carrying the signature of Principal Dunlop.[15] It is generally considered as the most powerful statement of republican theory in the early years of the Dutch Republic.

Acquisition of books by gift is a haphazard means of providing Library material required for university teaching and study. An area obviously important in Glasgow was patristics, and it is noteworthy that the Library possessed a considerable number of works by early Christian theologians printed in France in the seventeenth century. Of 150 volumes in sections D and E (Greek and Latin Fathers respectively) twenty-seven were printed in Paris, seventeen between 1605 and 1678. The works of Cyril and Synesius of Cyrene (Paris, 1631; D:2:10) and of St Epiphanius (Paris, 1622; D:2:12) were both edited by the Jesuit Denis Petau. Glasgow Divines needed patristic texts, and while some works were acquired by gift – e.g. Isidore of Pelusium, *De interpretatione divinae Scripturae* (The Interpretation of Holy Scripture), Paris, 1638 (D:5:6) from James Law – it is equally obvious that some were acquired by purchase. In an analogous area, the 1691 catalogue lists 219 volumes of 'Comment. Refomati' (sections L-M), but also includes 132 volumes of 'Comment. Pontificii' (sections N-O), rather more than half of which date from after the *Nova Erectio* of the 1570s, such as the commentary on Ecclesiastes by the Jesuit Juan de Pineda at O:2:7, 'Pineda in Ecclefiafton in fol: Edit: Antwerp: 1620' (Fig.6), also acquired by gift from James Law in the 1630s; Law purchased the work in Edinburgh for £12. Of course, the acquisition of Roman Catholic material, whether by gift or purchase, does not imply acceptance of its principles; the aim may well have been to use the material as a means of refutation as if for target practice.

Conclusion

A full history of the Library at the end of the seventeenth century requires more than a study of the 1691 press catalogue of Glasgow University Library. But the catalogue nonetheless reveals an institution heavily geared towards the perceived needs of its users, who were in the vast majority studying or teaching Theology and Divinity, with well over half the Library devoted to their requirements. The catalogue also reveals a Library in a state of development, with works being moved around to ensure better use of shelf space, or to be placed, in the eyes of the librarians or users, more appropriately. The Library was soon to enjoy (or dread?) the right to claim all UK publications by the copyright deposit arrangements agreed in the Copyright Act of 1710. Copyright deposit imposes heavy burdens on a library, both in the claiming of publications from publishers, but also in the obligation to catalogue large bodies of material; the eighteenth century librarians may well have viewed the new privilege with mixed feelings.[16] The rearrangement of the stock begun in the last decade of the seventeenth century nonetheless reflected a traditional approach to the arrangement of library material. It is an unprecedented mercy that in subsequent rearrangements before the redaction of Arthur's catalogue of 1791, and on the relocation of the Library to Gilmorehill in the 1870s, the evidence of the 1691 pressmarks was not effaced. The snapshot here provided is all the more focused by the survival of this vital information.

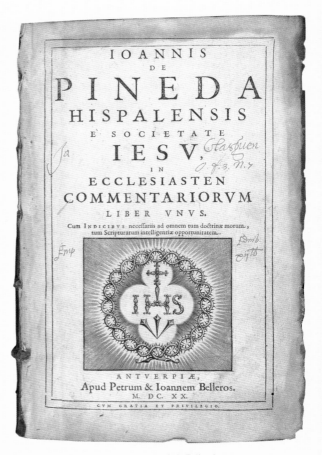

Fig. 6: *Pineda in Ecclesiaſton* in fol: Edit: Antwerp: 1620, with ownership marks of James Law, Archbishop of Glasgow. Archives & Special Collections [BI2-d.7 title page]. Reduced.

* This study is based on work in progress. Any conclusions drawn are subject to revision, especially any statistical observations. It is based on the state of the Library at the point when it was deemed appropriate to undertake a new listing of the Library's holdings: insofar as can be judged, therefore, additions demonstrably made after about 1700 are not taken into account, but total accuracy in this matter is impossible. This said, the exposition of the catalogue's methodology is fundamentally uncontentious, as is any analysis of provenances based on observation of the books surviving from the 1690s.

1 Snell is recorded in the *Oxford Dictionary of National Biography* as having made more than one donation to the Library; the first in 1661, might have included Brian Walton's polyglot Bible of 1657 (AP:3:1-6);. A duplicate of this edition (A:1:1-6) was evidently disposed of after the publication of Arthur's catalogue in 1791, where both copies are listed. A lengthy provenance statement mentioning Snell is found in all six volumes. Most of the books listed in AP date from later than 1661. There is currently no means of knowing when these books arrived; Snell died on 6th August 1679.

2 This does not mean that some, or even most, of the works listed in BA-BS were not present in the 1690s, only that there is no means of knowing without a systematic examination of the books listed, which has not yet been possible. On the enlargement of the Library in 1691, see p. 65.

3 The 4,222 volumes include about forty manuscripts, which are not further discussed here.

4 A bibliographical unit may be defined as a publication which requires a single entry in a library catalogue, reflecting the intention of the printer or publisher in planning, financing and printing the work or works in question.

5 About 400 volumes have been examined; about 3,800 modern catalogue records have been located in the on-line catalogue, frequently clarifying the situation.

6 It is acknowledged that these figures are susceptible to change as more analysis is achieved, but they are indicative of the general situation.

7 Switzerland was not, of course, uniformly Protestant, but most of the production represented was from Geneva, Basel and Zurich. The same applies to modern Germany.

8 In this role the Quaestor would now be called the 'acquisitions officer'.

9 AM:2:11-12; the copy acquired in 1577 was apparently disposed of as a duplicate some time after the publication of Arthur's catalogue. The copy now shelved at Sp Coll Bh9-c.2-3 cannot be that acquired in 1577 because it carries the ex-libris 'Ex libris Gaspardi Guyant Mellocensis. 1670'.

10 Quaestor's book, 1678-1680 (GUAS GB0248).

11 The series remained in use for an extended periods, and was copied in other countries: see, for example, Ovid's *Heroides* (Crispin, 1795).

12 Wrongly described as a folio.

13 The 1691 entry does not mention the Dauphin, but the modern catalogue record adds the information.

14 As so often, John Durkan's views were not recorded in print, but carried authority! A typical Baillie donation is A:4:7: Biblia Italica Vers: Jo: Diodatini 4to – Edit: 1607. Now shelved at Sp Coll Bk5-e.14; printed by Jean II de Tournes in Geneva. Baillie's motto is apparently derived from the ancient Greek rhetorician Isocrates.

15 B:5:10; 'Empt: publicis Academiae sumptibus An. 1691'.

16 See 8 Ann. c. 21 or as 8 Ann. c. 19. *An Act for the Encouragement of Learning, by vesting the Copies of Printed Books in the Authors or purchasers of such Copies, during the Times therein mentioned.*

Chapter 2

The Eighteenth Century – Enlightenment Emerges

A hand-coloured plate from *Select Views of Glasgow and its environs*, engraved by Joseph Swan, 1828, showing the Adam Library on the left, behind the tree. © The Hunterian, University of Glasgow 2016.

Andrew Hook
University of Glasgow

Intellectual Progress and International Reputation

In the history of Glasgow University no century is more important than the eighteenth. It was then that the decisive changes occurred that meant that the University was finally shedding its medieval past and moving into what we still see as the modern world. It is in the eighteenth century that English finally replaced Latin as the language of instruction in every course. It is in the eighteenth century, 1727 to be precise (Brown & Moss, 2001: 19), that the old system of pedagogy, according to which regents taught students across a range of subjects, was replaced by one in which specialist professors were separately responsible for the teaching of individual courses and subjects. It is in the eighteenth century that a new curriculum in the Arts, taken by the majority of students, was established that would remain largely unchanged well into the nineteenth century: two years of Latin and Greek, Rhetoric (including Logic), Ethics (Moral Philosophy), and Natural Philosophy including Mathematics, Physics, Astronomy, and Geography. A chair in Mathematics had been created in 1691, and the early eighteenth century saw the emergence of a wide range of new professorships, many of them funded by the Crown. Chairs in Greek, Humanity, Oriental Languages, Logic and Rhetoric, Moral Philosophy, Natural Philosophy, Ecclesiastical History, Law, Practice of Medicine, and Anatomy and Botany were all in place by 1727. In other words it was in the eighteenth century, with student numbers rising from around three hundred at its opening to approximately one thousand at its closing, that the University began to take the shape with which we remain familiar.

There is another reason, however, for seeing the eighteenth century as pivotal in the University's history. Glasgow University's contribution to the Scottish Enlightenment was as important as that of Edinburgh. What we need to remember is that around 1700 Scotland's reputation, in so far as it had one internationally, was of a country marked by poverty, economic backwardness, and violent religious controversy – whereas by 1800 Scotland was seen throughout the Western world as a model country in terms of Progress and Improvement. It was the calibre of the intellectual and cultural achievement of the Scottish Enlightenment that produced this dramatic change. All the Scottish universities contributed to the Enlightenment movement, but a group of distinguished professors within the Glasgow Faculty in the eighteenth century gave the institution a level of intellectual distinction greater than it had ever enjoyed in the past – and a status that is at least comparable to that of the University today. As a result the University began to attract students not only from the Glasgow area, but also from the rest of Scotland, including the Highlands and Islands, from England and Wales, from Ireland, from the West Indies, from the Americas, and even from Russia. (Two future Professors of Russian Law at the University of Moscow, Ivan A. Tretyakov and Semyon E. Desnitsky, studied for their first degrees at Glasgow and disseminated the ideas of the Scottish Enlightenment in Russia.)

Who were the men responsible for Glasgow's growing distinction? A key figure was the Ulster-born philosopher Francis Hutcheson (1694-1746) – sometimes described as the founding father of the Scottish Enlightenment – Professor of Moral Philosophy from 1730 until his death. His most famous pupil was the legendary economist Adam Smith (1723-1790), Professor of Logic and subsequently of Moral Philosophy 1751 to 1764. Smith's successor in the Chair of Moral Philosophy was Thomas Reid (1710-1796), who held the position until 1781. Reid went on to gain a European reputation as the founder of the Scottish common-sense school of philosophy that was widely seen as successfully countering the subversive scepticism of David Hume. An eminent contemporary of Adam Smith was John Millar (1735-1801), Professor of Law from 1761 to 1800, a highly influential early economic and social historian, often seen as a founder of the subject that became sociology. Glasgow's reputation in science and medicine became equally distinguished. William Cullen (1710-1790), who would be a key figure in making Scotland the world's most renowned centre for medical education in the eighteenth century, was Professor of the Practice of Medicine from 1751 to 1755. (He then moved over to Edinburgh University.) Joseph Black (1728-1799), the Bordeaux-born son of an Irish wine merchant, occupied the same Chair between 1757 and 1766, when he followed Cullen in moving to Edinburgh. However, the discoveries

The Author of the Wealth of Nations, 1790, Adam Smith by John Kay, caricaturist and engraver. Archives & Special Collections [BD6-d.3].

Francis Hutcheson, oil by Allan Ramsay. © The Hunterian, University of Glasgow 2016 [GLAHA 44025].

Dr William Cullen in his study, 1789, by John Kay, caricaturist and engraver. Archives & Special Collections [Sp Coll BD6-d.3].

Professor Joseph Black lecturing, 1787, by John Kay, caricaturist and engraver. Archives & Special Collections [SP Coll BD6-d.3].

that brought Black lasting fame – latent heat, specific heat, and carbon dioxide – had all been made in his Glasgow days. Between 1756 and 1774 his friend and collaborator, the engineer and mathematical instrument maker to the University, James Watt (1736-1819), while not a member of the Faculty, was closely associated with the University's outstanding record of research and teaching in science and medicine.

The Library's Equivocal Role

What then was the role of the University Library in helping or facilitating this transformation of Glasgow's status into that of a major seat of learning and research? The answer is in fact a somewhat equivocal one. Early in the century the Library's future seemed assured. An immediate cultural benefit of the Treaty of Union of 1707 was the Copyright Act of 1710 which stipulated that the libraries of all the Scottish universities had the right to a copy of each work entered at Stationer's Hall in London (Dickson, 1888: 12). But this apparently highly significant development never delivered on its promise and may well have been considered a mixed blessing by librarians of the day. The Quaestor's book for the earliest post-Copyright Act years (in Scotland the Quaestor was the Regent or Professor responsible for the University's finances including those relating to the Library) records that in 1711 and 1712 payment had to be made for the binding of books 'got by Act of Parliament', and also for the services of the person in London 'who collected and sent the books got by Act of Parliament' (Dickson, 1888: 13; Hoare, 1991: 27). In other words Glasgow, and presumably the other Scottish universities, quickly found that they had to foot the bill incurred in translating the promise of the Copyright Act into actual books on their libraries' shelves. Given the low level of funding available for the University Library, the result was that throughout the eighteenth century, and in the early nineteenth century, expensive works or books with plates were rarely procured, while over the entire period, the Glasgow Library seemed uncertain over how far it should accept cheaper items such as fiction and poetry in English. From a 1732 Glasgow Library list of copyright acquisitions during 1731, we gather that the system then in place involved a twice-yearly delivery to the University's London agent of items claimed from Stationers' Hall. However, actual shipping to Glasgow occurred much less frequently. The list for 1731 contains ninety-seven titles – mainly religious works but including nine English Literature titles, and ten History books (Nairn, 1959: 30). However, the relative failure of

Rev. Thomas Reid, oil by Sir Henry Raeburn, 1796 © The Hunterian, University of Glasgow 2016 [GLAHA 44012].

the 1710 Copyright Act to enhance substantially the size and quality of the college library explains why the new Copyright Act of 1837, replacing the Stationers' Hall privilege with a fixed annual payment of £707 to Glasgow – the highest sum awarded to any of the Scottish universities –, was at the time generally welcomed. Moreover, as these compensatory grants reflected the extent to which universities had previously availed themselves of legal deposit copies (*CHL*, II: 350), Glasgow had clearly profited from the scheme despite its disadvantages.

It is nevertheless perhaps not unfair to say that throughout the eighteenth century the University Library was almost as much a problem as an asset. Its modest size had been recognised as an issue in the seventeenth century – a report in 1664 had described the Library as 'verie small for ane Universitie' (Dickson, 1888: 10). In 1691 the collection amounted to a modest 3,300 volumes (Emerson, 2015: 6). Most of these works concerned religion or philosophy, and were largely in Latin, though John Locke's *Essay Concerning Human Understandin*g of 1689 (dated 1690) and his works on education and government were acquired in 1695 (Archives & Special Collections GUA 26778, 1695, pp. 99, 102). Books in English on science, history and literature did begin to appear early in the eighteenth century – alongside a three-volume edition of Locke's collected works and philosophical books by Descartes, Malebranche, and Pufendorf (Emerson, 2015: 6, 7). Nonetheless library expansion proceeded quite slowly for much of the century. As late as 1760, only 5,643 volumes were on the Library's shelves (Dickson, 1888: 31). By comparison the private library of Archibald Campbell (1682-1761), the 3rd

Duke of Argyll – a man whose interests outside politics grew to include almost every aspect of the Scottish Enlightenment –, amounted to 13,000 volumes and over 9,000 titles. This library passed subsequently into the possession of his nephew, the future Prime Minister John Stuart, 3rd Earl of Bute, and at the time of his death in 1792 the collection amounted to around 30,000 works (Emerson, 2013: 105). By then the University Library had grown substantially, but at around 20,000 books listed in Archibald Arthur's 1791 printed catalogue (see below) was still considerably smaller than this private library.

Limited Growth, Acquisitions and Influence
The explanation of the Library's modest size is clear enough. It struggled constantly over funding. There was no regular or established source of money for the purchase of books. In the early years of the century, when it came to decisions about book purchases, the professor responsible for Library expenditure (the Quaestor) had to work with all the Regents and subsequently with a library committee of four, which included the university Principal (Dickson, 1888: 53). Being responsible for the collection of student fees for examinations, matriculation, and graduation, the Quaestor would have been well aware of the financial problems facing the University as a whole – problems which would continue through the eighteenth century. As late as 1784, for example, the administration resolved that 'measures be taken to reduce the expenditure on the publick library' (ibid.: 15). In fact the gradual increase in the Library's holdings was in no way exclusively the result of the 1710 Copyright Act. The 'Quaestor's Book' reveals that books were bought at auctions, from widows disposing of their 'umquwhile husband's' collection, and by

Design by William Adam for the Old College Library, 1732. Archives & Special Collections [BUL/6/56/12].

1764 engraving by Robert Paul of Glasgow from the South West – 'one of the most beautiful small towns in Europe'. Archives & Special Collections [Bh13-x7].

Regents or others visiting Edinburgh or London or even continental countries. Then gifts of books had always been important in building up the collection. In his history of Glasgow University, James Coutts even asserts that 'for a considerable time after the Reformation more books were obtained by gift than by purchase' (Coutts, 1909: 251). In the eighteenth century, however, individual donations of books, while still remaining significant, appear to have declined. Nevertheless in 1753 the Duke of Argyll gave eight volumes of Leupold's pioneering treatise on mechanical engineering *Theatrum Machinarum* (1724); Robert Simson (1687-1768), the distinguished Professor of Mathematics and author of hugely influential

mathematical textbooks, bequeathed a valuable collection of nine hundred mathematically-related volumes, and in 1797 Thomas Reid presented over sixty works that were new to the Library (Dickson, 1888: 14). Bequests or gifts of cash also contributed to the Library's book-purchasing power.

In the eighteenth century, such gifts or bequests to the Library are often of special interest. The University's Principal John Stirling (1666-1738) gave the equivalent of £166 in 1727 – no doubt in recognition of his university's need to build up its library. In 1730, a Glasgow merchant and alumnus, John Orr of Barrowfield, gave £500, the interest of which was for the purchasing of 'such antient Greek and Latin books as have been wrote before the year of our Lord Three Hundred and Fifty, by authors of known esteem and repute' (ibid.: 51). Orr's trading ventures may well have extended as far as the colony of Virginia where, as the eighteenth century went on, the commercial link with Glasgow and the Clyde was of increasing importance. It is thus not surprising that in 1770 Robert Dinwiddie, the Scottish former Governor of Virginia and Glasgow alumnus, should have bequeathed the Library £100. (The University had awarded him an honorary LL.D. degree in 1754.) The interest from the endowment was to be used to buy books.

Of even greater significance is the bequest of £100 by the Whig Thomas Hollis (1720-1774) in 1774 and subsequent gifts by his great friend, the radical dissenter Thomas Brand (later Brand-Hollis: 1719-1804). The wealthy Hollis family had earned a reputation as keen supporters of liberal education, and the promotion of English political ideals of freedom and tolerance. An elder Thomas Hollis, a successful English merchant, became a generous benefactor of Harvard University, establishing chairs in Divinity and Mathematics and Natural Philosophy. His namesake grand-nephew became an active political philosopher. With his friend Thomas Brand, he toured Europe in mid-century, meeting French philosophers and Italian painters. Back in England he commissioned several paintings by Canaletto. A friend of William Pitt and John Wilkes, he became a Fellow of the Royal Society in 1757. Hollis was committed intellectually to what he saw as the tradition of English liberty and individual rights. Thus he strove to have the work of English thinkers who promoted such ideals of government reprinted and distributed to libraries in Britain, Europe, and eventually America. (Hollis sided with the American colonists in their dispute with the mother country, and also became a major benefactor of Harvard University.) The scale of Hollis's gifting of books to European and North American libraries is extraordinary and unprecedented: he may well have distributed as many as 4,000 volumes (Reddick, 2010: 11). Dickson, commenting on Hollis's £100 gift to the Glasgow Library tells us he 'is described as specially attached to civil and religious liberty and as having spent much on editions of the writings relative thereto of Algernon Sydney, Milton, Locke, and Ludlow' (Dickson, 1888: 52).

The main London publisher of works by these figures – and others including Bacon and James Thomson – in editions which Hollis favoured, was the Scot Andrew Millar – and Millar as it happens was a close friend of William Leechman (1706-1785), Principal of Glasgow University from 1761 until his death (Budd, 2015). This perhaps makes it even more likely that Hollis's pounds would have been spent on Millar's editions. Hollis's friend Thomas Brand, also a Fellow of the Royal Society, had been a pupil and admirer of Glasgow's Frances Hutcheson. Brand shared Hollis's radical political views including his support for the American revolutionaries. Thus when Hollis died in 1774, Brand inherited his estate – and added his surname to his own. Unsurprisingly, Brand-Hollis continued the tradition of support for the University of Glasgow Library. In his accounts as Quaestor between 10th June, 1781, and 10th June, 1783, Thomas Reid records a £10 donation by Mr Hollis – and in 1804 he gifted £100 to be spent on books 'relating to government civil history or the mathematics' (Dickson, 1888: 52).

Why, you may ask, are the Hollis gifts to the Library of special interest? Because they can be seen to shed light on the nature of the wider intellectual and cultural experience available to many Glasgow University students for much of the eighteenth century. It seems that from the teaching and influence of Francis Hutcheson onwards, the 'Glasgow' philosophy was to some degree supportive of a politically and socially progressive, broadly liberal, ideology. The Ethics and Moral Philosophy courses taught successively by Hutcheson, Adam Smith, Thomas Reid, and Archibald Arthur all appear to have been sympathetic to the notion of the civil and religious freedom to which Thomas Brand was so powerfully committed. In other words, the two Hollis's donations to Glasgow's Library would have resulted from their sense that the University's culture was one sympathetic to their own. If further evidence of this commitment at Glasgow to a broadly liberal world view is required, then one can point to the early enthusiasm for the French Revolution felt by so many of the University's major figures: Thomas Reid, John Millar, John Anderson, Archibald Arthur, and George Jardine.

Still more telling, however, – and forever to the credit of the University – is what transpired in the Senate meeting of 1st February, 1792. On that day the Senate unanimously approved a proposal to address the House of Commons in favour of a bill abolishing the African slave trade. The text of the petition to Westminster, the first to reach London from a Scottish institution, is eloquent and moving. The slave trade is described as 'an existing evil of infinite magnitude' – one which 'comprehends in it the most obvious violation of the feelings of nature, of the principles of morality, and of those doctrines and duties inculcated in the Gospels which form the basis of our most holy religion'. 'Deeply penetrated by the cries of justice and mercy', the Senate hopes to see 'banished from the face of the earth' this 'infamous Traffick'. The Clerk of Senate was instructed to transmit a copy of the petition to 'Mr Wilberforce', 'that it may be presented by him to the House of Commons at the time he may judge most proper' (Archives & Special Collections, SEN 1/1/2 1792, Senate meeting minutes, pp. 136-37).

The Senators subscribing to this attempt to influence Parliament in favour of abolishing the slave trade were Dr Archibald Davidson, as the University Principal, Dr Robert Findlay, Professor of Divinity, Mr John Millar, Professor of Law, Mr Patrick Cumin, Professor of Oriental Languages, Dr Thomas Reid, Professor of Moral Philosophy, Mr John Young, Professor of Greek, Mr Patrick Wilson, Professor of Astronomy and Clerk of Senate, Mr George Jardine, Professor of Logic, and Dr James Jeffray, Professor of Anatomy and Botany. Of this group, Principal Davidson has been identified as supporting the Tory party in Scotland, but Millar, Reid, Wilson and Jardine were all political radicals (Emerson, 2015: 28).

Thirty years before the foundation of the Glasgow Anti-Slavery Association by William Smeal, such early support for the anti-slave trade cause in a city where (initially covert) trade with sugar and tobacco plantations in Virginia, Carolina and New Jersey began in the 1670s is clearly a reason to admire the Glasgow moral philosophical tradition. More controversial perhaps is the part it may have

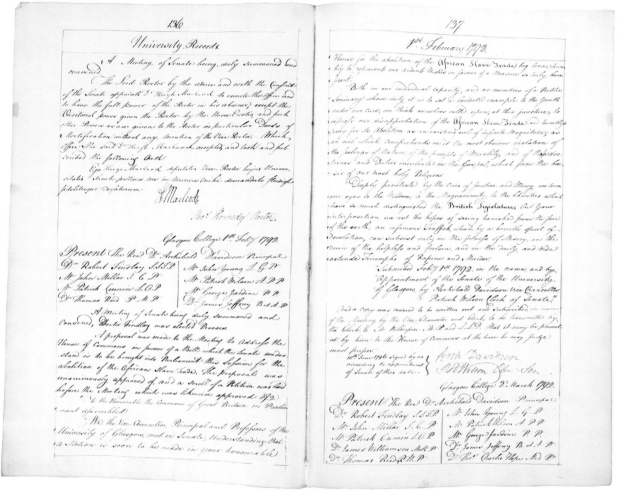

Extract from University of Glasgow Senate minutes regarding a petition to the House of Commons against the slave trade, 1st Feb. 1792. Archives & Special Collections, SEN 1/1/2 1792, Senate meeting minutes, pp. 136-37.

played in historical events that played out a few years later, when in 1798 a Republican rising broke out in Ireland led by the Society of United Irishmen. The heartland of this revolutionary movement, based on the radical principles of the French Revolution, was in Presbyterian Ulster, and among its founders, alongside the legendary Wolfe Tone, was the medical practitioner William Drennan (1754-1820), son of Thomas Drennan – a long-term Ulster friend of Francis Hutcheson. William Drennan received his M.A. from Glasgow in 1772, and among the Society of Irishmen's leaders were no fewer than ten Presbyterian ministers – all of them Glasgow graduates. Of course it is no more than speculation, but may not Glasgow

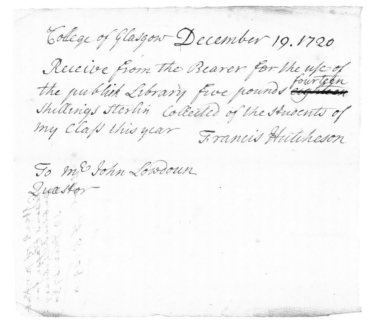

Stent of Francis Hutcheson's class for use of the public library, 19 Dec. 1720. Archives & Special Collections [GUA 58021/2/5].

Two students destined for stellar careers sign the Student Library Receipt Book for 1762-63: freshman James Wilson (1742-1798), one of the founding fathers of the USA, a signatory to the Declaration of Independence and in 1790 the first Professor of Law at the College of Philadelphia, and a founder of the Supreme Court of the United States; and second-year student 'John Tretyakoff', i.e. Ivan Tretyakov (c. 1735-1776), the future Professor of Russian Law (1767-73) at the trailblazing University of Moscow, founded 1755. Archives & Special Collections [SP Coll Acc2587].

University Library have provided the libertarian, Brand Hollis-style reading material concerning the nature of civic government that perhaps influenced their future conduct and beliefs?

While the foregoing discussion suggests that in the eighteenth century the University Library was less important than it might have been in consolidating Glasgow's growing reputation as an intellectual centre of excellence, there is on the other hand a sense in which the Library indisputably made a major contribution to the University's increasing distinction as a centre for scientific teaching and research. This was not a question solely of the book collection. Rather, from early in the century the University's collection of scientific apparatus and teaching materials appears to have been housed in the Library. Thus long before the hugely important Hunterian collection was received by Glasgow University, its Library was already in possession of scientific instruments, microscopes, globes, compasses, coins, and printing types (Emerson, 2015: 8, 9).

Library funding, however, remained a problem throughout the entire century. No doubt the size and scale of the book collection did continue to increase – partly at least because of the gifts and legacies described above – but library expenditure remained largely modest. Dickson tells us that a 1773 report declared that £177 had been spent on books and binding during the previous four years (Dickson, 1888: 53). Then the payment of debts incurred by the Library appears to have been a perennial problem.

In 1712 the Faculty directed Doctors of Medicine 'to pay ten pounds sterling for the degree' and 'appoints one half of the ten pounds for the use of the Library and things relating to medicine' (ibid.: 49). In 1768 the library committee was instructed to reveal how much the Library owed – and how its debts should be paid. But clearly the problem remained unsolved, resulting in the 1784 financial cutback noted above.

Student Access and Library Regulations

Fortunately, the continuing financial problems of the University Library in no way prevented the eighteenth-century professoriate from recognising that it needed improvement in a variety of ways. As the century went on, proposals for major changes kept being brought forward – even if their implementation often proved problematical. As early as 1712, rules (nineteen in total and still in Latin) over student access and use of the Library, charges, and related issues, were revised and amplified. Students subscribing to the Library had to sign a statement saying they would 'keep, obey and observe all the above-mentioned Laws of the said Library,' and 'thankfully pay the above specified summes of money as we shall be found liable thereunto' (Archives & Special Collections, GUA 26778, 20th December 1712, pp. 118-21). Exactly how much students should pay to have access to the Library always seems to have been a debatable issue. In the previous century a system had emerged in which the student body was divided into three social classes which determined how much individual students paid as University fees at matriculation, examinations, and graduation. This system of distinction by rank, which presumably also applied to library fees, appears to have been breaking down in the eighteenth

century. The 1712 rules revision concerned library payments, fines, times of opening and closing, and the need for professorial approval when the borrowing of books was in question. Even so, student access to the Library does appear to have been quite limited. One provision meant that students should have access to no book 'but what is proper to their present studies, and none which may have a bad influence upon their principles or morals' (Dickson, 1888: 61). That principle would have been very easy to enforce had a 1718 Faculty resolution that the 'great inconvenience,' caused by the Library's policy of lending books, should be ended simply by abandoning the practice altogether! It is hard to imagine what the students must have been up to for such a ban to be imposed by the Librarian Alexander Carmichael, but in any event the decision was rescinded a few months later – because (surprise, surprise) it 'was likely to prove very prejudicial to the students'. Nonetheless, students still needed a note from the Principal or their professor to be allowed to borrow a book (this remained the case for most of the century) – and books had also to be returned within a fortnight (Dickson, 1888: 62).

That the state of the Library remained a problem is evident from the report by the Visitors of the Library in November 1719. It finds that 'many of the books are much spoiled'; some are rain-damaged; some missing books have been recovered but not all; the catalogue locating where books are is not in good order. Hence a new catalogue is needed, and the alphabetical catalogue 'being torn in several places must be renewed' (Archives & Special Collections, GUA 8506, Report of the visitors of the library, 5 Nov. 1719). Nevertheless, Mr

Carmichael 'hath approved himself faithful and diligent in his office'. (It should be noted that that 'office' was limited in scope: as 'Librarian' the person occupying this position was responsible for the day to day running of the Library – but the Quaestor, a much more senior figure, remained in charge of the Library's finances.) Mr Carmichael was a son of Gershom Carmichael, the University's first Professor of Moral Philosophy, and as we shall see below, the Carmichael family would soon be centrally involved over the issue of how exactly the Library should be run.

In 1768 the rules and regulations of the University Library were once again revised. This time eighteen regulations were set out (Archives & Special Collections, GUA 26751, Schedule of laws and subscription rates relating to College of Glasgow Library, 1768, pp. 10-12). The first three specified the precise duties of the Librarian. Rule four concerned student behaviour: students may not 'loiter in the Library when they have nothing to do in it'. All matriculated students could borrow books 'provided they shall pay two Shillings in the Year to the Library Fund'. Professors still have to approve borrowings by members of their class, and loan periods are now spelled out: two weeks for undergraduates, four weeks for those with an M.A. degree, six weeks 'if a doctor'. The fine for failing to return a book by the due date was set at two pence per night. Books had to be returned in good condition: 'any person [who] shall write upon, scrawl or abuse, or blot' a volume will have to repay its price, and anyone lending a borrowed book to 'any other person whatever' will be fined ten shillings. Finally, the old system of library inspection was expanded:

the university Principal and Professors will take turns as 'Visitors of the Library', making weekly inspections to ensure that the Library is functioning as expected. And on an appointed day each May – by which all books have to be returned – the Library Committee will conduct an Annual Visitation.

However, in less than a year the Library found itself having to deal with a situation not anticipated in the 1768 regulations. In February, 1769, it was discovered that books were missing from the Library. The committee set up to investigate the situation reported that the books had probably been stolen: 'Suspicion of Theft landed upon Will Forrester Student in the Greek class and John McKechnie Student in the Latin class' (Archives & Special Collections, GUA 26644, Senate meeting minutes, 1st February 1769, p. 21). At first the two students denied the charges, but in the end admitted their guilt: 'They have now confessed and signed their Confessions' saying they had taken 'a great number of books at different times' which they 'disposed of to different Persons for money' (Archives & Special Collections, GUA 26644, Senate meeting minutes, 6th February 1769 – 9th February 1769, pp. 23-24). The consequences for the two were severe. They were deemed to have forfeited 'all Right and Title to their Bursaries' and fined five pounds sterling. Worse still, they were to be 'publickly expelled this University with all Marks of Ignomiy, which Sentence is to be executed […] on Saturday next at eleven o'clock' (Archives & Special Collections, GUA 26644, Senate meeting minutes, 9th February 1769, p. 25). At this point Forrester and McKechnie disappear from history, but one imagines their public humiliation, though marginally less punitive than that imposed on Patrick Wilson for the same

Extract from University of Glasgow meeting minutes regarding expelled students, 9th Feb. 1769. Archives & Special Collections [GUA 26644 pp. 24-25].

offence in 1691, would have been considered as an effective deterrent over any future putative theft of library books.

Near the end of the eighteenth century, library regulations were addressed yet again, but the changes this time were relatively minor. In December, 1796, the need for students to behave themselves in the Library was underlined: 'the Librarian has the fullest powers from Faculty to preserve the strictest order and decorum in the Library' (Archives & Special Collections, SEN 1/1/2, Senate meeting minutes, 2nd December 1796, p. 232). (Perhaps too many students were still choosing to loiter inside.) The student subscription was raised to 'five shillings at least'; the loan period for student borrowings was now three weeks

The Adam Library, Old College. Thomas Annan, c. 1870. Archives & Special Collections [Photo B26].
Following pages: Hunterian Museum, left, and the Adam Library from *Select Views of Glasgow and its environs*, engraved by Joseph Swan, 1826. The Hunterian, University of Glasgow 2016. [GLAHA 17688].

(two pence a night remained the fine for exceeding that limit) and a student could borrow three books at a time. (Faculty members could borrow up to twenty.)

Library Administration

Issues over student access to, and payment for, the Library, controls over borrowing, and student behaviour clearly kept recurring throughout the eighteenth century. But there were other equally pressing concerns. One was that of how exactly – and by whom – the Library should be run. At the opening of the century the position of University Librarian remained a junior and temporary post, usually held for a four-year period by a recent

University graduate. At times in the early decades of the century, however, it looked as though the post of Librarian had become something of a family business: between 1716 and 1736 all four sons of philosophy professor Gershom Carmichael (1672-1729) occupied the position, but an attempt to install Alexander Carmichael as a permanent librarian failed despite his having been appointed to the post on a temporary basis on three separate occasions. Even more oddly, as a result of the original 'mortification' (or endowment) by Thomas Hutcheson of Lambhill in 1641, the library appointment was a joint one, shared between the University and Glasgow Town Council who took it in turn to fill the post.

The first attempt to move away from this anomalous arrangement occurred in 1732. In January of that year the Senate agreed unanimously that the post of Librarian should become permanent, and in October the Town Council concurred. In December a new contract was drawn up by the Senate committee, and presented to the Town Council. At this point, however, things began to go wrong. In January, 1733, the University Principal announced his opposition to the change. Glasgow's Provost Andrew Ramsay was also among those who objected. In November the controversial Principal, Neil Campbell, supported by the Professor of Divinity, John Simson, maintained his opposition arguing that the suggested change would mean rejecting the wishes of the original donor. Answers in turn were drawn up to these objections, but in the end, in November, 1735, it was agreed that 'advocates should be consulted'. The result was that in February, 1736, the Lords of Session suspended the new contract (Archives & Special Collections, GUA 26639, Senate meeting minutes, 20th January 1732 – 16th February 1736, pp. 12-67). Soon afterwards William Craig was appointed to succeed Alexander Carmichael for the traditional four-year term. Given the somewhat tenuous reasons advanced for the Principal's dissent, one may speculate that his opposition had more to do with the role of the Carmichael family than with the rejection of change in itself. In any event, over thirty years later, in 1769, a committee was set up to consider a new footing for the post of Librarian, but again no progress was made. It was not until 1782 that Glasgow University finally agreed that the efficient administration of its library required the presence of a permanent librarian. Under the new arrangement, the old Hutcheson Bursary would continue to be awarded to a recent graduate, but it would no longer involve any significant Library duties, while the old Town Council's role was bought out for the sum of 200 marks meaning that the University now had the exclusive right to appoint the Librarian (Hoare, 1991: 34-35). Since 1774 Archibald Arthur (1744-1797) – who in 1796 would eventually and briefly succeed Thomas Reid as Professor of Moral Philosophy – had proved such a successful holder of the part-time position that he had been re-elected to the post by both the University and the Town Council. Thus it was Arthur who in 1784 became in theory Glasgow University's first full-time Librarian. In fact, when Reid subsequently preferred to concentrate on writing rather than teaching, Arthur also had to assume Reid's teaching duties and in 1794 this double workload obliged him to resign his librarianship (ibid.: 35). Only in 1827 did the post of University Librarian become full-time and permanent.

Library Premises

At the opening of the eighteenth century, the University Library seems to have been housed in a single room within the college. Clearly, as the University expanded its curriculum and the student body increased in size, this provision became more and more inadequate. Hence, in 1726 the Duke of Montrose, then Chancellor of the University, determined that a gift of £500 made five years earlier by the wealthy politician and philanthropist James Brydges (1674-1744), 1st Duke of Chandos and Chancellor of St Andrews University, should be used to build 'a fit house for the library' (Dickson, 1888: 45). In January 1732, a Faculty committee was set up to oversee all aspects of the building of the new

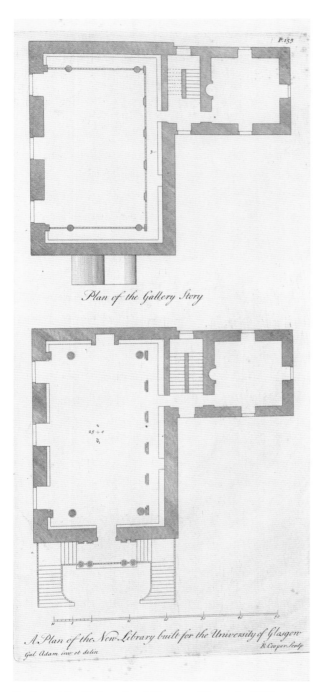

Plan of the Gallery Story

A Plan of the New Library built for the University of Glasgow

Gul. Adam inv. et delin.

R. Cooper Sculp.

Design of the University of Glasgow Library by William Adam showing sections, published in *Vitruvius Scoticus*, 1750. Archives & Special Collections [SP Coll e11].

library. Its design was soon entrusted to William Adam, then Scotland's leading architect (and father of Robert). At first progress was swift. In June, 1732, according to Faculty minutes, the builders were paid thirty-four shillings for wine drunk at the laying of the new building's foundation stone. How lovely it is to imagine Glasgow's distinguished professors, standing around, glasses of claret in hand, toasting the birth of their brand new library! However, this event proved to be something of a false dawn. William Adam had not taken long to satisfy the Library Committee with an elegant design for the new building. 'What I have in view,' wrote Adam, 'is not only Conveniency But a Magnificence Joined with Simplicity. I am not Affecting gaudy ornaments that would run to great Expense'. In a second letter to the Committee he assured his members that as long as his Library plan was exactly executed then 'you may reasonably Esteem it one of the best pieces of its kind in Britain' (Haynes, 2013: 30-31). However, both execution – which appears not to have followed Adam's plan in every detail – and expense soon became major problems. Progress was extremely slow, and in the end, more than a decade would pass before the new building was complete. While construction went on, the existing library books were distributed among the professors' houses – which must have made student use of the library more than usually difficult. However, with books restored, William Adam's new Library finally opened in 1744.

Cataloguing and Other Improvements

From a user's point of view, a library is only as good as the quality of its catalogue – or catalogues. The eighteenth century happily saw important developments in this crucial area of the college library. Such earlier catalogues as existed seem to have been only lists of books purchased or donated, or descriptions of shelf contents. In 1741, however, a committee was appointed to plan a new library catalogue, and in 1744, just as William Adam's newly reconstructed University Library opened, preparation of alphabetical and press catalogues began (Haynes, 2013: 31; Dickson, 1888: 33). These appear to have been completed by 1750, but they were not accessible in printed form. The need for more to be done to make the Library more reader-friendly was recognised once again in 1776. Back in 1771 yet another committee had been set up 'to enquire into the state of the Library, its funds etc. and to consider what measures [were] best conducive to its further improvement' (Archives & Special Collections, SEN 1/1/1, Senate meeting minutes, 15th April 1771, p. 14). No report of this committee appears in the Senate minutes, which perhaps explains why on April 1st, 1776, a new committee, consisting of the polymath scientist John Anderson (1726-1796) – well-known for his commitment to 'useful knowledge' and expanding the diversity of the student body –, Thomas Reid, and Patrick Cumin, Professor of Oriental Languages since 1761, was once again established to consider the state of the Library (Archives & Special Collections, SEN 1/1/1, Senate meeting minutes, 1st April 1776, p. 141).

This time there was no delay over the committee's report. Exactly one week later it was available – suggesting its members had long agreed what needed to be done. On April 8th it reported that further new space was required to improve the shelving and display of the books, and that a new alphabetical catalogue was needed – which

Old Library To New Library

In 1691 the Library Room was lengthened, by taking away the Bibliothecarius' chamber, and seven new cupboards installed, all with wire casements, rather than chains for security. In his *Short Account of Scotland*, and its libraries, published in 1702, Thomas Morer praises its use of wire-fronted cupboards and commends Glasgow University: 'The Library is well digested, and the Books so order'd, (not as at Edinburgh, where they are Marshall'd and distinguished according to the benefactors), but as the Sciences direct 'em'.

To meet the need for more books and storage the Senate, in 1732, finally approved the plans by architect William Adam for the New Library, a temple design, elegant and practical. Adam wrote 'you may reasonably Esteem it one of the best pieces of its kind in Brittain'.

In operation by 1744, it had a deep basement with two large teaching rooms, well lit by basket-arched windows and heated by stoves. Above, the beautiful 2-storey library room had a columned gallery around three sides. The fourth side, again amply lit by large round-headed windows, faced east over the gardens. The entrance was to the north side of the room and there was a marble fireplace in the south gable, as Adam insisted. A small room for the librarian and an inside staircase projected to the west.

Later there was an extension to the west that linked it to the main east range of the Inner Close.

Courtesy of *BUILDING KNOWLEDGE: An Architectural History of the University of Glasgow, 2013.*

should, if necessary, be printed. To help with this task, editions of the printed catalogues of 'the great libraries in Britain, such as the Advocates and the Bodleian' should be given to those involved. Under pressure from Anderson and other colleagues, Faculty agreed to the enlarging of the library space, the rearranging of the shelving of books, and the provision of new catalogues (Coutts, 1901: 281). The key figure involved in making all this happen in the following few years was the Archibald Arthur who, as we have just seen, would become the first permanent custodian of the University Library in 1784. As a scholar, Arthur's range of knowledge was exceptionally wide even for a period in which the degree of specialisation we take for granted was quite unknown. At different points in his career, before focusing on Moral Philosophy, Arthur had lectured on Logic, Humanity, Botany, and Church History. In going about the daunting task of compiling new catalogues, such a cross-disciplinary background must at least have been of some assistance. The two-volume catalogue of the Library's 20,000 books was finally published by Andrew Foulis in 1791. Involving both alphabetical and shelf listings, the catalogue appears to have been modelled on Edinburgh's Faculty of Advocates' library catalogue originally prepared by Thomas Ruddiman (1674-1757), the well-known classical scholar, philologist, printer and publisher. In 1787 the Glasgow Faculty recognised the scale and quality of Professor Arthur's endeavours by awarding him £200 (Dickson, 1888: 33).

The Foulis Press and Foulis Academy

Only three years before the opening of William Adam's new library, an event had occurred which would prove to have a significant impact upon the Library and its use. In 1741, after spending two years in England and France with his brother Andrew, Robert Foulis (1707-1776) returned to Glasgow and set up what was initially a bookselling business but soon also involved printing and publishing. Having successfully petitioned the University, in 1743 the firm of Robert and Andrew Foulis was appointed its official printers. The brothers quickly established themselves as the publishers of high quality editions of a range of books: classic works in Greek and Latin; books in French

Robert Foulis, *Notices and documents illustrative of the literary history of Glasgow during the greater part of last century*, 1886. Archives & Special Collections [Mu24-c.2 frontis].

and Italian, both in the original languages and in translation; standard works by major English authors; and new books by professors at the University. Unsurprisingly, large numbers of these books were donated to the University Library.

A few years later, Robert Foulis began to plan the expansion of his business in a new direction. In 1754 with the support of both the University and individual Scottish patrons, he opened an Academy of the Fine Arts. This bold and ambitious venture quickly proved a success and continued to flourish for twenty years. Students of the Academy were taught painting, drawing, engraving, moulding and modelling. The painter and illustrator David Allan (1744-1796), famous for his historical genre work, and James Tassie (1735-1799), the highly popular engraver and modeller, best known for his many miniature medallions of the rich and famous, both trained there. The University's key contribution to the Academy's success was its agreement to provide rooms in the College to house its various activities free of charge. However, the most important

The interior of the Foulis Academy of Fine Arts, c. 1761. Oil by David Allan. © The Hunterian, University of Glasgow [GLAHA 43390].

space made available under this arrangement was actually in the new Library building: the floor above the Library itself became the Academy workshop in which its students had room to engage in work on the different arts on offer. In September 1771 one of the University's most famous alumni made a point of visiting this room. James Boswell's book *An Account of Corsica* (1768) had made General Paoli, the Corsican patriot hostile to the French *ancien*

régime, famous throughout Europe. When Paoli visited Scotland in 1771, Boswell escorted him to Glasgow and on September 6th, together with the Polish ambassador Count Burzyuski, they visited the University. Various professors, including Thomas Reid, John Anderson, and James Moor – Professor of Greek – conducted them through the University, their tour including visits to the Foulis brothers' printing establishment and the Academy of Fine Arts in the Library building.

The Foulis Brothers

The sons of a maltman, Robert and Andrew Foulis were educated at the University and then toured England and France over 1738 and 1739 developing their knowledge of fine libraries and art studios. From the Continent they despatched books to London for retailing. On their return home, Robert established a bookshop in the High Street in 1741 (in premises later absorbed in the College's expansion), ten years before John Smith & Son started in the city. A year later they established the Foulis Press, printing, binding and publishing in many languages. The following year they were appointed as Printers to the University. The Foulis Press earned its international reputation, setting new standards in design, printing and engraving, and producing over 700 separate editions. The brothers were described as the 'Elsevirs of Britain', after the famous family of Dutch printers.

The University accepted proposals from Robert for teaching the Art of Design in the University, and provided accommodation in the Library for the brothers to open their pioneering academy of Art and Design in 1753, predating the foundation of the Royal Academy in London by fifteen years. Many of the teachers of painting, sculpture and printmaking came from the Continent, and the Academy taught men and women.

Exhibitions of work took place in the Library, and in the open in the quadrangles. The Foulis Academy ran for over twenty years and the Foulis Press continued to 1800. Many of the elegant engravings and fine books are in Special Collections at Glasgow University Library, the Mitchell Library, and at Edinburgh University Library.

The visiting party was served with food and wine in the Library (Coutts, 1909: 305).

James Boswell, son of Lord Auchinleck, is of course among the most notorious of Glasgow's eighteenth-century alumni. However, the two professors who accompanied Boswell, Burzyuski and Paoli on their tour of the University were equally flamboyant characters. Anderson ('Jolly Jack Phosphorous' as he was nicknamed) seems all too often to have been at loggerheads with most of his fellow faculty members – which explains why in his will he set out plans for an entirely new higher education institution he wished to found. Today's University of Strathclyde is the long-term result of Anderson's planning. James Moor (c. 1712 – 1779) was equally controversial. It seems that pastoral concern and loyalty to a former employer prompted this cantankerous tutor, while still only the University Librarian and no Jacobite himself, to travel to London on a vain mission to plead for clemency for his patron, senior and former student, William Boyd (1704-1746), 4th Earl of Kilmarnock, who had been captured at Culloden (Hoare, 1991: 33-34; Chambers, 1841: IV, 25). Such exceptional behaviour must have raised eyebrows at an institution firmly situated in an evangelical Presbyterian environment where the previous year professors had combined to pay the wages of a fifty-strong company of pro-Hanoverian soldiers. One leading contemporary scholar of eighteenth-century Glasgow observes: 'Episcopalian and Jacobite intellectuals were all but absent from the city after 1690' (Emerson, 2015: 136). Then again, despite being a protégé of Professor Hutcheson, a founding member of the Glasgow Literary Society, and a collaborator with the Foulis brothers over their celebrated editions of Greek and Latin classic texts, Moor too seems to have regularly fallen out with most of his University colleagues. However learned, he was argumentative and obstreperous, and on at least two occasions was formally disciplined: for a tavern brawl with Professor

John Anderson – Another place, another Library

Born in 1726, John Anderson, the liberal educator and promoter of a second university in the city, graduated with a Glasgow M.A. in 1745, became tutor and then in late 1754 Professor of Oriental Languages, additionally being the first to introduce French classes. From 1757 until his passing in 1796 he was Professor of Natural Philosophy, concentrating on physics and encouraging experiments, practical mechanics and inventions, acquiring the nickname 'Jolly Jack Phosphorous'.

Anderson also promoted vocational evening classes in the city for working class men and women, and gave voice to the need for a new place of practical learning. He said that the University of Glasgow was the wrong place for that.

In 1796 he bequeathed most of his estate to form a new institution which would specialise in practical subjects – 'a Seminary of Sound Religion; Useful Learning; and Liberality of Sentiment'. This emerged as Anderson's Institution or University, which is now the University of Strathclyde. He also bequeathed his collection of over 2,000 books to form its library.

Anderson justified the attaching of his name to the proposed institution, writing it would have 'a better title in my name on account of the property bequeathed, than Mr Stirling's small Donation of Books had to perpetuate the name of Stirling's now Extensive Library, in consequence of large subscriptions to it'. Anderson's will stipulated the structures and purposes of his later University, including, from his experiences: 'The Professors in this University shall not be permitted, as in some other Colleges, to be Drones, or Triflers, Drunkards or negligent of their duty in any manner of way'. His former university colleagues disputed some of the charges!

The number of books bequeathed in 1791 by Walter Stirling, starting the city's Stirling Library, was (only) 804, in contrast to Anderson's 2,000. Strathclyde University's Andersonian Library today, in Cathedral Street, has around 865,000 print books, 570,000 electronic books, and has purchased over 105,000 serial electronic titles

---

assaulting a student with a candlestick. In 1774 he took early retirement from his Chair – but kept his College house and salary!

Congestion and Class Libraries

On the face of it, it is surprising that just over twenty years after its inauguration it was decided that more shelf space was required in the Library. Particularly given the increasing size of the student body, should the New Library not have been designed with expansion very much in mind? Or did budgetary considerations, as ever, prevail? One possible explanation for such apparent short-sightedness was the emergence of class or Faculties' libraries in the mid-1720s.

Back in 1725 it had been resolved 'that for the encouragement of students in the Humanity class, particularly in the furnishing them with the use of books proper for them, and which cannot be easily had in this place, the Faculty allows a soume, not exceeding

Professor John Anderson, oil by William Cochrane. Courtesy of the University of Strathclyde.

twenty-five pounds sterling, belonging to the Library be applied for the said use', and 'that the books to be purchased in the first place be a

William Hunter, 1764-65. oil by Allan Ramsay. © The Hunterian, University of Glasgow.

competent number of Ciceros and Livies at the easiest prices, and of the ordinary editions, and that twenty-two pounds sterling be employed upon these books' (Dickson, 1888: 26). There is much of interest here. Does the reference to the unavailability of such books 'in this place' mean that the Old College library had never been seen as providing copies of basic texts for student use? Or is the suggestion that students were finding it hard to get hold of basic Latin texts in Glasgow bookshops? Then, in the context of the Library's perennial shortage of funds, the figures proposed here seem quite large. And what would that outstanding three pounds be spent on? Virgil or Ovid perhaps? In any event, the relatively precious nature

of these Humanity class texts is suggested by the elaborate rules and regulations that students borrowing them had to observe. The books had to be kept in a separate cupboard of their own; the Humanity Professor had to personally sanction each loan; the borrower had to hand over the price of the individual volume (presumably returned when the book was handed back); a loan was normally only for one month – but could be renewed, once the librarian had checked that the book had not been 'spoiled' in any way; and for a month-long loan the student had to pay one fortieth of the book's price (ibid.: 26). The relatively small number of students in the class probably explains this system's success.

Soon the Humanity class example was being followed both by other Arts subjects and by classes in Anatomy and Medicine. What this means is that throughout the eighteenth, and on into the nineteenth century, the University Library came increasingly to coexist with a range of separate class or subject libraries. The result inevitably was what must often have been complex issues over funding, duplication of stock, and library use and membership. Certainly the existence of these class libraries explains why as late as 1768 only around a hundred students chose to subscribe to the University Library. Yet another factor working against library membership becoming the norm for undergraduate students was the emergence of textbooks tied to individual classes or courses. Members of a class would buy their own copy of this book, and presumably many students felt that owning such books for their classes meant that library membership was an unnecessary luxury. Whatever the reason, it is

College Green showing the Library. Thomas Annan, reproduced in *University of Glasgow Old and New*, ed. William Stewart, 1891, 15. Archives & Special Collections [Old & New No. 15].

clear that throughout the eighteenth century probably a majority of students did not subscribe to the University Library.

Finally, it must be acknowledged that an account of Glasgow University Library in the eighteenth century with only a fleeting reference to its Hunterian collection will surprise many readers. After all, even today the Hunterian collection probably remains the University Library's most celebrated possession. William Hunter himself, leading anatomist, medical teacher and physician, of course lived, practised and died in the eighteenth century.

Thus it was in 1783 that he bequeathed his wonderful and unrivalled collection of manuscripts, books, coins, anatomical and natural history specimens, to the University of Glasgow, which he had attended from 1731 to 1736. However, for most of his career Hunter (1718-1783) had worked in London, and after his death his collection remained in that city. In fact it was only in 1807 that the Hunterian collection moved to its permanent home in Glasgow. Hence its importance in terms of the growth and celebrity of the University Library is a nineteenth-century story to be told in the next chapter.

Chapter 3

The Nineteenth Century – Industrial Expansion and Migration

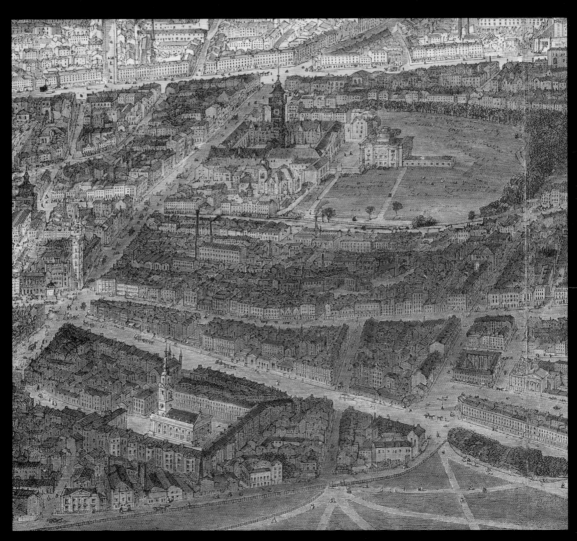

Bird's-eye view of the Old College site *circa* 1862-1863, from Thomas Sulman, 'Glasgow', *Illustrated London News*, 1864. Maps [C18:45 GLA10].

Nigel Thorp
University of Glasgow

Collections

When the Library's first printed catalogue, by Professor Archibald Arthur, was published in 1791, the book stock was around 20,000 volumes (up from around 5,600 in 1760), mainly acquired out of the University's own funds. This came to be known as the 'Old Library'. In the course of the nineteenth century various class and departmental libraries which originated before 1800 were transferred to the main Library as supplementary collections to the 'Old Library': much of this took place after the Compensation Fund was introduced in 1836 to replace the provisions of the Copyright Act. Particularly important were the collections forming the Anatomy and Medical Class Libraries, the Greek and Latin Class Library, the Ethics Class Library, and the Mathematical and Natural Philosophy Class Libraries. In 1818, however, Professor James Jeffray (1759-1848), Regius Professor of Anatomy and Botany, protested against the meagre allowance for procuring books on medical subjects for the General Library, which led to the medical professors and students raising £600 for books in a separate medical library (Coutts, 1909: 519).

By 1826 the Old Library contained over 30,000 volumes, increasing to 40,000 by 1838 (Dibdin, 1838: II, 714), with 3,000 volumes in the medical library (Coutts, 1909: 555). However, Allan Maconochie, appointed in 1843 as Professor of Civil Law and teaching the law of Scotland as well as Roman or Imperial law, was aggrieved at how little coverage there was for Law and correspondingly grateful to the Faculty of Procurators for admitting law students to their library. This led Professor Duncan Harkness Weir (1822-1876), Professor of Oriental Languages, and Clerk of Senate from 1855 to 1876, to secure a grant of £200 for the purchase of law books, to be held in a separate law library (Coutts, 1909: 391).

By far, the star attraction at the beginning of the new century was the arrival of Dr William Hunter's famed bequest to Glasgow, where it was housed in Scotland's first purpose-built public museum. Visitors flocked to it.

The library of Dr William Hunter (1718-1783), doctor and professor, born in East Kilbride, educated at the University, the leading anatomist and physician of his day, and Physician Extraordinary to Queen Charlotte, is the best-known of the Library's rare book and manuscript collections (*CHL*, 2006: II, 355, 401). His collection relates to exploration, travel and astronomy, fine art, numismatics, medicine and the natural sciences. About one third of the 10,000 books, which include 534 incunabula (books printed before 1500) and over 2,300 volumes with sixteenth-century imprints, are to do with medicine, and around two thirds of the 650 manuscripts are medieval or Renaissance in origin.

Hunter's extensive collection includes his own anatomical and medicinal studies (with a set of illustrations by Jan van Rymsdyk) and the medical and scientific papers of his mentor Dr James Douglas (1675-1742), who was Physician Extraordinary to Queen Caroline. For Thomas Dibdin in the 1830s, 'Of all the

Dr William Hunter, enamelled miniature. © The Hunterian, University of Glasgow 2016 [GLAHA 42408].

Library-visits paid by me in Scotland, whether to public or private collections, this, to the Hunterian Library, was by far the most gratifying' (Dibdin, 1838: 722).

Hunter's collection had remained in London in his house in Windmill Street after his death for the use of his assistant William Cruikshank (1745-1800) and of his nephew, Dr Matthew Baillie (1761-1823), and came to the University in 1807.

Held in the Hunterian Museum, the library (including the manuscripts) was not, however, under the administration of the University Librarian. The Hunterian Museum, with its Art Gallery, is now home to one of the largest museum collections in Britain reflecting Hunter's interests in art, archaeology, coins, anatomy and medicine, scientific instruments, natural history, rocks and minerals.

In later years the Keeper of the Hunterian, the geologist and zoologist John Young (1835-1902), Regius Professor of Natural History from 1866, worked extensively on a catalogue of the manuscripts, which was completed after his death by P. Henderson Aitken and published in 1908. The introduction to the catalogue, by Frederick Orpen Bower, FRS, the distinguished professor of Botany from 1885 to 1925, notes that Young's whole attention was focused on the manuscripts,

which may explain why the printed books did not receive similar attention at the time, but they were later added to the general catalogue. The Hunterian books and manuscripts were moved into the care of the University Librarian in 1905 (Galbraith, 1909: 25; Heaney, 1997, in Stam, 2001: I, 340).

For the period 1845-1863 there is a record of donations to the Library, listing some 750 publications, or around forty per year (Special Collections, MS Gen. 1089). In addition to 'the author', the donors include expected sources such as the Home Office, the British Government, and Lincoln's Inn, but also numbers of foreign dignitaries, like Prince Demidoff of Russia, and overseas bodies (e.g. the Universities of Uppsala and Utrecht, Frederick's University in Norway, Saint Petersburg Academy and Observatory, the Medical Board of Bombay, the East India Company, the Bombay Geographical Society, the Smithsonian Institution, and Melbourne Public Library). Clearly, the University's international reputation was continuing to rise.

Following the University's move to Gilmorehill in 1870, the Library grew substantially, to over 136,000 volumes by 1888, with 13,000 more in the Hunterian Library and 7,000 in Divinity Hall (*CHL*, 2006: II, 347-51; Dickson, 1888: 31-32). By the end of the century the Library held 175,000 volumes (Coutts reckoned 200,000 in 1909), but with many of these being volumes that contained several pamphlets or separate works, the total number of publications approached 220,000, a ten-fold increase over the century (Coutts, 1901: 51). Much of this development took place under the guidance of William Purdie Dickson, Professor of Biblical Criticism from

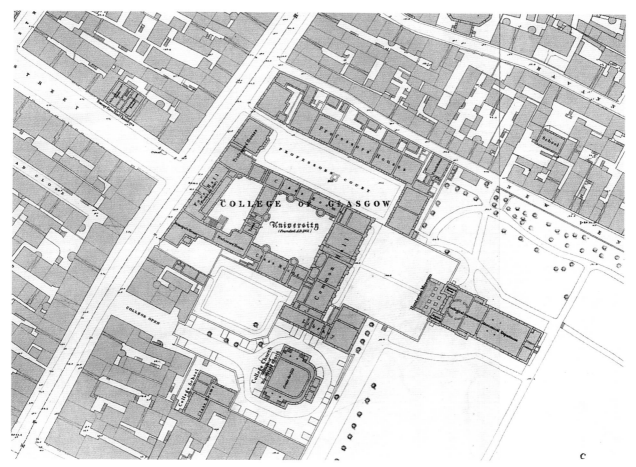

Close-up of detailed Old College layout in the High Street from Ordnance Survey Town Plan, 1857 series. GULMOPS [OS Town Plan 1857-58, Sheet VI.11,12].

1863 and subsequently Professor of Divinity, acting as Curator of the Library from 1866 to 1901, overseeing the work of the Librarian.

In 1888 Dickson became President of the Library Association, and for the Association's visit to Glasgow that year he published *The Glasgow University Library: Notes on its History, Arrangements, and Aims*, the forebear of this illustrated survey. From the earliest donations

in 1475, he outlines the history of the Library in three sections: donations and small payments on matriculation and on graduation, 1577-1709; privilege under the Copyright Act, 1710-1836; and purchase of selected books under the Compensation Fund, 1837-1888 (Dickson, 1888: 4). He notes the Library had received nearly two-thirds of its contents over the previous fifty years, including almost everything it had of modern Continental literature and science, with

The Hunterian Museum. Thomas Annan, reproduced in *University of Glasgow Old and New*, ed. William Stewart, 1891, 16. Archives & Special Collections [Old & New No. 16].

a straightforward system in place for professors to make recommendations for purchase to the Library Committee, and suggestions by other readers being entered in a book kept in the Library for the Committee's assessment.

Important collections donated in the nineteenth century include the bequest of 350 volumes in 1847 from the founder and secretary of the Maitland Club, the esteemed bookseller John Smith of Crutherland, of John Smith & Sons, the oldest booksellers in the English-speaking world (whose shops continue on academic sites including Glasgow University). His collection additionally includes a unique series of Glasgow pamphlets bound in 118 volumes (*CHL*, 2006: II, 353). This was followed in 1869 by the collection of 970 volumes of botanical literature formed by George A. Walker-Arnott (1799-1868), Professor of Botany, together with some seventy volumes in an extensive herbarium: these were purchased by the University from the Walker-Arnott trustees, with half the £700 cost being met by private subscription (Dickson, 1888: 21).

William Euing a major benefactor to the Library, from *Memoirs and Portraits of One Hundred Glasgow Men*, MacLehose, 1886. Archives & Special Collections [Sp Coll Mu22-x.5-8].

William P. Dickson, Thomas Annan, *Memorials of the Old College of Glasgow*, 1871. Archive & Special Collections [Photo B16].

William Purdie Dickson

William Purdie Dickson, Curator of Glasgow University Library from 1866 to 1901, was the University's Professor of Divinity and Biblical Criticism, 1863-1873, Professor of Divinity, 1873-1895, and Dean of Faculties, 1896-1900. A son of the manse, he was born in 1823 in Pettinain, Lanarkshire, attended school in Lanark, and studied classics as a prize-winning scholar at St Andrews University. His wife was the daughter of the acting Librarian of Edinburgh University, and her brother John Small became Librarian there from 1847 to 1886.

During a period as preacher at Grangemouth, he made a catalogue of books in the Public Library before being ordained as a minister in Cameron, Fife, in 1851. He was later Examiner in Classics at St Andrews and prepared 'Suggestions towards the Improvement of the University Library at St Andrews'.

After coming to Glasgow in 1863 as Divinity Professor, he made his mark as the Library's one and only Curator, a life-long appointment made in 1866 until his passing in 1901, rearranging all the catalogue records in a single alphabetical sequence, based on Jewett's Smithsonian rules of 1853, and producing other finding aids. Dickson won praise for his translations of Theodor Mommsen's *History of Rome and Provinces of the Roman Empire*. He was Convener of the Education Committee of the Church of Scotland from 1875 to 1888, in which year he was President of the Library Association. The William Dickson Prize for Divinity students was created by him and his wife.

One of the most substantial donations is that of the 15,000 volumes bequeathed in 1874 by the Glasgow insurance broker William Euing (1788-1874): a general collection of 12,000 volumes, and his collection of bibles, psalters, prayer books and hymn-books, and English broadside ballads, amounting to 3,000 volumes, including an overall total of 168 incunabula (Coutts, 1909: 455). Under the terms of Euing's will, books could be sold, with the 'proceeds falling to be applied partly to the provision of accommodation for the books retained, partly to their binding and repair, and partly to the purchase of other works in lieu of those sold' (*GPL*, 1966: 18). In 1874, some 1,800 duplicates from the Euing Collection were indeed sold to the Corporation of Glasgow for the newly formed Mitchell Library, with other library duplicates also being donated. Euing's music collection, with 2,500 volumes of early printed music, was originally bequeathed to Anderson's University (now the University of Strathclyde), where he had founded a Lectureship in Music

and which published a catalogue of the collection in 1878, noted for a number of idiosyncratic details. Not many years afterwards, Glasgow city librarian Thomas Mason gave his assessment of the value of the catalogue as being 'open to some question', but 'its virtues as an irritant, to

Florida Jay from *The Birds of America; from original drawings by John James Audubon,* 1838. Archives & Special Collections [Hunterian Cd.1.1-4 plate 87].

such persons as desire to consult the treasures it pretends to describe, are unmatched' (Mason, 1885: 177). The collection was transferred to Glasgow University Library in 1936.

The 8,000 volumes in the library of Sir William Hamilton (1788-1856), Professor of Logic and Metaphysics in Edinburgh University, were purchased by twenty private subscribers in Glasgow for £2,000 and presented to the Library in 1878, being kept in a separate room for consultation by students of Philosophy (Dickson, 1888: 23-24). The core of the collection consists of works on logic, aesthetics and the history of philosophy, and on Greek and Latin classical texts, with 150 editions of Aristotle alone, and thirty-two editions of the works of the famous humanist, George Buchanan (1506-1582).

Other donations noted by Dickson include a gift of some 800 miscellaneous volumes from the library of Frederick Eck, a Swiss partner in Antony Gibbs & Sons, British merchants and bankers, noted for the guano trade with South America. In later life Eck bought the Hollybush estate near Dalrymple, and his widow, originally from Glasgow, made the donation. The musical library of Thomas L. Stillie, comprising about 760 volumes, was bequeathed in 1884, and many books on engineering, mining, religious literature, Oriental literature, anatomy and physiology were gifted by a number of other families and individuals (Dickson, 1888: 24-25).

Despite this growth in donations, Dickson emphasised the need for an increase in annual funding, from the existing £750, to not less than £1,000 for current publications, especially 'the transactions of learned societies, scientific journals, and other forms of periodical literature, which are indispensable to research' (Dickson, 1888: 68-69). He made a more specific appeal for an increase in the Library's limited resources, noting in particular that university libraries in the United States were growing far more quickly, with Harvard being able to spend £8,000 annually, and Cornell receiving £140,000 from a single donor (Dickson, 1889: 15-16). In 1890, Dickson reported that the Library received many gifts from other universities and societies without being able to give anything in return, and he suggested that catalogues should be prepared of the Hunterian Library and of the Euing Bibles, these inventories also serving as potential gifts (Dickson, 1890, para. 7). Yet in the face of Dickson's efforts the University took advantage of the commutation of the compensation grant in 1890 to reduce its Library's funding (Heaney, 1997; in Stam, 2001: I, 340).

In the closing years of the century at least some further financial support was forthcoming, with a capital donation of £500 in 1894 from the Bellahouston Trust, followed by an annual donation of £100, to improve the holdings of scientific journals (Heaney, 1997; in Stam, 2001: I, 340). As Henry Heaney observes:

Dickson continued as curator and chaired a newly constituted committee as one of three members nominated by Court, the governing body. In 1897, making international comparisons, he issued The University Library: What It Is and What It Might Be. *As professor emeritus he was incensed by the University's refusal to meet its Library obligations. Rejecting a well-argued case for more shelving, the Court recommended a public appeal by the Library. Dickson replied that appeals were the Court's responsibility and that its suggested target of £60,000 was quite inadequate.*

Nevertheless the Library stock continued to grow, albeit too slowly for Dickson's liking. In 1892 William Thomson, Lord Kelvin (1824-1907), presented a collection of 3,500 pamphlets, chiefly on scientific matters. In 1895 the widow of John Veitch, Professor of Logic in the University from 1864 to 1894, presented his compilation of some 400 volumes, mostly early printed editions of medieval scholastic philosophers and including twenty-nine incunabula. A collection of almost 4,000 volumes and 1,800 pamphlets, largely of theological literature, was donated in 1900 by the trustees of the Rev. Alexander Robertson (d. 1899). Other donations were made by the British Museum and by Public Departments in Britain, its colonies, and the United States, as well as other universities and libraries, societies and scientific institutions, both at home and abroad.

Copyright and Funding

The Copyright Act of 1710 established that the Library was entitled to receive a copy of each work entered at Stationers' Hall, but the Library experienced difficulties in getting publishers and printers to acknowledge its right to free copies of books. In 1774 the bookseller John Murray had been appointed to receive books for the University from Stationers' Hall, for which he received an honorarium of one guinea a year (Dickson, 1888: 13). Many of the books recorded as having been bought between 1783 and 1815, however, should have been delivered under the Copyright privilege. Dickson observes that 'books were procured with ease in inverse ratio

of their value, and continuations, periodicals, and works with expensive plates, especially if issued in parts, were either not procured at all, or supplied imperfectly' (ibid.: 16).

In 1825 another London agent, Mr Elliot, was appointed to act for the University in securing the compliance of publishers in delivering books at Stationers' Hall for the Library (Coutts, 1909: 377), but this arrangement did not last very long.

A Royal Commission report on Scottish universities in 1831 showed that Glasgow University Library was deficient both in its contents and its administration. There was no stock-taking of holdings, and the absence of control over lending resulted in professors borrowing as many books as they wanted, returning them at any time or not at all, with an example given of one professor who between 1796 and 1827 had not returned 132 of the items he had borrowed (Miller, 1985: 47).

By modification of the Copyright Act in 1836, legal deposit was surrendered at the Scottish universities and commuted into a Compensation Fund, the Treasury making to Glasgow an annual fixed payment of £707, based on the estimated value of books procured on an average of the three preceding years (Mackie, 1954: 266-67; Miller, 1985: 52). This compensation appears to be the largest sum provided to a Scottish university, exceeding that of £630 for St Andrews, £575 for Edinburgh and £320 for Aberdeen. Five professors now met quarterly in committee to approve new orders, which largely reflected personal interests. Under an 1862 ordinance, the committee regulated the selection, ordering, loan, return, and preservation of

Steamboat on the Clyde near Dumbarton from William Daniell, *A Voyage round Great Britain 1813*, Vol.3.
Co-produced with Richard Ayton, London, 1814-25, Vol. 3. Archives & Special Collections [Sp Coll f54 p.16].

books, the approval of books held for reference only, library membership, and an annual stock inspection. Revealingly, the number of books bought from the Compensation Fund in little more than the first fifty years, 1837-1891, was 58,000, whereas the number of books received from the Stationers' Hall privilege during the preceding 125 years, 1710-1836, was just under half that number, at 28,000 (MacKenna, 1973: 240).

It was normal for books to be supplied in sheet form from the printers, and Senate added an annual grant of £100 for binding (Dickson, 1888: 50; Miller, 1985: 52-53; Fox, 2014: 132). When the firm of MacLehose was appointed in 1865 to deliver British and foreign books, they were engaged to bind them as well. MacLehose became the University printers in 1872.

At the beginning of the nineteenth century the Library revenue from all sources was about £100 a year, with the subscriptions from readers amounting to £23; annual interest received from legacies was about £43, increasing only slightly to £52 by the 1880s (Dickson, 1888: 50, 52).

In 1876 Dickson gave evidence to the Scottish Universities Commissioners that the Library needed an annual purchase grant of £1,000, rather than the £700 received at the time (Dickson, 1889: 6). He reported also that the Library did not have sufficient staff, as the numbers were kept at the lowest level possible in order to enable the purchase of more books. The expenditure on staff was £506, compared with £744 in Edinburgh, and at least £200 more was required 'to pay the librarians at a rate at all adequate to their attainments' (Dickson, 1888: 69).

The Library's funding for purchases was not, however, increased for some years. As Dickson wrote in a pamphlet he published in 1889, *The Glasgow University Library: A Plea for the Increase of its Resources*, 'while the University has received of late years numerous and liberal contributions for buildings, new Chairs and other teaching appliances, scholarships and bursaries, no addition has been made for fifty years to the resources placed at its disposal for the increase and maintenance of the Library – its most important possession, of common and permanent interest to Professors, Graduates, and Students' (Dickson, 1889: 3). There was a varying annual grant from the General University Fund of around £750, but the bulk of this was for salaries and binding, and the total sum available for the purchase of books was only around £550 (ibid.: 4). Dickson noted how few periodicals there were at Glasgow University Library compared with Oxford, and stated that Glasgow should double or treble the existing representation. The comparison with universities in the United States was even worse, with Glasgow receiving around 250 transactions and periodicals, as against 435

at Cornell University and over 1,000 at Johns Hopkins University in Baltimore. Dickson also examined university libraries in Germany and Scandinavia, where the holdings were in general several times greater than those at Glasgow, and noted that the library expenditure for each student was over £1 at Heidelberg, and over £3 at Strasbourg, whereas at Glasgow it was only 7s. 6d. Despite the recent move to new buildings at Gilmorehill, accommodation was a further issue, as the Library was 'seriously hampered' by the lack of additional cases or shelving in all the rooms, prompting Dickson to suggest the fitting-up of the Old Reading Room, for an outlay of £600-£700 (ibid.: 8-9, 12-13, 19).

Dickson recorded that he was authorised by the Senate to spend £100 annually on making up defects in the catalogue as opportunity occurred, but he added that the need to meet current demands meant that he was not able to fill more historical gaps (Dickson, 1888: 68).

Librarians repeatedly mentioned the importance of acquiring foreign publications, and the rules of 1820 directed that 'the money got from the students be employed first and principally in making up the deficiencies in the Memoirs of Foreign Academies, which ought to form a part of every university library, and which belong to all departments of science; and, secondly, that the sums paid by students in different faculties be applied to the purchase of books in these departments, the largest expenditure being on those which are most expensive and where there is most deficiency' (Dickson, 1888: 15).

In late 1834 the students themselves pointed out to the Earl of Derby, then Lord Rector, the defective state of the Class Libraries and suggested that other classes should follow the example of the students of Theology, having the power to elect 'a committee from their own body to manage the funds and select suitable publications' (Dickson, 1888: 18). Lord Derby then wrote to the Principal, Duncan MacFarlan, in January 1835, reporting that the students had suggested that the supply of foreign works should be supported by the curators of the Library being 'authorised annually to realise a

sum of money by the sale of works of no public benefit to the students, and especially of the large stock of novels and romances, which they are prohibited, by a regulation, the propriety of which they admit, from borrowing' (ibid.: 17).

Dickson later made a substantial increase to the figure he felt was necessary for the Library budget, raising it to £2,750, with no less than £500 needed for arrears of binding, and more support being needed for staff, including an

Watercolour by Mrs Jemima Blackburn, appearing on the left, showing the removal of the animal specimens by horse and cart from the old Hunterian Museum in the High Street en route for Gilmorehill. Courtesy of Allan Blackburn and family.

West Quadrangle looking North, showing the outside of the Library. Thomas Annan. Archives & Special Collections [Old & New, No. 26, reproduced in *The University of Glasgow Old and New*, ed. William Stewart, 1891, 26.]

increase in the salary of the Librarian, which was below that in other institutions (Dickson, 1890: paras. 8-10).

Given his decades of energetic support of the general purposes of the Library, it is nonetheless somewhat surprising to see that, as late as 1899, Dickson argued against giving students free access to the stacks of the Library by asking rhetorically: 'Why should he [i.e. the typical student] be brought into contact possibly not merely with rubbish, but with garbage? Why should he have to run the risk of being distracted, perplexed, and, it might be, led astray amidst the possibilities of a large and miscellaneous aggregation?' (Dickson, 1899; *CHL*, 2006: III, 340). Eventually, in an untidy compromise, a new regulation permitted access to the shelves for approved students, but only in their own subject area. Other books had to be fetched by library staff (Heaney, 1997; in Stam, 2001: I, 340).

Fees

At one point in the early part of the nineteenth century, the contribution from fees allocated to the Library constituted almost the only fund in the hands of the Senate. When this body was called upon in 1840 to pay the very considerable costs (£1,684) of an unsuccessful legal action with the Faculty of Physicians and Surgeons over the degree of Bachelor of Surgery, its only recourse was to use the assets of the Library, which was not only robbed of its revenue but compelled to pledge some of its books as security for a loan, and for many years the library funds had to be used to pay off the interest and the reduction of the principal, with the liability ending only in 1857 (Miller, 1985: 53}.

From 1818 one half of the money from medical degrees was to be spent on the purchase of medical books, which as a result of an 1834 modification of this instruction went partly to the University Library, and partly also to the Medical Library. By 1834 this sum amounted to £2 out of the £15 then charged for the degree.

The annual six shillings paid by students from 1818 for access to the Library was increased under the rules for 1820-1822 to seven shillings for the winter, with an additional 3s. 6d. during the summer, and students then had a right to borrow books on depositing a reasonable sum before taking them out. Three shillings out of the seven paid by each student were later made over to class libraries (Dickson, 1888: 27).

A number of students nonetheless complained in 1832 to the Rector, Henry Cockburn, that while the subscription of seven shillings was strictly enforced for 'gown and theological students', and in addition the theological students paid seven shillings a year to the library connected with the Divinity Hall, this levy was evaded by the great majority of law and medical students. The general arrangements on the payment of fees lasted, however, until the Commission of 1858 merged all such payments in the uniform matriculation fee of £1, entitling students to use the Library. Members of General Council using the Library paid 10s. 6d. from that date, as did those admitted as Special Readers (Dickson, 1888: 49-50).

Dickson commented in 1888: 'It has been suggested that the deposit of a pound may act as a hindrance; but it has not of late years been made a matter of practical complaint, and it affords the best means of securing the due return of books' (Dickson, 1888: 65). The earlier thefts of books from the Library, which in 1691 earned Patrick Wilson three months in prison and expulsion from the University, and a recurrence in 1769, had evidently not been entirely forgotten (Durkan, 1977: 123).

By 1876 in keeping with the advance of knowledge, scientific periodicals alone were five times more numerous than they had been thirty-five years earlier, something particularly overwhelming since the role of a University Library was to maintain an extensive series of the transactions of learned societies, and scientific journals. What had changed since the early years of the century, however, was that the previous payment of specified sums to the Library from graduation fees and matriculation fees had been discontinued. Large sums of money had come to the University for buildings, new Chairs, scholarships and bursaries, but hardly any were passed to the Library. By the

1880s the situation was becoming intolerable, the Library's funding for purchases having been effectively frozen at around £750 per annum for the previous fifty years.

Following the introduction of the Humanity Class library around 1725, other small libraries had been constituted for other Arts classes, and also for Anatomy and Medicine, Mathematics, Natural Philosophy and Ethics. Dickson noted in 1888, that 'considerable difficulties were experienced in connection with their management', and that while one professor, in his evidence before the Commission in 1827, thought them 'valuable and manageable', another, Professor Walker, 'disapproved of them because of the difficulty of keeping the books and taking charge of them' (Dickson, 1888: 26). Before long, the contents of the class libraries were merged partly with the General University Library and partly with the Reading Room.

The only survivor retaining a separate existence in the late nineteenth century was the Divinity Library, which had been founded in about 1744 and was supported 150 years later by an annual payment of 2s. 6d. from each reader via the Matriculation Fund. Dickson noted that it 'has suffered much from loss of books and other difficulties incident to its administration' and took the view that it also would work more conveniently and efficiently 'in connection with the general library' (Dickson, 1888: 27).

Catalogues

Prepared under the direction of the Librarian William Fleming (1794-1866), a supplement to Archibald Arthur's 1791 printed catalogue of the Library was published in 1825 taking account of the acquisitions made in the interim. Some fifteen further printed supplements followed between 1837 and 1860, but the inconvenience of having to consult so many sources led to the creation of a single alphabetic series made by cutting up two copies of the printed catalogue and supplements, with three manuscript supplements for books added between 1858 and 1862. In 1866, in his capacity as Convenor of the Library Committee, Dickson submitted the outlines of a plan for making a full inventory and preparing a new catalogue, as well as listings by pressmark and classification. The Senate supported the proposal and conferred on Dickson the special appointment of Curator to put it into effect, but it would be some twenty years before he found time to complete all the work required. Dickson oversaw the whole process, checking all titles listed against the books, and preparing them for printing in four columns on one side of the paper, so that the individual titles could be cut into slips as required and pasted into the appropriate volumes. The shelf-marks from the old arrangement of books were printed on the inner margin, and the outer margin was reserved for the new shelf-mark and donors' names. Some 20,000 cross-references between authors and other contributors such as editors were also included. Additional columns were inserted in the bound volumes to allow new titles to be inserted.

This guard-book catalogue enabled the full content of the library to be recorded, thus minimizing unnecessary purchases that would later prove to duplicate existing holdings. It was intended that it could be updated every twenty years or so and, remarkably, it was still in use in the early 1980s. In 1888 this catalogue ran to twenty folio volumes.

A set of titles was used for making a classified catalogue, allowing the arrangement of books according to subjects, following the division of Faculties and Chairs, in twenty-five volumes, all provided in addition with indexes, and in 1888 it was expected that the process would need five or six further volumes to be completed. Glasgow's city librarian Thomas Mason had wanted to include 'an accurate and adequate description' of the Library's treasures in his survey of *Public and Private Libraries of Glasgow*, 1885, but the authorities declined because the Library was still in the throes of the cataloguing process (Mason, 1885: 7). This inability to cooperate with Mason's project was perhaps fortunate, since, once the cataloguing process was complete, Dickson noted that, as well as showing 'at a glance' what the contents of most departments of the Library were, the classified catalogues could also be seen, 'unhappily, to suggest to the expert its manifold shortcomings' (Dickson, 1888: 25).

It was recognised that although the comprehensive catalogue was vital for academic and professional readers and for Library staff, the students needed something more concise, combining author and subject entries, concentrating on the most recent and most useful books likely to be asked for. A handy catalogue of some 20,000 entries, including a list of journals and other periodicals received, was accordingly compiled by James Lymburn, the Librarian from 1878 to 1905, and issued to students from 1887 at the price of one shilling.

There was still, however, a call for the development of separate class libraries, such as that for students of Moral Philosophy, for which a list of desiderata was drawn up in 1895 by William Ker and Robert Balloch and a

From *The Glasgow Herald*

An additional free public library?

As the subject of the necessity of Glasgow having an additional free public library has been much discussed of late at some of our public meetings, and as the examples of Manchester and Liverpool have been cited to show how superior to Glasgow these towns are placed in respect of libraries, I beg leave to say that, so far from the said towns possessing each respectively public and institutional libraries of greater extent than Glasgow, that, on the contrary our city libraries contain more volumes of books than the libraries of Manchester and Liverpool put together. What a splendid library is contained within the walls of our university, and how little advantage does the public of Glasgow derive from it. – SENEX

Glasgow Herald, 1st November 1860

Professor Bradley's declaration

The annual meeting in 1890 of the Stirling's and Glasgow Public Library referred to Glasgow City Council still being dilatory in agreeing to form a Free Library, to be paid for by local ratepayers. When visiting Liverpool, Professor Bradley often heard that city describe itself as the Second City of Empire, which made him say there:

'Don't talk about being the second city of empire until you have a university such as the University of Glasgow. Perhaps I might say here "Don't talk about being the second city of empire until we have a great free library like the library in Liverpool."'

Glasgow Herald, 9th April 1890

catalogue then published in 1899. In addition, special catalogues were issued for periodicals, and separately for a number of individual collections, including the Euing, Hamilton, Simson and Walker-Arnott collections.

Following an ordinance of the University Commissioners, a check of holdings was ensured by an annual recall of books in April, which was seen as a means of reducing losses ('from which the Library has greatly suffered in its earlier history') to the minimum. The general recall ensured that, if any books had been lost, they were 'easily traced and recovered from, or replaced by, the losers' (Dickson, 1888: 39).

A decision was also made in 1882 to buy the new catalogue of the Library of the British Museum, but when it was published in 1884, the Universities of Edinburgh, St Andrews and Aberdeen were found to have received free copies. There followed a campaign supported by the industrialist, politician and future Rector Joseph Chamberlain, James Balfour and Archibald Primrose, 3rd Earl of Rosebery, who were all trustees of Glasgow University, and the Library was also provided with a free copy.

Reading Room Facilities

By 1827 there were 458 students (out of a total student population of 1,027) who subscribed to the rules of the Library allowing them to make use of its services, whereas in 1768 there had only been around a hundred who did so. On the recommendation of the Rector, the celebrated poet Thomas Campbell (1777-1844), who noted that in German universities 'the library rooms were constantly half filled with students', a Reading Room was established for them from 1827, and in 1833 the Senate resolved that additional accommodation should be provided for their benefit, allowing them to consult books within the Old College library in a dedicated Reading Room, furnished with a special collection reserved for the use of readers

(Dickson, 1888: 27-28; MacKenna, 1973: 22-23). The special collection was obtained partly from the aggregation of the class libraries, and partly by purchase.

Under the regulations of 1796, professors could borrow twenty volumes, and students three volumes, with a fine of twopence per night imposed for every book kept out more than three weeks, though in 1818 the regulations reduced the entitlement of students to two volumes. Library hours were from 11 a.m. to 2 p.m., and the days for giving out books on loan were Monday, Wednesday and Friday, while Tuesdays and Thursdays were designated days for receiving returns. When a Commission was set up in 1826, a petition signed by twenty-six students raised three grievances: (1°) that the payment of seven shillings for access and a deposit of £1 was especially hard for the poorer students; (2°) that for some unknown cause the Deputy Librarian declared himself unable to give to the students many valuable modern publications in science and literature; and (3°) that works of narrative fiction and drama in English were prohibited, while they were permitted in foreign or ancient languages. Two students examined in support of the petition claimed that there was only one catalogue that they were allowed to use, and they might have to wait an hour before they were given access to it. Rather side-stepping the issues in his reply, the Librarian, William Fleming, simply stated that the regulations on the payment of penalties were not enforced.

Undergraduate access to the Library had at one time been given as a privilege for seniority, after a personal interview with the librarian

(*CHL*, 2006: III, 339). A Royal Commission in 1852 examined the different practices of university libraries in allowing access to collections, including whether books could be borrowed, as they could at Cambridge, or not, as at Oxford (*CHL*, 2006: III, 323-324), but there was apparently no move towards general entitlement allowing undergraduates to access collections at Glasgow. Graduates were given permission to use the library from 1857 – a facility that was naturally extended to Arts postgraduates and Research Fellows when the University admitted them in 1889 (Coutts, 1909: 404, 460, 555).

Cartoon by Alexander S. Boyd showing the Balfour v. Aberdeen Rectorial Campaign of 1905, from *Glasgow Men and Women, a selection from the sketches of Twym*, London, 1905. Archives & Special Collections [Mu23-x.4].

New provision was made from 1870 with the University's move to Gilmorehill. In his re-evaluation of the Library in 1889, however, Dickson referred to 'the imperfectly lighted Reading Room' as 'the most conspicuous failure of the new buildings'. This led to the provisional occupation of the Museum Lower Hall, with accommodation for 300 readers (Dickson, 1888: 47; MacKenna, 1973: 24). This change of use, however, removed the Lower Hall from the purposes of the Museum, reducing its provision to display collections, and this situation could only be addressed by providing either a new Reading Room, or a new museum building to allow the Library to remain in the lower hall.

Students had their own views as well, and a letter to *the Glasgow Herald* from one of them in the first year at Gilmorehill complained of the cold: 'The general Reading Room is so cold that unless one gets near the fire – which, by-the-by, is no easy matter – he [the average student] has to sit wrapped up, just as one requires to be in such weather out of doors'.

In the 1880s the Reading Room held about 2,200 volumes, with a substantial number of works of reference provided at his own expense by lawyer, bibliophile and Dean of Faculties, Dr Alexander McGrigor (1827-1891), following recommendations by professors in their respective departments. To prevent crowding, on entering the room each reader received a tally designating which table he should sit at, and he was required to return it when he left. These Reading Room regulations were introduced in 1884 as a result of numerous complaints about noise and disturbance.

By 1887 the number of students using the Reading Room was 1,136, while 483 students borrowed books from the General Library, and the number of other borrowers (Professors, Assistants, Members of General Council and Special readers) was 184. Students of Divinity had a class library of their own, and students of Law continued to have access to law books in town (*CHL*, 2006: II, 359; Dickson, 1888: 65). A new student union, the Students' Representative Council, was formed in January 1885, and in 1895, after representations from the SRC, the Library Committee lengthened the opening times of the Reading Room by one hour (Moss, Munro, Trainor, 2000: 79, 81).

Student life, apart from studies and fees, now embraced the many clubs and sporting associations formed at Gilmorehill and included the hectic Rectorial campaigns.

Buildings

The most significant event for the Library in the nineteenth century, as indeed for the University as a whole, came with the move of the entire campus from the High Street in the city centre to Gilmorehill in 1870.

The industrialisation of the city in the first half of the nineteenth century provoked the Principal, Dr Duncan MacFarlan (1771-1857), to deplore the environment of the college before a Select Committee of the House of Lords, and in the view of the Superintendent of Police, James Smart, the area around the High Street had become one of the worst districts of the city for the character of the inhabitants, with crimes and disorder occurring on a daily basis.

Such views encouraged a move to the cleaner and more fashionable West End, which had been developing apace since the early 1840s. An initial scheme for transferring the University to an entirely new site was approved by Parliament in 1846, but it came to nothing. In 1863, however, the University agreed plans to sell the whole of its site on the High Street to the City of Glasgow Union Railway Company, for £117,500, with further financial support coming both from public subscription (£82,450 from 150 subscriptions) and from a matching Parliamentary grant (Mackie, 1954: 267; Dickson, 1888: 51). The University was soon to purchase some forty-three acres of the lands of Gilmorehill for £65,000, and, after a competition, architect George Gilbert Scott was commissioned to draw up plans, with the building work beginning in 1866.

BLOCK PLAN OF THE NEW BUILDINGS.

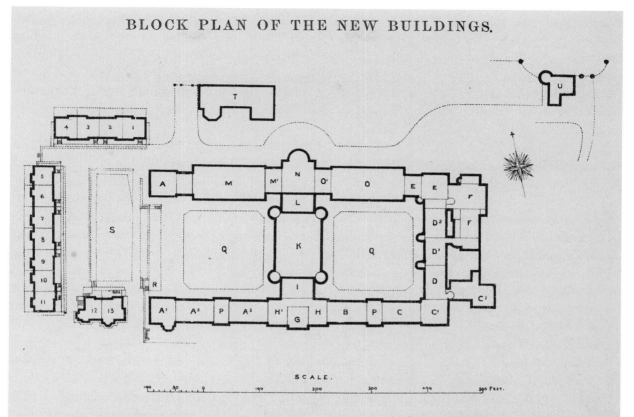

SCALE.

A. Greek, Logic, and Moral Philosophy Class Rooms in the three floors.

A^1. Latin, Mathematics, and Engineering and Mechanics.

A^2. English Literature and Astronomy (in Attics, Engineering and Mechanics Work Rooms).

A^3. Physical Laboratory, (and above the Archway P.) Natural Philosophy Class Room and Apparatus Room.

B. Law Class Rooms and Examination Hall (also above P.).

C. Hebrew, Church History, and Biblical Criticism Class Rooms (in Attics, Divinity Hall Library), and in part Chemistry.

C^1. Chemistry Class Rooms, Divinity Hall.

C^2. Chemistry Laboratories (and in part below D.).

D. Medical Jurisprudence Class Room and Laboratory, Midwifery Class Room, &c.

D^1. Physiology Laboratories and Class Room, Practice of Physic Class Room.

D^2. Botanical Laboratory, Materia Medica Class Room. In Attics over D, D^1 and D^2., Natural History Store Rooms, &c.

EE. Natural History, Surgery, and Hunterian Anatomy Collections.

FF. Anatomy Class Room and Laboratories, &c., extending also below D^2 and E.

G. Tower, Principal Entrance, Clerk of Senate's Office, &c.

H. Staircase and Corridor.

H^1. Senate Room and Corridor.

I. Matriculation Office, Cloak Room, Randolph Hall.

K. Cloisters and Bute Hall.

L. University Court Room, Antiquities Room, Hunterian Coins Room, Randolph Staircase.

M. Library Halls, Upper and Lower.

M^1. Library Service Room and Ante-rooms.

N. Students' Reading Room below, Central Hall of Hunterian Museum above.

O. Hunterian Museum Halls, Upper and Lower.

O^1. Ante-rooms, &c., of Museum.

PP. Entrances to East and West Quadrangles (QQ).

R. Old College Stair.

S. Professors' Court and Residences of Principal and Professors (1 to 13).

T. Students' Union.

U. North East Lodge, Naval Architecture Class Rooms.

Block Plan of the New Buildings, including M: Library Halls, Upper and Lower, and M1: Library Service Room and Ante-Rooms. Archives & Special Collections [RX 152, p. xxxiv].

The Library was to hold 20,000 square feet of shelving, enough to accommodate a further fifty years of collecting at the 1864 rate. Service rooms were to be provided for Library staff for the first time, and as well as a cloakroom and toilets, there was to be a reading room for a hundred readers (Haynes, 2013: 57-58).

The costs of the move from the High Street were of course substantial. According to Haynes:

> *The total cost of the project in 1877, including the land purchases, was estimated at £427,856, of which the larger ticket items of construction were as follows: the 25 classrooms at £95,000; the Museum and Library at about £36,000 each; the Hunterian Library and the Student Reading Room below it at £21,000; the tower/administration block at £32,000 and the stairs and corridors at £30,000.* (Haynes, 2013: 77).

The Gilmorehill buildings were far from complete when the University moved in and work stopped in May 1871 when money ran out, with the tower lacking its upper levels and the Great Hall complete only to ground level (ibid.: 79-80). The final full cost of the new building was £500,000, equivalent in today's value to £267 million, and that the fundraising campaign – which lasted until the 1880s – raised £280,000, equivalent to £150 million today, from donations, but excluding government grants. In the Report of the Scottish Universities Commission in 1877 it was recommended that the outstanding deficit of almost £20,000 should be met in part by the sale of the coins in the Hunterian Museum and rare books from the Library, even if the actual debt could be cleared

by some other means. Fortunately, although Professor John Young advocated the sale of coins, the following year the debt was found to be somewhat lower than expected, at £12,575, and the priceless collections were kept (Mackie, 1954: 286).

In the new campus the Library was located on the north side of the west quadrangle (in the section of the Gilbert Scott building subsequently occupied by the staff dining rooms, telephone exchange and part of the Hunterian Museum), and the old Adam building in the High Street was pulled down in 1887. The area set apart for the Library included a ground floor, an upper hall with gallery, and an excavated basement of half the breadth, together with some smaller rooms at each end. There was shelving for 100,000 volumes, with room for a total of 180,000: this was estimated by Dickson to provide enough space for the following fifty years, but was followed by an almost annual request to Court for the provision of more bookcases (Heaney, 1997; in Stam, 2001: I, 340).

Following the move to Gilmorehill, some 3,000 books were laid aside as duplicates, and while some were sold, around 2,000 books were selected by the librarian of the Mitchell Library, which had opened in its initial location in 1877 (Dickson, 1888: 71).

Several difficulties followed the move. Dickson and the Librarian of the day, Robert Spears, had stated in a planning memorandum that the new library 'should be isolated as far as possible, so as to diminish the risk of fire, and constructed throughout with special precautions against that risk' (ibid.: 46). The new building was not

Robert Spears, 1843-1878, University Librarian, 1867-1878. Archives & Special Collections [UGC87/5/1].

isolated, however, but had class-rooms and a building annexed to it, and the risk of fire was not thought to be reduced by the provision of an open shaft with a wooden staircase leading from the basement to the second floor. Dickson and Spears had also asked that the building should be heated with hot water pipes and well ventilated, only to find that the heating was provided by hot air flues, some of which lay beneath the basement and which brought in the dust and sooty smoke of Glasgow, not to mention occasional moisture evaporation from water in the underground chambers; and this system was not replaced by hot water pipes for some years. They had also recommended that light iron galleries should provide access to the upper shelves on the ground floor, but these were not built, with the result that a large area of space for the storage of books could not be used. Finally, they had further advised that the bookcases should be a uniform size, so that books could easily be moved from one case to another, only to find that the transfer of books from one case to the next was hampered by there being a difference of several inches in the height of alternate cases. In addition, they had suggested that the reading room should be well provided with light, but daylight entered the original room from only one end, so that for much of the winter it was necessary to use gas, which was not good for the general air quality of the room (ibid.: 47).

Women's Education

The Protestant Reformation in Scotland had stressed the need for universal education, regardless of social class or gender, with John Knox insisting on the spiritual equality between women and men, but it was only in the latter part of the nineteenth century that the admission of women to Scottish universities was seriously considered (McDermid, in Purvis, 2000: 96). Indeed the introduction and development of higher education for women has been the most significant event for the University and Library since the move to Gilmorehill.

The professorial triumvirate of John Nichol, Edward Caird and his elder brother (and later Principal) John Caird had already campaigned for the education of women from the 1860s, and lectures for women began in Glasgow in 1868 under a scheme launched by Mrs Jessie Campbell of Tullichewan (1827-1907), the wife of a prosperous wholesale draper, but there were no courses which offered degrees or diplomas. In 1877 the Association for the Higher Education of Women in Glasgow and the West of Scotland was founded under the Presidency of Queen Victoria's daughter, Princess Louise, Marchioness of Lorne. In 1883 the Association was incorporated as a college, and in 1884 the classes held by Queen Margaret College were moved to North Park House, purchased by Mrs Isabella Elder, a noted philanthropist and supporter of women's education, which now took the name of the college.

Professor Edward Caird
cartoon from *The Bailie*.
Archives & Special
Collections [Sp Coll Bh12-d].

The first Head of College was Janet Galloway (1841-1909), who was succeeded in 1909 by the suffragist Frances Melville (1873-1962). In 1892 the Scottish University Commissioners, under the powers of the Universities (Scotland) Act of 1889, allowed women to matriculate at the University, and in 1893, one year after the College merged with the University, the Library arranged for the loan of reference books to Queen Margaret College. Initially, the trailblazing female students were heavily outnumbered (131 women matriculated as students in 1892-93, alongside 2,049 men), but their presence grew steadily. Having attended University courses taught at Queen Margaret College, no fewer than four women became the first to graduate in medicine at any Scottish university in 1894; the first female Glasgow Arts graduate, Isabella Blacklock, followed a year later; and Ruth Pirret, the first female BSc, graduated in 1898. The first women were appointed to the University's teaching staff in 1908, when female students finally won admittance to the Library at Gilmorehill (to the slight unease of the Librarian James L. Galbraith, who chose to delegate to a female colleague the task of overseeing women readers' behaviour). By 1914 women accounted for almost a quarter of full-time Glasgow students, and by 1919-20 the number of women students had increased to 1,027 (Moss, Munro, Trainor, 2000: 76, 109). Today with over 27,000 Glasgow students the average female to male ratio among new entrants has reached 60% to 40%. This gender gap, found throughout the world, is not yet matched anywhere by the distribution of leadership roles in wider society.

Librarians

A number of 'Keepers of the Old Library' appointed by the Council into the nineteenth century continued to receive income from the Hutcheson bequest of 1641, but these appointments were 'grace and favour' sinecures rather than active posts and the recipients had no part to play as Glasgow University Librarians.

By 1800 the salary for the Librarian appointed by the University had been increased from £22 a year, with some extra allowance for entering additional books in the catalogue, to £40, including remuneration for entering the additions (Coutts, 1909: 328).

Holding the post of Librarian for twenty-eight years from 1795 to 1823, Lockhart Muirhead was appointed Professor of Natural History in 1807 and supervised the removal of the Hunterian collection from London. He later became the first Keeper of the Hunterian Museum in 1823 (Hoare, 1991: 41). According to Mackie (1954: 267), he was seen in relation to the Library as a 'part-time' Curator. He was nevertheless probably the first serving Librarian to sit on Senate, albeit by virtue of his Regius Chair rather than as Librarian, and, unlike his immediate predecessor William McTurk but like Archibald Arthur before him, can be seen as a transitional figure, marking a break in the

First Women Graduates

Thanks to the formation of Queen Margaret College some years earlier, in July 1894 Alice Cumming, Margaret Dewar, Marion Gilchrist, and Dorothea Lyness became the first women to graduate in Medicine from a Scottish university.

Alice Cumming was the daughter of a medical doctor in Glasgow.

Margaret Dewar was the daughter of a tea planter in Ceylon. She became a hospital doctor at Dumfries, followed by Gartnavel, and then a surgeon at Sheffield before moving to the United States.

Marion Gilchrist was the daughter of a farmer in Bothwell. She was an active suffragette, and an early motoring enthusiast. She became a general practitioner in the West End of Glasgow, then an eye surgeon at the Victoria Infirmary and at Redlands Hospital for Women.

Dorothea Lyness from County Antrim was also an active suffragette, and doctor at Glasgow's Royal Samaritan Hospital for Women. In 1913 she was awarded the Silver Suffrage Hunger Strike Medal for Valour and Cat and Mouse.

They were quickly followed by more graduates in Medicine and then the first women graduates in Arts, then Science, and after the turn of the century in Education, Divinity and finally Law.

Completed in 1871 for John and Matthew Bell, proprietors of the Glasgow Pottery, North Park House and its extensive grounds on what became Queen Margaret Drive were purchased in 1883 by Isabella Elder, widow of the shipbuilder John Elder, as the home for the women's college, Queen Margaret College. She continued to offer moral and financial support for the development of higher education for women and also endowed two Chairs at the University of Glasgow. Teaching continued until 1934 at the College, which became the home of BBC Scotland in 1935, and all classes were transferred to University of Glasgow premises at Gilmorehill. Women were segregated in the Library reading room until the 1950s.

Some of the first female students, 1890-1895. Archives & Special Collections [DC233/2/22/2/71].

Margaret Dewar, MBCM, one of the first female graduates, 1894. Archives & Special Collections [DC233/2/22/2/9].

Marion Gilchrist, MBCM, the first female medical graduate in Scotland, 1894, Archives & Special Collections [DC233/2/22/].

sequence of brief tenures as Glasgow University Librarian while prolonging the local tradition whereby Library duties were combined with those in other academic fields, albeit almost invariably at different stages in a person's career.

William Fleming (1794-1866), appointed Assistant Librarian from 1818 to assist in measures for exacting contributions from students, became Librarian in 1823, holding the post until 1827.

He would subsequently become Professor of Oriental Languages in 1831, Vice-Rector in 1836 and Professor of Moral Philosophy in 1839, a post that he held until his death in 1866 and which earned him the nickname 'Moral Will' (Coutts, 1909: 377; Hoare, 1991: 41).

Fleming was followed by William Park, first an assistant, then sub-librarian for eighteen months in 1826-27, and Librarian from 1827 until 1845, initially at a salary of £70. He is thought to have been the last Librarian to be required to provide the full security of £2,000 for the faithful discharge of his duty. His salary was raised in 1830 to £85 (Coutts, 1909: 404).

Park was in turn succeeded by Nathaniel Jones, 1845-1863, previously assistant librarian to the Faculty of Physicians and Surgeons of Glasgow, with a salary of £84, half paid by the Faculty and half by the Senate, and the requirement for security reduced to £1,000. Jones was also appointed Registrar of the General Council in 1858.

While the subsequent tenure of Robert Scott, 1863-67, as Librarian seems to have been unremarkable, his successor, Robert B. Spears (1843-1878), previously an Assistant Librarian, worked assiduously on cataloguing during his eleven years as Librarian. A Glasgow confectioner's son, he was appointed University Librarian at twenty-four in 1867, two years after matriculating to read English and Mathematics to which he soon added Mental Science and Logic studied at the Glasgow Athenaeum. Despite poor health, he prepared a report for the Library Committee on the 'very imperfect' state of the catalogues he had inherited, which

led to William Purdie Dickson proposing his plan to Senate for re-organising and re-cataloguing the Library. Spears was in charge of the important move of the Library in 1870 from the Old College to Gilmorehill, 'without the loss of a single book', and contributed a paper on the Library's catalogues to the first conference of librarians held in London in 1877 (Hoare, 1991: 37).

Having served as an Assistant Librarian since 1867, James Lymburn assumed the role of Librarian in 1878, holding the post until 1905 (Coutts, 1909: 377, 455; Dickson, 1888: 58-59; Hoare, 1991: 41). He supervised the general arrangements for shelving and general cataloguing, while Dickson organised the classified cataloguing, and in 1887 he compiled the select catalogue of 20,000 books and periodicals for student use. Yet despite his also being 'an inexhaustible mine of information' on the Euing Bibles, Dickson noted in 1889 that the Librarian of Glasgow University received only half the salary of his counterpart at Edinburgh (Dickson, 1889: 20; Galbraith, 1909: 31). In 1900 the total number of Library staff was still only ten (MacKenna, 1973: 24).

In general terms, the turn of the century was marked by what Principal Robert Herbert Story (Professor of Ecclesiastical History, 1886-1898, and Principal, 1898-1907) saw as a crisis of funding, increased by falling student numbers, and in 1900 he launched an appeal to overcome both. As well as new buildings, extra teaching staff and up-to-date equipment, he sought to provide further support for the Library, including a new Reading Room for the students. The international status of the University was

Lord Kelvin's Inventions Jubilee Celebration held in the Library, 1896, from *Cassier's Magazine: Engineering Illustrated* Vol. XVI, July 1899, p. 148. [Photo by Field, Glasgow].

nonetheless celebrated the following year by the Ninth Jubilee celebrations of 1901 (Moss, Munro, Trainor, 2000: 92-97).

Chapter 4

The Twentieth Century –
War, Peace and Opportunity

Glasgow International Exhibition 1901, showcasing progress and power.

Part 1 (1901-1919)

Nigel Thorp
University of Glasgow

The death of William Dickson in 1901 marked a significant moment in the history of the Library. With around 400,000 books in 1902, as well as periodicals, pamphlets and continuations, the main collections were supported by departmental and class libraries administered by heads of department but under the control of the University Librarian (Mackie, 1954: 302). These satellite libraries had expanded owing partly to the cramped conditions of the main Library, which was already full, with the annual intake occupying the equivalent of 140 shelves, and 28,000 volumes of journals scattered round the building. The Library sub-committee recommended that steel stacking should be put in place, but this advice was not acted on for twenty years, making Glasgow the last Scottish university to adopt it (Heaney, 1997; in Stam, 2001: I, 340). The development of University departments, discussed below, also contributed to the resurgence of class and departmental libraries with the attendant problem of duplicated holdings.

Unsurprisingly, funding was also a continuing issue. The Library still received the annual donation of £100 from the Bellahouston Trust, mentioned above (Chapter 3), and the establishment of the Carnegie Trust for the Universities of Scotland would provide substantial further support for the Library. The Trust was set up in 1901 with funds of US$10 million, half the income to be used in support of university facilities and research, including buildings, and half to be used for supporting students of Scottish birth or extraction (Coutts, 1909: 472; Moss, Munro, Trainor, 2000: 97, 107-08; and Brown and Moss, 2001: 54, 72-73). The initial annual grant from the Carnegie Trust for the Library was £480, but despite this grant, the Bellahouston grant and balances carried forward, total expenditure in 1903 came to only £1,450, with just £600 available for new purchases, and the Library was judged to be under-funded. Within a few years the Carnegie grant more than doubled, to £1,000 a year, but even at that level, funding was still insufficient (Coutts, 1909: 455; Heaney, 1997, in Stam, 2001: I, 340).

An example of the way in which thrift prevailed is the purchase of a manually-operated book hoist, costing £49, instead of an electric model costing £180. (An elevator costing £615 was later installed in 1919.) 'Occasionally technology triumphed more quickly: a telephone, priced at £10, was preferred to a £3 speaking tube, to link the library and the reading room, in which readers were now allowed to study their own books "if essential for their convenience"' (Heaney, 1997; in Stam, 2001: I, 340). The concern for preserving the book-stock is evident in one of the regulations in 1910 which prescribed that 'When a book is taken from the shelf, dust must be blown off the edges before it is opened': in 1914, however, in preference to paying £24 for a vacuum cleaner, approval was given for an extra attendant 'to dust the books in a systematic fashion'. Clearly labour was cheaper than mechanisation at the time, yet war mobilisation left that cleaning post (and several others) unfilled, and in 1917 a machine was bought for £26.

There was a continuing commitment to ensure that historical collections in the Library were fully catalogued. Dickson's demise was followed in 1902 by that of the Keeper of the Hunterian Museum, Professor John Young, which led one of Glasgow's leading bibliophiles, the lawyer and antiquary David Murray (1842-1928), to point out to the University Court that the 12,000 printed books of the Hunterian Library still needed a proper catalogue, the absence of which had led to the purchase of expensive duplicates, as Dickson himself had noted. In 1905 the newly-appointed University Librarian, James L. Galbraith, was accordingly designated Keeper of the Hunterian Books and Manuscripts, and a catalogue of the printed books was subsequently undertaken by the sub-librarian, Mungo Ferguson (Bunch, 1975: 77). Professor Young's catalogue of the manuscripts, completed by P. Henderson Aitken, was eventually published in 1908. Following his protracted nervous breakdown, Galbraith resigned in 1916 and Ferguson continued as sub-librarian, with the post of Librarian left vacant. He stayed in this post up to his death in 1924, and his catalogue of the printed books was published posthumously in 1930 (Hoare, 1991: 38). The post of Librarian remained unfilled until 1925.

In a lengthy petition written in 1913 before his illness, Galbraith deplored the damage inflicted on the Library holdings owing to students' increasing access to books, citing the example of an article on insanity having been cut out of the *Encyclopædia Britannica* and commenting: 'To overlook the effects will be to earn the reproach of succeeding generations'. Neither he nor the Library Committee had a solution to the problem of wear and tear (Heaney, 1997; Sp Coll, MS Gen. 552 / 8).

Jubilee and Expansion

Thanks largely to a series of generous grants by the Carnegie Trust, and a positive response to the University's Ninth Jubilee Appeal of 1901, the University expanded considerably in the early years of the century, with numbers of departments being located in premises separate from the Gilbert Scott Building housing the central Library, including Botany, Chemistry, Physics, Physiology, Pharmacology, Hygiene, Pathology, Engineering and Astronomy. A substantial growth in publications led to the recognition that access to library resources needed to be considered from the point of view of where departmental collections were most appropriately located. By 1912 the University Court had for a couple of years been distributing £250 a year to various departments in support of their departmental libraries, but it then announced that the annual sum available was to be severely reduced to just £20. The Library Committee analysed the distribution of resources and how the management of other universities dealt with this issue, contacting universities in Scotland, England, America, Canada, Italy and Germany to do so. The necessity of having departmental libraries was well established, but overlapping procedures could lead to direct competition with the central Library, so that there was an obvious need for co-ordination. The experience of American universities in particular supported the view that the best solution was to have departmental libraries administered as part of the central Library. The Committee report concluded that departmental libraries were indeed necessary at Glasgow University, but that they should be co-ordinated with the main Library. Numbers of examples given in the report show that some of the practice at the time was rather less formal,

Humanity Class 1901-1902 with male and female students on the Lion and Unicorn Staircase.
Archives & Special Collections [PHU80/76].
Overleaf: Colour drawing of *The Glasgow International Exhibition, 1901*, by its architect James Miller.

with Professor Graham Kerr, in Natural History, writing: 'We have a considerable working library in my Department, the bulk of which consists of my private collection. It is my intention that this should remain in the Department when I disappear from the scene'.

There were nonetheless numbers of additions to the central Library collections in the early years of the twentieth century. Adding to the scientific pamphlets which he had donated to the Library in 1892, Lord Kelvin, who died in 1907, also presented some 1,100 letters from his correspondence, including some from the

leading scientists and physicists of the time, among them George Boole, H. C. Fleeming Jenkin, J. P. Joule, James Clerk Maxwell and P. G. Tait. A collection of some 700 poems and letters of two Renfrewshire poets, Robert Tannahill (1774-1810) and William Motherwell (1797-1835), was deposited in the Library by Capt. D. S. Robertson in 1907. Another Glasgow bibliophile and alumnus, the physician and magistrate William Gemmell (1859-1919), bequeathed his collection of editions of the Dance of Death to the Library in 1919, together with his chronological list giving full descriptions and bibliographical notes.

R. I. A. ARCHITECT, GLASGOW.

GLASGOW INTERN

ONAL EXHIBITION, 1901.

GILMOUR & D

West Quadrangle prior to addition of the Arts wing and Memorial Chapel in the 1920s. Archives & Special Collections [PHU11/12/1].

This late-medieval allegory was particularly resonant for a society emerging from the horror of the Great War (Kurtz, 1934: 276; Carey, 1999: 288; Wiegand, 1919).

Despite embarking on an ambitious building programme and creating more than twenty new Chairs during his lengthy time as Principal, from 1907 to 1929, Sir Donald MacAlister was faced with the consequences of WWI, which by 1916-17 saw the male student population decrease to 40% of the pre-war level. By October 1918 the University's Roll of Honour recorded 3,363 names of those who had died. Funding was in short supply, but a special grant of £48,000 was made in 1919-20, together with a non-recurrent grant of £21,000, to restore the University to its pre-war condition for expenditure on services and books (Moss, Munro, Trainor, 2000: 133, 148). After the end of the war the Government provided regular and systematic financial support for universities for the first time (MacKenna, 1973: 24), so that MacAlister ultimately presided over a period of spectacular growth in academic departments, whose development was strongly supported by the Library. In addition, the University Chapel was one of several important new buildings completed during his time in office.

Part 2 (1920 to 1999)*

John Hume
University of Glasgow and of St Andrews

No historian of the University Library from the First World War until the Millennium will fail to note the profound changes which have taken place not just in library practice, but also in the academic and cultural mores of British society. The notion of universities as 'Ivory Towers' in which the teaching of an intellectual elite combined with a little gentle research and academic speculation within a collegiate community is long outdated, and the University Library has had to meet the challenges inherent in the ever changing academic, social and economic environment of the wider University. Fortunately, successive Library administrations have been very effective in tackling these challenges.

The 1920s: Sober Reconfiguration

Library Committee papers reveal the growing significance of class libraries (numbering twelve by 1920) and continuing concern about losses of books. Noting twenty-six volumes missing from the English Class Library, the sub-committee on class libraries for 1920 reported that 'The losses have been abnormal, owing to the difficulty of supervision by a reduced staff during the war, and to the irregularity of arrival and departure of undergraduates on service'. In an attempt to recover the lost books, their titles were being advertised on all the University notice-boards. Yet the Logic and Moral Philosophy Library was reported as being in good working order, with the books all catalogued and indexed by subjects, including chapters. As for losses,

the Committee felt impotent: 'Unless free consultation and access were stopped, which would be a still greater evil, there does not seem to be any way of preventing what the Committee deplores'. In 1922-23 a new alphabetical catalogue was in progress and a card index of recent accessions was available on the counter. The practice of garnering important accessions to the Library's collections would continue for most of the twentieth century.

The same year D. A. Ferguson presented to the Adam Smith (Economics) Class Library 'an almost complete collection of German paper money covering the depreciation of the German currency and continuing till the establishment of the Reichsmark'.

More importantly, in 1924 the Acting Librarian, Wilson Steel, accompanied by the Master of Works, John Stitt, visited the university libraries of Edinburgh, Aberdeen, St Andrews, Cambridge, and London, the Bodleian Library, the London Library, the British Museum Library, the Westminster Library, the Mitchell Library and the Technical College Library, to look at ways of increasing the capacity of their premises. Some had roller racking, but in most cases steel shelving had been inserted into existing spaces, to divide them into two or three floors, each measuring not more than seven feet in height, so as to obviate the use of ladders. Accordingly, Wilson Steel suggested that quotations be sought from the Art Metal Construction Co. of America and the Art Metal Equipment Co. of London for a system for the division of the lower hall of the Library into three floors, at a height of six feet eight inches, with a gated top floor of five feet four inches for storage of society publications and other books not generally kept on open shelves. At that time the Library had about 253,000 volumes, a number only exceeded by its counterparts at the London School of Economics, Aberdeen, Edinburgh, Oxford and Cambridge.

Installation of the proposed steel shelving began during 1924. With much vacuum-cleaning of the Lower Hall some 85,000 volumes were temporarily moved from its west end to the Examination Hall while the work was undertaken. In all, 110,000 volumes were moved and replaced. While a new ladies' cloakroom was to be created in the basement for staff members, the Library Committee did not approve steel shelving in the basement, which was to be used for obsolete and duplicate books, and also rejected the idea of installing steel shelves in the upper gallery.

The same Committee resolved to spend a sum annually to modernise the Music collection and make it more useful for teaching purposes, resulting in the acquisition of the collected works of Mozart (seventy-three volumes), Haydn, Liszt and Wagner.

In the summer of 1926 the 85,000 volumes moved to the Examination Hall were transferred to the newly erected steel shelves in the west end of the Lower Hall, and 65,000 volumes were transferred in wooden cases to the Examination Hall while the new shelving was installed in the eastern half of the Lower Hall. In the Upper Hall windows had been inserted into the roof, and fourteen large arc lamps suspended from the ceiling. This development was the first substantial alteration to the Library since its

completion in the 1870s, and was an effective investment – the shelving continued in use until the new Library was completed in 1968.

By this time a new Librarian had been appointed, William Ross Cunningham, previously of the Public Record Office. During his twenty-six years of service he would work with no fewer than four Conveners of the Library Committee. One of his early actions was to seek approval for the appointment of a library clerk for the class libraries in Classics, English, History, and Philosophy. He reported on the departmental libraries (as opposed to class libraries) in, for example, Physiology, Anatomy and Pathology, pointing out that, while the cataloguing of current accessions was not a problem, back cataloguing was. Administration of loans would need a very considerable increase in staff, and he wondered if working books should not be lent. A Library Assistant was soon appointed to deal with both aspects of cataloguing, tackling back cataloguing in instalments. Book orders for Class and Departmental libraries were to be routed through the main Library. Yet despite this attempted closer integration of class and departmental libraries with the main Library the problems with satellite libraries proved intractable and perennial.

In counterpoint to such preoccupations, in 1927 the Glasgow lawyer, antiquary and bibliographer David Murray offered the University Library the bulk of his superb collection of antiquarian books and manuscripts, including student notes, local histories, museum studies and legal texts, all then stored with MacLehose, Jackson and Co. the University printers. The collection was to be kept separate from other material, in closed and locked cases, to be available to all and to be catalogued.

Anticipating future developments, members of the teaching staff at the Royal Technical College (now part of the University of Strathclyde) preparing students for the BSc in Pharmacy now asked the University Court for rights of membership of the Library.

The 1930s: Developments amid the Depression

As noted above, the administration of class and departmental libraries continued to exercise the Library Committee, which submitted a broad review of these facilities to the University Court. It was noted that, though useful and necessary as scarcely fifty reading spaces remained in the main Library, these libraries – now numbering thirty-three in all – had grown up in a 'fortuitous, piecemeal and haphazard fashion'. Distinguishing between departmental and class libraries, the Committee identified eighteen of the former, used mainly by teaching and research staff and needed primarily for consultation. They might thus be described as 'apparatus' rather than 'literature'. On the

Upper Hall of the Library in the 1930s. Archives & Special Collections [Photo A49/129].

Interior of Round Reading Room pre 1965. Archives & Special Collections [Photo A49/119/1].

other hand, the fifteen class libraries existed to provide numerous copies of standard works and meeting places for students working on the same subjects. Conversely, in the Committee's view the University Library 'must supply for [all readers] necessary books (unduplicated) and, ideally, it must lay down in each generation books representative of that generation, which succeeding generations will be glad to find conserved for them'.

The Committee's recommendations to Court were, in summary:

a) Departmental Libraries. These should report to the Library Committee. There should be sparing acquisitions, periodic ruthless weeding out, and dispatch to the University of books no longer useful for their specific purpose.

b) Class Libraries. Practices within this group should be standardised. Book orders should be channelled through the University Library, which should also have an advisory and consultative role. Obsolete books should be weeded out, and any duplication of periodicals avoided.

It also concluded that 'most of the class libraries are very poorly housed and that they have a well-founded claim to facilities for their work which has never hitherto been adequately recognised'. The Committee speculated that the Students' Union Building (now the McIntyre Building) might provide suitable accommodation, but here one can, in retrospect, see the genesis of the Round Reading Room built in the late 1930s.

Indicative of the different mores of interwar Britain, the Library Committee noted, firstly, in 1931 that the Senate of Aberdeen University had ruled on the admission of the University Librarian to its number, and that the Library Committees of the Scottish Universities were composed of six Senate members plus three members appointed by the University Court, and observing that the Librarian was subject to the superintendence of the Library Committee, it concluded that 'the status of the [Glasgow] Librarian was amply established and would not be improved by admission to the membership of the Senatus'. Another item of interest is Librarian William Cunningham's intimation to advertise the vacant post of Assistant Librarian at a salary of £300, increasing annually by £20 to a maximum of £400, as follows: 'Candidates (men only) should be graduates of a British University and have library experience. They must be under 35 years of age'.

As an aside, despite the cutting edge research in forensic pathology led by Professors John Glaister senior and junior the annual report on class and departmental libraries for 1937-38 included the following: 'Forensic Science: The collection is extensive, but much of it was found to be in a wretched state of repair and very badly arranged. The obsolete or obsolescent books of the collection are mostly either in a tattered condition or are of a quite infantile character'. A later Report on departmental and class libraries commented on the loss of books needed by Senior Honours students from the French Class Library, adding that 'the other losses are of more psychological than pecuniary importance, being mainly novels whose titles announce, or appear to announce, some erotic interest'.

Included with the Library Committee papers of the 1940s, an undated Committee Report gives useful background to the construction of an innovative new undergraduate Reading Room located on the north side of University Avenue on the site of New Hillhead House as part of Sir Hector Hetherington's ambitious 1936 building programme:

One of the most urgent needs of the students is a properly equipped Reading Room. The present Reading Room is in a part of the buildings which belongs to the Hunterian Museum, and the Keeper of the Museum is very desirous to claim his own. Moreover it is very undesirable both that the small funds at the disposal of the University Library should be expended in placing students' text books in the Library and that the Library books should receive the kind of handling which they must receive from the students which require to use them daily.

To get over these really serious difficulties a new Reading Room is most urgently needed which would be permanently devoted to that purpose. Moreover such [a] Reading Room should be furnished with an ample library of books of reference and ordinary text-books for the use of the large number of students who spend their time between the classes in the College buildings, or are too poor to buy anything but the most ordinary text-books for themselves.

Completed in just over one year, albeit retarded by the outbreak of war, the award-winning building opened in November 1939. The Librarian, William Cunningham, confirmed that Dugald MacArthur would be in charge of the new Reading Room, with two existing and two new male assistants. The room would be open from 10 a.m. to 10 p.m. This new facility was the first new building for the congested Library since the move to Gilmorehill nearly seventy years earlier. It was immediately successful. In 1939-40 the number of Library members rose from 913 to 2,213, and the number of books borrowed from 9,421 to 40,861. The class libraries of the Classics, Philosophy, English, History, Spanish and Celtic Departments were transferred to rooms in the gallery of the building.

Operationally, the Library now allowed the lending of theses, one year after receipt, for consultation by approved individuals in other institutions. The authors would be notified of such loans.

WWII: Overcoming Hard Times

The outbreak of the Second World War very quickly hit Library acquisitions, the rate of which dropped significantly owing to the virtual impossibility of buying and receiving books and periodicals from abroad. Before the war the Library had subscribed to 228 German periodicals. When hostilities commenced, the

Library Committee decided that only necessary scientific periodicals should be bought – thirty-four in all. In May 1940, however, their supply through Holland ceased. On the other hand money due to enemy book agents was paid to the Custodian of Enemy Property.

Library membership fell slightly as men enlisted, though conversely 1939-40 saw a 'marked increase' in the number of women members. Several members of the Library staff enlisted for war service. The RNVR enlisted Dugald MacArthur, as a Sub-Lieutenant, returning to Library duties in 1942, and R. Ogilvie MacKenna, as a Paymaster Sub-Lieutenant, becoming an Instructor Lieutenant, RN. S. G. Stewart joined the army, becoming a Captain in the Highland Light Infantry and Arthur C. Wood became a coder.

A Chemistry Departmental Library opened in the new Chemistry Building. The French Class Library moved into No. 2 University Gardens, though French books were now difficult to obtain. In view of the continued risk of bombing the Director of the British Museum, Sir John Forsdyke, took protective custody of four important Hunterian manuscripts, which were placed in a bomb-proof and air-conditioned repository in the West of England.

Library Special Readers included several men involved in the war effort, including a civilian on the staff of Anti-Submarines Captain Fairlie, an officer in the Polish Army, and three Admiralty chemists working in the University. There was an increase in the number of cadets in the Royal Artillery, RAF and Royal Engineers using the Library and Reading Room. Staff hours

Fruits of the 1960s developments as seen today: the Mackintosh House, Hunterian Art Gallery, University Library, and the Fraser Building. Photographic Unit [GUPU 15-007-001].

increased, and holidays were curtailed from 1st June 1942, as required by the Ministry of Labour. By 1943 nearly half of the members of the Reading Room were women. Special Readers now included five Polish teachers resident in Glasgow and one 'Mr William Crosbie, artist'.

By 1944 the Library had the greatest membership in its history, 1,572, of whom 602 were women. In preparation for peacetime conditions it was agreed that scientific books and periodicals should be supplied through John Smith and Son Ltd, while foreign books should be procured and reclaimed through Braun-Riggenbach Booksellers, Basel, though it was still proving impossible to obtain books from Germany. Other signs of progress were the mounting of an exhibition of books and other items relating to the anatomist Vesalius and, more mundanely, the resumption of the routine cleaning of books. As a foretaste of the future it was reported that:

During the summer a Microfilm reader was set up in the Teaching Staff Reading Room. Arrangements are being made to obtain films from the ASLIB film bureau. The present reader is of a simple type. It is proposed to obtain a more elaborate and expensive reader after the war, when film technique will have developed.

Also, a new medical library had been founded as a gift from relatives of Dr Archibald Acton (a former house-physician at Stobhill), who had been killed in action off North Africa while serving as a Surgeon Lieutenant in the Royal Navy.

Post-War Recovery amid Austerity

The most substantive item of the 1945 Library Report related to acquiring items held up by the war, noting measures taken to obtain those parts of American periodicals lost in transit during hostilities. After the war the focus of the University began to change from preoccupation with undergraduate teaching to scientific, technical and social-scientific research. Early instances of this trend emerge in a report on class and departmental libraries, where it was noted that the Court had made a grant to Professor J. Monteath Robertson for literature on X-ray diffraction and crystallography for inclusion in the Chemistry Department Library, and that books on arc-welding had been acquired for the Engineering Department Library. A multi-disciplinary Modern Languages Library was created in University Gardens and the Professor of Italian concluded his report on his Department's involvement by 'expressing very sincere thanks for the expeditious manner in which my Class Library was removed and installed'.

By 1948 usage of the Library was increasing, with record membership (2,590) and seventy Special Readers. As research units continued

to develop, the Department of Economic and Social Research, established in 1946, created a new Departmental Library. Other new research areas with implications for Library holdings were Genetics and Soviet Studies as a sub-division of Russian.

More Library funding was needed, as balances accumulated in previous years eroded. This age-old issue dominated the post-war years. Another concern was the need for improved retiring accommodation for Library staff. Another issue which would reverberate down the years emerged – the rising cost of journals, in this case of American periodicals, affected by the devaluation of the pound in 1949. Increased funding from Court and a grant from the Carnegie Trust for the Universities of Scotland temporarily solved the problem. Most significantly, the final Report of William Cunningham, the retiring Librarian, stated:

> *The Library Committee joined with six additional representatives of the Senate and two of the Court to form a Library Policy Committee charged with the task of considering the construction of a new Library, or the re-adaptation and extension of the present Library.*

Although Cunningham resigned with effect from 31st March 1951, he continued to manage the Library until 1st September 1951, when Ogilvie MacKenna became free to take up the office.

The 1950s: Growth and Confinement

In the first annual report of MacKenna's tenure he commented that expenditure was up by 40%, mainly on periodicals, deducing that an income of £15,000 p.a. would be necessary to maintain the central Library during the coming quinquennium (the five-year planning regime then used in university funding). Special efforts were made to develop holdings of periodicals, reflecting the move away from monographs, especially in scientific disciplines. The Euing Music Collection, transferred from the Royal Technical College in 1936, was being catalogued. Another signal of returning normality after the War was the recognition of the Reading Room as an important inter-war building:

The Reading Room building won for its architects (T. Harold Hughes and D. S. R. Waugh) the bronze medal of the Royal Institute of British Architects for the best building erected in Scotland during the last fourteen years. A medal and plaque were also presented to the University at a ceremony in the Reading Room on 2nd February 1951.

The following year MacKenna's 'Summary Report on Class and Departmental Libraries' highlighted the success of the Child Health Library at Stobhill Hospital for examination and research purposes, while the Main Committee Report commented on the expanding needs of the recently-founded research departments. Among gifts were volumes presented by the Universities of Belgrade, Bologna, Geneva and Uppsala to mark the fifth centenary of the founding of the University.

By 1953 annual expenditure was greatly outrunning income, despite the establishment of book-selection sub-committees. A most important addition to the 417,605 volumes in the Library was the newly purchased Dougan

Collection of the work of D. O. Hill and other early photographers from about 1843 to about 1860, assembling 'a most impressive volume of work whose level of artistic merit has probably not since been surpassed, and which in its subject matter provides an important range of illustrative material for students of Scottish culture in the early Victorian period'. This acquisition, one of the glories of the Library's Special Collections, reflected MacKenna's aim of strengthening the Library's collections of local history and political economy.

In the increasingly cramped Library 'more shelf room was needed for books, more room for readers and more working space for library staff', although somehow three new offices had been carved out of existing space, and forty new places for readers had been arranged in the upper hall around 'handsome oak tables made in the University workshops'. The problem of inadequate shelf room was exacerbated by the rigid press-mark system for locating books. In apparent dismay the Librarian described his problems as 'too much like bailing with a thimble in a sinking boat'.

Good news and bad again followed in 1953-54. Expenditure was exceeding normal revenue. New steel shelving was behind schedule, and even when complete would only accommodate about 14,000 volumes, 'equal only to the normal increase of a year and a half'. Notable purchases included microfilms of *The Times* for 1840-1948 and 173 photostats of General Roy's Survey of Scotland, supplied by the School of Scottish Studies in the University of Edinburgh. 'The most notable gift of all was a collection of the private papers of James McNeill

Presentation drawing by William Whitfield of the Library and Art Gallery, 1961.
Archives & Special Collections [GUA 78064].

Whistler, presented by Miss Rosalind Birnie Philip to supplement the splendid collection of Whistler paintings which she handed over to the University in 1935'. The Librarian's statement concluded, however, that 'Despite many mitigating considerations, it cannot be regarded as a satisfactory state of affairs that less than one fifth of the undergraduate population should find it worthwhile to make use of the Library'.

In 1954-55 'Serious disruption was caused by rewiring in connection with the changeover of the University's electrical supply from Direct Current to Alternating Current, and by the installation of new heating and lighting systems'. By then a decentralised book store at No. 7 Bute Gardens was being fitted out.

A new library (with two full-time librarians) was established in the Veterinary Hospital at Garscube, complementing that in the Buccleuch Street Veterinary School, merged with the University in 1949.

At the end of the session the Sub-librarian, Wilson Steel, retired after more than fifty years' service before becoming Librarian of the Glasgow School of Art. If his most visible local legacy was the steel shelving, 'for whose design he was very largely responsible when serving as Acting Librarian in 1923 and 1924', of more lasting importance was, however, his strengthening of the Library's Fine Arts collection in the years before the establishment of a lectureship. Yet, in MacKenna's view, his greatest contribution was his personal influence on his colleagues of two generations – his balanced outlook, unfailing commonsense and powers of judgment – and his even temperament, 'which radiated calm in times of stress'.

The financial problems facing the Library grew, with escalating book prices and the end of free presentation copies of learned societies' publications. Among increased microfilm purchases was a subscription to the microfilm edition of *The Glasgow Herald*, on the grounds that it offered a better chance of preserving the journal permanently. More importantly, the decision was taken to classify the Library fully, beginning with the Education section and using a system in operation in University College London (UCL), which was in turn based on one used in Leeds University for thirty years or more.

A report on the choice of a scheme of classification was presented in 1957. It stressed the desirability of being able to accommodate new concepts. Having examined the Dewey (1876), Universal Decimal, Library of Congress (1904), Colon and Bliss schemes, it concluded that these were too complicated in notation. Using the name of the subject as the header, the UCL scheme was flexible and suited to the pattern of teaching in Glasgow. As compared with the system traditionally used in the Library, the UCL system meant that an individual book was no longer linked permanently to one particular shelf.

The balance of funds at the year-end in 1958 was lower than at any time since before the war. The impact of this financial pressure was severe. The need for additional staff could not be met, and the remodelling of the basement was postponed, despite the recognition that the existing staff facilities had been designed for less than a quarter of the present staff. Shelving and reading space were becoming seriously inadequate.

Another emerging problem was the dispersed nature of teaching departments in Medicine, with the recognition that a strong central collection needed to be developed. Though the system of class and departmental Libraries was working fairly well, the Professor of Medieval History was against having a specialist subject library, regarding it as 'siloisation' and arguing that 'No real progress can be made unless the present system is radically altered, so that undergraduates have access to a general undergraduate lending library, served by Library staff'.

On a more positive note, re-classification of the Education section had been completed and two important bequests had been received. The late Emeritus Professor Thomas K. Monro's collection of the printed works of Sir Thomas Browne (a seventeenth-century English physician and author) was exceptionally almost complete. The other collection, from the estate of Sir John Stirling Maxwell of Pollok, was of books on Emblem literature – 'the most complete representation ever assembled of this special facet of sixteenth- and seventeenth-century thought and culture, and undoubtedly one of the most important gifts by which the Library has been enriched throughout its long history'. Begun by the donor's father, this collection is an important component of Special Collections, and has been enriched by further acquisitions from time to time.

Already anticipating the next round of funding, serious forward planning was on the agenda:

Although it is virtually certain that a beginning on the new library building will not be made during the current quinquennium, we ought to make some mention of the project in our estimates for the period, partly to help prepare the ground for a start not later than 1963, but still more because a great deal of preparatory work must be put in hand in the immediate future.

Noting that the Library had only an author catalogue, the Library Committee urged the immediate preparation of a subject catalogue, requiring by its estimate at least five cataloguers and an organising supervisor. Also identifying other desirable cataloguing projects, it stressed the impending need to replace the existing bound guard-book author catalogue, which was becoming worn. Other aspirational suggestions included the need for evening opening, a binding shop, a photographic department, more cleaning, more microfilm readers, and additional staff accommodation.

The planned basement improvements were not implemented; instead the Library appropriated the house at No. 1A The Square, formerly occupied by the Master of Works, although 'Despite this welcome development, the need for a completely new library building remains as urgent as ever'. The Engineering Class Library relocated to the new South (James Watt) building, and a few other class and departmental libraries had to be closed briefly 'because of the disorderly behaviour of those using them'.

In 1959-60 Court provided money to replenish reserves, and the annual grant met the year's expenditure. Opening hours were extended from 10 a.m. – 5 p.m. to 9 a.m. – 9 p.m. Classification was proceeding, and a conservation bookbinder was appointed to deal with decaying leather bindings, although he soon had to go on National Service. At a special meeting the Library Committee agreed on the chief requirements to be met in the design of a new library building.

The 1960s: On the Move Again

The Library began the new decade in upbeat mood: 'It is pleasant to report for once without an expression of foreboding about the Library's financial position'. The annual recurrent grant in 1960-61 increased to £35,000, making it possible for the first time in ten years to avoid drawing on reserves to make ends meet. A new post of Keeper of Special Collections was created. No. 1A The Square had been converted to accommodate cataloguing, classification and acquisitions staff. In preparation for the construction of a new library to be designed by the architect Raglan Squire and principally his associate William Whitfield, 'the Court agreed to send Librarian MacKenna on a visit of two or three months to the United States to collect information and impressions that would be of help in the detailed planning (now becoming imminent) of the New Library building'. This overshadowed everything, as colleague Elizabeth Rodger observes:

MacKenna's main attention was given to the planning of a new library building – undoubtedly his greatest achievement. He was among the early advocates of developing reader services in university libraries, and his brief to the architects in 1962 specified that

Robert Ogilvie MacKenna

A Glasgow graduate (a First in Classics), a proud Paisley Buddie and a prominent Scotland cricketer, Ogilvie MacKenna was University Librarian from 1951 to 1978, a hugely significant period for the Library. He had already been on the Library staff: he first joined under Dr W. R. Cunningham (another first-class Classicist) in 1936. He served in the RNVR during World War II, and retained something of the manner of a naval officer – perhaps reflected in his observation on 'the most important of all the functions which a book can perform, namely that of a detonator, setting off in the mind of a reader a train of independent thought'. He moved to the Brotherton Library at Leeds University, under the redoubtable Richard Offor, who within a couple of years sent him on to become Librarian of King's College, Newcastle: he had already developed his view that 'any library is first and foremost a collection of readers'. While at Newcastle, in 1950, he was a founding member of the Standing Conference of National and University Libraries (SCONUL), which confirmed his ideas of a research library with a fundamental remit of serving its users.

Cunningham's retirement in 1951 opened the door for him to return to Glasgow. He attracted great loyalty from his staff, not least because of the trust he placed in them, giving them more responsibility – the staff structure devised to match the new building allowed a measure of initiative that was effective and much appreciated. The new staff he was able to appoint included more women than before – known affectionately as 'MacKenna's Babes' – and provided, for the first time, specialist staff for the Hunterian Library and the other special collections which are such a feature of the University Library. He encouraged his senior colleagues to take up librarianships elsewhere,

Robert Ogilvie MacKenna, 1913-2004, University Librarian, 1951-1978.

all part of the Glasgow Diaspora. His successor Henry Heaney called him 'an outstanding leader in the library profession' and many fellow-librarians can echo those words. He passed on in 2004, aged 91.

The 1968 building was planned by MacKenna from the start both to serve the whole University's reading community, and to develop the concept of specialist subject divisions. It was quickly remarked by both library and architectural professions as a major creation, even though (to MacKenna's sadness) it was never completed as originally designed. It stands high on Hillhead Street, balancing the Gilbert Scott tower on Gilmorehill: a fine memorial to MacKenna and his innovative ideas.

'the emphasis must be on bringing books and readers together, with the library staff acting as intermediaries'. The confined site available on Hillhead Street meant that the new library had to be a high-rise building. MacKenna made a special feature of this by organising the library as a series of carefully co-ordinated subject libraries. What evolved as Glasgow's special type of 'subject specialisation' owed a great deal to his vision and flair.

A detailed statement of requirements, including the brief to the architects, was then prepared by the Librarian, and forwarded to the University Grants Committee. As Haynes observes:

In order to gain the approval of the building's main funder, the University Grants Committee, the scheme needed to be divided into two stages. Stage I comprised the core block and two-storey western office annexe, both of which were built. Stage II was to be a mirror image adjoining to the north, but in the event this would not be built. (Haynes, 2013: 170).

Meanwhile the membership and use of the Library increased and the Reading Room teemed in the evenings. By now there were eighty-one class and departmental Libraries, twenty-six of which had accommodation problems. Anticipating eventual amalgamation, the Library Committee commented prophetically that 'All these experiences serve to underline the need to regard departmental libraries in the long term as no more than ancillaries to a central library designed and equipped to cover all subjects adequately, and to allow for natural growth over the years'.

Gifts of books and historic letters continued to be received each year. New acquisitions ranged from microfilm of the records of David Livingstone's Zambesi expedition, and a collection of letters relating to the Paisley-Ardrossan Canal, 1817-46, to the library of Sir Denis Brogan, the noted scholar in the field of American studies and one of the great benefactors of the Library, amounting to 6,000 volumes over and above his annual gifts to the Library. An ambitious programme of cataloguing in Special Collections was being implemented, including an inventory of incunabula, and a bibliographical teaching unit was established in the basement of the Reading Room, with two nineteenth-century hand printing presses.

The Librarian, R. O. MacKenna, and staff on steps of the Library, 1978. Archives & Special Collections [Photo A49/113/1].

The pace of change was speeding up. With the imminence of a new building, correspondence ensued on the need for a book conveyor, extra passenger lift accommodation and an ancillary message system. Meanwhile the prospect of more rapid British university expansion following the Robbins Report led the Committee to take two precautionary steps, asking Court to expedite Library Stage II and to make provision for a larger extension. A sub-committee was set up to look at additional Reading Room space, and staffing arrangements for the New Library were put in hand.

Following the Librarian's fact-finding tour of the United States in 1961, in September 1964 he 'visited libraries in Germany and Scandinavia in company with William Whitfield, the architect of the new library building'.

Five months later the Library Committee rather over-optimistically reported:

An important landmark in the Library's history was passed on February 15th, 1965, when the contractor took possession of the site and actual work on Stage I of the new building began. Progress thereafter, despite one or two awkward setbacks, was rapid, and there is every hope that this stage will be ready for occupation before the end of 1967. The starting date for Stage II, however, is not yet known, though it is earnestly hoped that it may follow immediately on Stage I. Even more urgent, in the Committee's view, is the need to make a beginning on the Fine Art department and gallery, which is to share certain facilities with the building now in course of erection, and to be physically linked to it.

The Report further commented that 'With the prospect of the new building thus imminent, lively interest in the affairs of the Library became widespread', particularly among the Faculties of Arts and Science, and the Association of Lecturers and Assistants.

Construction of the new building proceeded throughout the year at an impressive rate, but there were one or two annoying setbacks – in particular an unexpected difficulty over the foundations of closely-adjoining buildings in Hillhead Street, which necessitated costly piling, and continuing uncertainty over planning permission to close Hillhead Street, which prevented a start being made on the entrance porch and approach stairway. Consequently the Library move to its new premises seemed unlikely before summer 1968. The Committee continued to urge an early start to the erection of the new Art Gallery 'which is to occupy the area immediately to the south of the new library, and will, indeed share a common entrance with it, and another link through the photographic laboratory'. Unsurprisingly, the strain on existing facilities was 'almost intolerable'.

More cheerfully, a meeting had been held with the Basic Sciences Building Committee about library facilities in that block (now the Boyd Orr Building). The Librarian noted a change in reading habits, with an increase in pressure on the Library's congested facilities out of all proportion to the rise in its membership and which would only intensify by the summer of 1967.

Because only Stage I of the new building was ever in hand, the Library Committee's Report in 1967 suggested retaining part of the Old

Library for storage, reading space and so on, pending the hoped-for construction of Stage II. With the continuing expansion of the University, Library membership was 138% higher than a decade before, and some 90,000 volumes a year were being issued. Similarly the Reading Room was issuing over 89,000 volumes, nearly twice the number of a decade before.

The 1970s: Mini-Crises and Consolidation

By 1971, the Library was faced not only with prices of books and periodicals rising twice as fast as elsewhere in university expenditure but also extra demands caused by the expansion of the University itself; subsequently a sub-committee on economy in organisation and administration was set up to address the deteriorating financial situation. The Court agreed that £5,000 could be

The Library On The Hill

By August 1966 the reinforced concrete frame had risen to ten storeys and by the following May the towers were reaching their full height and the cladding was being fitted. Structurally the towers are isolated from the core to allow for differential movement.

The Library progressing committee selected a new Danish-manufactured cantilevered shelving system called 'Reska'. With standard steel components and shelves, the system was extremely flexible, allowing different lengths, heights and types of free-standing shelving. The Library was an early adopter of a system that is now widely used all over the world.

Work began on the huge task of removing, cleaning and transferring the 640,000 volumes from the old Library on 7th July 1968. A marker placed in every book indicated its location in the new building. The floors were arranged to accommodate related subject groups. Special Collections and the Hunterian Library were housed in the basement. Stage I of Whitfield's Library opened for use on 30th September of the same year, although building works continued into 1969. For the first time open access to the shelves was available to all students, where previously junior undergraduates had needed to order books through the catalogues.

The final cost of Stage I was just over £1m. Although Stage I was intended to be capable of operating without Stage II, in practice Stage I was immediately under pressure, most notably in housing only two unreliable

lifts for an eleven-story building, and in provision of just 925 reading spaces for a student population of nearly 9,000. Failings in the weather-proofing of the hilltop building, which is battered by the prevailing south-west wind and rain, have been resolved only recently. The tight budget militated against cooling and humidity controls for each floor, resulting in a build-up of heat in summer. The back wall of the building deteriorated quickly because it was intended to be internal, adjoining Stage II. The initial inadequate budget, untested building materials, subsequent performance issues, the omission of the planned Stage II, and changing needs and technologies have all played a part in the large number of subsequent alterations to the original design. The most notable of these were: 1972-79 new east-facing entrance in Hillhead Street (the original entrance faced south towards University Avenue) by Whitfield Partners; 1979-83 extension of the ground and first floors to the north by Walter Underwood & Partners to create a new 400-seat reading room; 1986 tiered addition on top of the 1982 extension, also by Walter Underwood & Partners; 1996-98 the addition of a storey on the core block with a curved roof by the Holmes Partnership to house Special Collections; and replacement of the opaque 'Profilit' glazing with blue-glazed curtain walling.

Courtesy of BUILDING KNOWLEDGE:
An Architectural History of the University of Glasgow, 2013.

used to purchase important works which might be permanently lost, and £1,750 was found for books for the Arts Faculty. Because book orders were easier to cut than periodicals, there was a disproportionate impact on Arts, Divinity and Law, and on undergraduates as opposed to research workers. A new quota system, for a time, also led to the purchase of cheaper books, which could adversely affect the acquisition of books of lasting worth.

On receiving complaints that the new building was being used by non-University readers, the Library introduced membership tickets. Already the accommodation was being stretched in the new building, which was only half the size originally planned. To ease this situation, the University allocated to the Library one floor of a warehouse which it had acquired in Thurso Street.

As a foretaste of future developments, a short-title list of science periodicals had been 'produced from punched cards by the computer line printer', as then was the normal means of computer input. By this time there were some 923,450 volumes in the main Library, Reading Room and branch libraries.

With universities facing many unprecedented challenges, there were four major preoccupations: (a) the need to extend the University Library building assuming normal growth of the University; (b) the continuing growth in the volume of world-wide publication and in postgraduate study, especially in the Arts; (c) a trend towards inter-library cooperation; and (d) the growing use of information technology and services, as computer science was applied to library needs. A four-phase timetable for automation was proposed, starting with computerised lists; then systems design, and mechanised systems; the accessioning of periodicals, etc.; and for the late seventies a possible introduction of on-line catalogues with small satellite computers sited in the Library and provision of multi-access points.

Observing 'that over the country as a whole too little is yet being spent on library resources, and that Glasgow comes out none too well out of comparisons' (since in 1967-68 Glasgow had spent £15 per student, Dundee £24, St Andrews £29, and Stirling, being very new, £55), the Committee recommended in 1972 that the annual budget should be not less than £235,000, rising to £395,000 at the end of a five-year period.

With Britain's entry into the European Economic Community, the University made £20,000 available to improve the Law collections, especially in the field of European Law. Unusually but sensibly, the Library recommended to Senate that Arts postgraduate students be encouraged to choose research topics reflecting the Library's strengths. Significantly, the number of submitted Glasgow theses more than doubled in four years from 164 to 341 in 1972-73.

The new Library was nearly at full capacity with average peak usage of table space at 83%. Increasing reader enquiries were handled by helpful staff. New technology was increasingly adopted. All was not positive, however, for the initial inadequate budget and untested building materials were beginning to result in performance issues: windows in the new

The Library under construction, 5th May, 1967. Archives & Special Collections [PHU15/2].

building started to blow out and the roof leaked where the towers joined the core. Moreover, 'The commencement of work on the construction of the Hunterian Museum Extension and Art Gallery had a considerable impact on the Library'. The original south-facing entrance was demolished, and a temporary alternative carved out pending the construction of an east-facing replacement by Whitfield Partners in Hillhead Street – which would wait until the completion of the new Art Gallery.

By the middle of the decade the infamous three-day week was followed by a flood of deliveries but, operationally, the number of books purchased dropped. An in-house bindery, set up a few years earlier, was proving very effective, the bookbinder having by then restored about 24,000 volumes. The book conveyor installed when the new building was opened was proving unreliable, with only 50% availability, and the Thurso Street store, with space for 55,000 volumes, was already two-thirds full. The General Assembly of the Church of Scotland donated the Trinity College library, amounting to 75,000 volumes and 14,000 pamphlets; notable gifts continued to be received including Whistler

The completed Library, February 1971. Archives & Special Collections [PHU 15/28].

correspondence; and the archives of the Citizens' Theatre were acquired.

The re-classification of the Library stock was completed, except for new topics. Physically, accommodation for readers was just adequate, but shelving was nearing saturation; any dreams of unlimited expansion were over. Weeding was proving necessary but time-consuming. Increased storage was squeezed into the Stage I building – 400 linear feet on each floor – and the bound volumes of *The Glasgow Herald* and of *The Times* were jettisoned.

Staffing was unavoidably cut through natural wastage. Once again control of expenditure was easier with books than with periodicals. Cataloguing proceeded apace despite the need to cancel or alter catalogue entries for books withdrawn from open-access shelves. Manpower Services Commission funding was secured to list large accumulations of unsorted donations. Membership was now over 15,000, and increased usage was hastening the disintegration of the guard-book catalogue. Vandalism was increasing, while in the Reading Room inconsiderate chatter compounded the disturbance due to construction work.

The Glasgow Diaspora

While many early librarians went on to become professors at Glasgow or Edinburgh, or to attain senior positions in the Church, it was only in the mid-twentieth century that a significant diaspora of senior Glasgow librarians began, filling Chief Librarian posts in universities throughout the country and abroad. All of these worked under R. O. MacKenna, as his deputy or in other senior posts – and not forgetting Wilson Steel, who became Librarian of Glasgow School of Art in 1955 after fifty years at the University Library. MacKenna's philosophy of university librarianship influenced many more, but the spread of his senior staff was quite remarkable.

The series of promotions of MacKenna's Deputy Librarians over twenty-five years shows how the Glasgow 'gospel' travelled:

Leonard Jolley, Librarian of University of Western Australia 1959-79.

Tom McCallum Walker, Librarian of University of Alberta, then of Calgary 1964-71.

James Thompson, Librarian of University of Reading 1967-87, then of Birmingham 1987-95.

John Simpson, founding Librarian of the Open University 1969-94.

Michael Smethurst, Librarian of University of Aberdeen 1972-86, then Director-General, Humanities, British Library (later Deputy Chief Executive) 1986-96.

Peter Hoare, Librarian of University of Nottingham 1978-93.

Elizabeth Rodger, Librarian of University of Sussex 1980-87.

Other holders of senior posts such as Superintendent of the Reading Room and senior subject librarians who moved on include the following (the first two began under W. R. Cunningham):

Douglas Walker, Librarian of University of Leicester 1960-82.

Dugald MacArthur, Librarian of University of St Andrews 1961-76.

Frederick W. Ratcliffe, Librarian of University of Manchester 1965-80, then of Cambridge 1980-94.

Elizabeth M. Moys, Librarian of Goldsmiths' College, University of London 1967-89.

Tom Graham, Librarian of University of York 1984-1997, then of Newcastle 1997-2008.

Ian Mowat, Librarian of University of Hull 1986-1991, then of Newcastle 1992-97, and of Edinburgh 1997-2002.

Sheila Cannell, Librarian of University of Edinburgh 2003-2012.

And other librarians who received their initiation through the Glasgow graduate trainee scheme which MacKenna promoted strongly, included:

Robert Butler, Librarian of University of Essex 1980-2014.

Margaret Coutts, Librarian of University of Kent 1994-2004, then of Leeds 2005-10.

As a measure of the respect the Librarian enjoyed, he was appointed to a University Grants Committee working party on capital provision for university libraries. Over the new Library's first nine years accessions were up by 43%, membership by 124%, photocopying up by 172%, loans by 68%, inter-library loans by 277% (incoming) and 74% (outgoing). All this had been achieved with an increase in the Library establishment of less than 5%.

In 1978, ten years after successfully overseeing the relocation and consolidation of his charge and following twenty-seven years of very distinguished administration, the Librarian Ogilvie MacKenna announced he would be retiring.

The major day-to-day preoccupations of staff were a revision of current subscriptions to periodicals, a review of priorities for services, the work of the Manpower Services Commission team, a study of automated data processing, and experimental extensions to opening hours. The Manpower Services cataloguing team inspected the Divinity Library and checked 39,408 items. Of these 46% were duplicates, some of which were offered for sale. Another group looked at some 30,000 donated books. Thirty MSC staff were employed, and of these sixteen found permanent employment within a year and a further nine immediately after; only five returned to the unemployed register, a highly successful result. Progress on automation was slow since a new computer generated a need for re-programming. However a tele-ordering system was introduced and ways of automating acquisitions were discussed with the Scottish Libraries Co-operative Automation Project (SCOLCAP) team, of which Glasgow University Library was a founder member. Microfiche catalogues of the Science Reference Library and of British Books in Print were purchased.

The cumbersome nature and status of the Library's ternary cataloguing systems – guard-book, supplementary and sheaf – were of increasing concern. First the supplementary catalogue was eliminated by passing slips to division heads for them to decide on re-cataloguing into the sheaf system or the withdrawal of the book. Emergency repairs to the disintegrating guard-book catalogue were necessary during the summer. Computerisation of the catalogue was investigated, and a working party considered specifications for a microfiche replacement for the sheaf and supplementary catalogues.

To make space for new acquisitions, a Stack Supervisor was appointed to manage the transfer of books to store. Most fortunately, news arrived that the University Grants Commission might fund a modest Library extension, and a working party immediately explored this possibility.

Appropriately, though the new street-level entrance would not be opened until the Art Gallery was completed, 'On the evening of September 30th, at a small semi-official opening ceremony the Librarian was invited to turn the key in the lock. It is a matter for debate whether this was his last official act as Librarian, or his first as Librarian Retired'. With characteristic modesty MacKenna concluded his final report by writing 'I should like to express my deep feelings of gratitude for the support and friendship offered to me by a long succession of Library Staff and by all the Chairmen and members of the Library Committee with whom I have worked. I hope that I have been in some measure successful in my efforts to make an acceptable return'. In his last session in post the Library held about 1,287,000 volumes, 251,445 of which were issued, and had 16,206 members.

As the Library entered a new era in 1978-79, the newly appointed Librarian, Henry Heaney, paid tribute to his predecessor, who was 'a senior statesman among academic librarians in the United Kingdom' and 'revered by his own staff'. Part of MacKenna's legacy was that the University Grants Committee had agreed in principle to seek funds to extend the ground

Various areas of the Library, 1968. Archives & Special Collections [Photo A49].

and first floors of the Library, as proposed in a feasibility study. Detailed planning of this extension would anticipate eventual development of the upper floors.

Court agreed to activate the Library's membership of SCOLCAP and specifically to fund the appointment of a Systems Librarian and the automation of catalogues. Glasgow would have the first major library to use the method of catalogue data input which the British Library had just begun to market. With price rises slackening the Library could return to Court £50,000 of its additional grant. Following the success of the MSC scheme in addressing the backlog in book handling, the Euing Music Collection would be re-catalogued under a Job Creation project. Meantime The Friends of Glasgow University Library, a society getting into its stride in 1976, were seeking to acquire early dictionaries.

In 1979-80 news was mixed. Court appointed a Progressing Committee to oversee the planning of the Library extension, and the Library Committee agreed that the ground-floor reading room in the extension should include a reserved loan collection. On the other hand there had been a cut of £40,000 in non-pay items, and a 3% cut in staffing estimates. As expected, new spiral staircases installed between pairs of floors reduced staffing in the evenings. Microfilm usage was increasing, and more readers had been installed, but the lack of microfilming equipment was reportedly a risk to collection items.

The 1980s: Steadfastness amid Vicissitudes
As Henry Heaney observed, the start of the decade was only superficially inauspicious:

The prevailing spirit of economy prompts an annual report publishing the usual statistical report without further comment. Yet to dismiss the 1980-81 session in cold numerical terms would be to ignore the real achievements that in the long history of the Library will prove more enduring than the effects of those cut-backs which now preoccupy our thinking.

Building of the Library extension designed by architects Walter Underwood & Partners started in April 1981, necessitating the transfer of more than 70,000 items to the Thurso Street store, for which shelving had been purchased from Strathclyde University and installed by temporary staff paid by Court. The Mitchell Library was storing oversize material. The recalculated third phase of the Library building was expected to begin in 1983, with a view to completing it in 1985-86, before which the newly completed 'second' phase could not be fully accessed. After only thirteen years the Stage I building was showing signs of age. The sub-basement was frequently flooded, and the roof continually leaked, as did the joins between the core and the towers.

Construction noise was proving a problem, but in the meantime the ground floor of the phase 2 extension was being used as a supplementary reading room, leading to discussion of the future of the old 1930s Reading Room.

A Working Party on the future of class and departmental libraries concluded that the main Library should be the priority, and that only off-campus libraries should cater for research use. Court funded the conversion of the guard-book catalogue (pre-1960) to microfiche. Despite difficulties with automation, most of the Sheaf Catalogue was expected to be computerised by 1983. The Universities of Strathclyde and Glasgow agreed on reciprocal rights for Library members.

Attended by 2,500 visitors, a three-day Library exhibition on computer-based information systems – IT82 – was opened by Sir Monty Finniston as part of 'Information Technology Year' 1982. With increasing computerisation, the University Equipment Committee approved the purchase of a Geac 8000 mini-computer and terminals to support an automated loan system and on-line catalogue, replacing the microfiche catalogue introduced in 1980. These computer systems were expected to be functioning by the summer of 1984, and would also be accessible through the University's mainframe computer.

Funding for acquisitions re-surfaced as a concern. As the Librarian commented, a 9% increase in grant fell far short of the sum necessary to maintain a steady rate of acquisition, prejudicing ability to support research. Periodical prices having escalated by 20%, he concluded that 'The Library must be recognised as requiring special treatment as long as book and periodical prices continue to outpace so markedly the general level of inflation'.

The gruelling but productive session 1983-84 finally saw 'the introduction of on-line automation to the University Library'. Featuring new access points by keyword and subject, the public access catalogue was installed for tests in February 1984, and was fully operational in March. Public response was enthusiastic –

too few, rather than too many, terminals had been provided and the sheaf catalogue needed to be converted into machine-readable form. The Library withdrew from the now redundant SCOLCAP in December 1983, and by June 1984 the loan system was also automated. The essential bar-coding of stock encountered some teething trouble.

Major effort was devoted to developing the new on-line cataloguing and lending systems and to planning for the occupation of the third stage of the University Library building in 1986. Construction was on schedule, but occupation planned for the end of June slid to the 10th of August 1986, involving readers being accommodated in other libraries.

However, the 1960s main Library continued to give trouble, demanding replacement of the south-facing large windows and refurbishment of flooring and paintwork. In the run-up to the opening of the third stage the gallery in the old Reading Room would be reorganised to provide an integrated multiple-copy medium-loan service, to be known as the Undergraduate Lending Library.

In other moves a Scottish Theatre Archive was created, funded by the Scottish Arts Council. It soon became a standing responsibility of the Special Collections department. In anticipation of the bicentenary in 1983 of William Hunter's death, an exhibition on his book collecting was prepared. Alasdair Gray kindly donated the manuscript (and other papers) of his monumental novel *Lanark*. And in connection with Whistler's 150th anniversary year the future Director of the Centre for Whistler

The University reflected in the Library windows. Archives & Special Collections [PHU15/41].

Studies, the Library's Deputy Keeper of Special Collections, Dr Nigel Thorp visited the United States. The number of items consulted in Special Collections showed a gratifying increase, from 6,235 in 1983-84 to 11,728 in 1985-86. To mark the tenth anniversary of the founding of The Friends of Glasgow University Library, Dr Kenneth Elliott organised a celebration concert drawing on items in the Euing Collection, complemented by a related exhibition.

There were plans to open catalogue access to other universities. Only a fifth of Library holdings had been computerised so far – post-1979 acquisitions and heavily-used earlier stock. Retrospective cataloguing was being explored with other institutions. Use of the computer search service was up by 83%.

To coincide with the opening of the extension in 1986 new subject divisions were created in Fine Arts, Music and Theatre, Divinity, and Law and Official Publications. An audio-visual suite was installed, with facilities both for playing and for listening. To most users' satisfaction a remodelled issue desk allowed returns to be made from outside the entrance control point. Also very successful with readers were the Undergraduate Lending Library, with borrowing up almost 50%, and the automated systems following the increase in the number of micro-computers from ten to twenty-six. However, more intensive staffing was needed, resourced from the fund for Special Collections purchases. The Geography Department's maps were transferred to the main Library. A consortium of university research libraries was formed to find a way to link databases and to improve the representation of large libraries.

The large south- and west-facing windows of the Stage I building were replaced during 1985-86 and the existing two internal telephone systems integrated into an all-University network. Computing power was increased with the acquisition of a new Victor computer to replace the Superbrain and facilities were further extended through ten Apple micro-computers, two image writers and a laser printer. Computer searches continually increased.

At £1,065,000 the non-pay budget for 1988-89 was £140,000 down from the previous year, journal spending was down by 10%, continuations by 20% and monographs by 50%. The allocation for the following year 1989-90 was to be £1,235,000, only £32,000 more than the grant of two sessions before. As the Librarian put it, 'Prolonged blood-letting on such a scale will have irretrievable effects'. In addition, there were cutbacks on staffing and reductions in opening hours. On the other hand, the Library's mini-computer was upgraded to a Geac 9000, and the short-loan collection was moved to the Reading Room.

The first postgraduate students were recruited to study the Library's notable collection of emblem books in Special Collections. Dr Nigel Thorp curated an international travelling exhibition of the Library's medieval and renaissance manuscripts, *The Glory of the Page*, accompanied by a fine catalogue.

The baseline for 1990-91 was set at 108% of the 1989-90 figure of £1,235,000, and inflation-proofed. The purchase funds for journals, books and continuations were amalgamated, but the number of books purchased fell 'catastrophically', from 12,700 in 1988-89 to 10,700. The annual report concluded:

> *One may well ask how much further the Library's ability to keep pace with monograph publications must decline before it surrenders any serious claim to serve its clientele. There is an even more urgent question: how soon will it be before necessary journal expenditure totally exhausts the funds available.*

As automation continued, hardware needed to be refreshed. CD-ROMs were sometimes used instead of books, and barcodes on matriculation cards allowed them to serve as library borrowers' cards and for telephone renewals. The expanding micro-computer cluster was transferred to the Reading Room basement.

The 1990s: Before Electronic Supremacy

In 1991 Henry Heaney noted an independent 1990 survey of some 2,500 British academics who were asked how well the libraries which they customarily used were currently supporting their research. In the published, but little publicised, report more readers from the ancient Scottish Universities commented that their libraries had markedly deteriorated in keeping stock up-to-date, in contrast to the 'greatly above average service which these particular libraries had hitherto provided'. In Glasgow the widely acknowledged need for improved funding led the Principal, Sir William Kerr Fraser, to announce in May 1991 that the baseline would be increased by 12%, with a top-up grant of £100,000, a decision warmly welcomed by the Library Committee.

Henry Heaney

Before coming to Glasgow, Henry J. Heaney had become Librarian of Queen's University Belfast, from where he first graduated in 1957, and latterly was Librarian of University College Dublin.

Henry Heaney inherited a library and staff markedly stamped with the 'MacKenna ethos' when he became the first non-Scot to be appointed Librarian and Keeper of the Hunterian Books and Manuscripts in 1978. He particularly insisted on using his full title as part of his normal description, reflecting an appreciation, understanding and knowledge of the many heritage collections entrusted to his overall care. His twenty years in office saw a profound change in both the University and its Library, particularly in the rise of electronic information sources and their delivery to users. Moreover, it was a time of significant addition to, and alteration of, the Library building despite the prolonged financial stringencies which were characteristic of the 1980s.

It is to his everlasting credit that his professionalism and foresight enabled these changes to be handled with tact and the sensible combination of an innovative approach based on an understanding of the best practices already in place. His vision helped place the Library in a stronger position as it entered the twenty-first century.

As a committed and influential member of the Standing Conference of National and University Libraries, now the Society of College, National and University Libraries, he did much to lay the groundwork for many of the collaborative activities now taken for granted. In addition, he ensured that Glasgow was a founder member of the Consortium

Henry Heaney. Archives & Special Collections [GUAS ip5/6/25].

of University Research Libraries and, as subsequent chairman, he was able to offer opportunities for libraries to work together in a time of restraint. Such services as COPAC – the union catalogue of the major libraries of the United Kingdom and Ireland – and the Statistical Accounts of Scotland Online were the direct result of his commitment. His pioneering involvement in Conspectus, an American system for recording the strengths of libraries' collections, reflected a foresight well ahead of his time in collection management.

Following the preparation of a Mission Statement in March 1988, a Vice-Principal was appointed with library services in his portfolio. Performance indicators were revised, and policies put in place for conservation, marketing and training. In line with changing attitudes in university administration, the Library was becoming a 'quasi-planning unit', with more delegation of responsibilities. Office automation and electronic mail was introduced. Only five years after completion of the phase 3 extension, library accommodation was reckoned to be at 85% of capacity – essentially full.

The Wolfson Foundation made a £10,000 grant for the conservation of the Stirling-Maxwell emblem books. To complement the BBC radio drama scripts recently deposited with Special Collections, the Jimmy Logan archive was acquired, through the N. S. Macfarlane Charitable Trust, while the Louis Sinclair collection of material on the Fourth International was also deposited. A Festschrift in honour of the previous Librarian, Robert Ogilvie MacKenna, was published as a special issue of the *Library Review*. In the Modern Languages Class Library, opened in 1959, staff

Library Services desk on entrance Level 2 in the main Library building, 2006. Photographic Unit.

Interior of the James Ireland Memorial Library, which holds the University Library's collection of dental books and journals. It is situated on the fourth floor of the Glasgow Dental School in Sauchiehall Street. Photographic Unit [GUPU 16-05-137].

Interior of the James Herriot Library, which holds the University Library's collection of veterinary medicine books and journals. It is situated on the second floor of the Mary Stewart Building on the Garscube Estate. Photographic Unit [GUPU 16-047-098].

wished to reduce the stock of printed volumes so as to create a 'multi-media learning area'.

By summer 1992 the Library had, for the first time, more than 20,000 registered readers as well as 5,000 visitors and had issued more than half a million loans. A three-year staff restructuring was planned, with subject divisions re-aligned into groups. A survey revealed that Library shelving would be completely full before possible space expansion could be identified, and therefore a pilot weeding programme began amid awareness that electronic publishing might well offer a parallel or better long-term solution as 'necessary competition for the printed page'.

As forecast, the Library budget for 1992-93 remained constant. But because of prudence in recommending monograph purchases a sizeable proportion of the 1991-92 book grant was unspent; Court accordingly withheld £150,000. Yet an extra £200,000 from Court for 1992-93 enabled most periodical subscriptions to be renewed, though the increasing price of journals was still a problem and the Library generally purchased multiple undergraduate titles in preference to periodicals.

A University Grants Committee report concluded that 'The character and efficiency of a university may be gauged by the treatment of the central organ – the library'. And in September 1992 'Quality in Higher Education', the first report of the national survey of one hundred requisite criteria, stated that after the first priority – which was the need for staff to understand the aims and objectives of the teaching programme – the second, third and fifth were all library-related: adequate access to library facilities; adequate library resources; and adequate teaching resources.

The 1993-94 Library Committee's report opened with a quotation from Jaroslav Pelikan's published 1992 lecture *The Idea of the University: A Re-examination*, delivered in preparation for Yale University's tricentennial celebrations:

> *The advancement of knowledge through research, the transmission of knowledge through teaching, the preservation of knowledge in scholarly collections and the diffusion of knowledge through publishing are the four legs of the university table, none of which can stand for long unless all are strong.*

To promote this solidity the national Joint Funding Councils' Libraries Review Group – the Follett Committee – was established 'to shape library and information services to meet the challenge of growth and to exploit new technologies and serve research needs'. Local new specialist units were established – Classification, Maps and Official Publications and Research and Technology Support – and new subject groups constituted – Arts and Humanities, Sciences and Social Sciences. A new Historical Collection was established off-site, and books published before 1851 were not to be lent. Readership in Special Collections increased by 78%. In March 1994 the Library's main conference room was renamed the 'R. O. MacKenna Room'.

During 1994-95 publication of the Follett report prompted two local initiatives. A bid was made to the Scottish Higher Education Funding Council for £1.9 million, which, with matched funding from the University's own resources, would allow Special Collections to move to a new building on the roof, with compact shelving. This development would allow areas in the entrance and basement to be remodelled for undergraduate study. Secondly, a non-recurrent grant of £1 million and a recurrent grant of the same amount would be sought for research collections, including a Humanities microfilming project. In part for the activities of Special Collections the University was awarded the Queen's Anniversary Prize for service to the public.

Postgraduate students constantly complained about the lack of needed periodicals. On Garscube estate a new Veterinary School library, the James Herriot Library, funded largely from faculty resources, was opened by Herriot's son, as his father had died the day before the event.

Midway through the decade the *Library Review* strongly commended the pioneering role of the University's subject librarians in liaising with academic departments. Innovation continued in other fields too: Reader Services was abolished as a separate department, and the Senior Management Team was renamed the Library Management Team. More materially, the changeover of the computer system to 'Innovative Interfaces Inc (III) Innopac' was completed, and the new catalogue was inaugurated by the Principal. The Adam Smith (Social Sciences) Library was also automated.

Detailed planning of the extension and of 'collateral change' was in hand. To prepare for the move of Special Collections into the extension eight temporary assistants were appointed. The Scottish Theatre Archive saw an 'overwhelming' influx of material, and issues of Special Collection items were up by more than 300%. The total number of bound volumes in the Library, including branch, class and faculty libraries and stores, reached 1.835 million by 1996.

With the creation of academic Planning Units most of the purchase grants had been transferred to them, a notable change. The Librarian, Henry Heaney, took early retirement in September 1998 preceded by a six-month period of study leave. Consequently, in March 1998 his colleague, Andrew Wale, took over, firstly as Acting Librarian.

The reorganisation of Levels 2 and 3 resulted in Level 2 being adapted to form a new undergraduate library to replace the Reading Room. Problems were encountered with the automatic doors and with overheating 'caused by insufficient understanding at the design stage of the heat generated by the number of computer terminals (as well as the body heat of users)'. On Level 3 a newly created electronic enquiry area was proving very popular. In relation to a new formula for distributing the Library grant, complex arrangements were made for allocating grants to subject areas. A reduced budget resulted in subscriptions to some serials being cancelled, and a system of tendering for book supplies was introduced. An electronic entry system for the main Library was successfully introduced. In line with the IT revolution, the Library was now subscribing to about 900 electronic journals, double the number of the previous year. E-journals were proving very popular.

Various areas of the Library and Reading Room.

Visits to Special Collections were significantly up, as were issues from the desk, unsurprisingly since the Royal Commission on Historical Manuscripts recognised that in its new home it ranked 'among the best-appointed university special collections departments in the United Kingdom'. Dr Larry Schaaf, a noted Glasgow photographer, was appointed a research assistant and produced an illustrated catalogue of the Hill Adamson collection of early photographs on CD-ROM. The scanned images were licensed to SCRAN (the online Scottish Cultural Resources Access Network).

In September 1999, slightly less than a year after his retirement Henry Heaney died from a stroke, aged sixty-four. In his tribute Andrew Wale wrote:

> *Mr Heaney inherited a well-run library with an assured place in the University and an experienced and committed group of staff. The twenty years which followed were an unprecedented period of uncertainty, both externally and internally. Henry did not find the new management environment congenial – a pattern of reviews leading to a continuous process of change management. His achievement was to leave an organisation which was respected within the University and beyond, and widely recognised as a major research resource as well as an innovator in the delivery of electronic information. He was a perfectionist, and those of us who worked with him remember his charm and kindliness. We remember also his dynamism and commitment, his enthusiasm and support.*

He had also served as a member of the British Library Board and the Follett Committee, which reviewed the Higher Education library system and changed the way this would develop. This tribute noted that the Library was in a state of transition, looking to a future whose parameters are far from fixed, and concluded that it was facing two fundamental problems: 'the rate of change in the world of information provision which continues to become faster and more complex year by year'; and the fact that 'many people are now carrying responsibilities which it is unreasonable to expect them to shoulder indefinitely'.

There was no sign of stability being re-established. Two major developments in the wider University would have implications for the Library: firstly, the creation of Crichton College in the campus of the former Crichton Royal Mental Hospital, where delays by the University were proving damaging; and secondly, a merger with St Andrew's College, the west of Scotland Catholic teacher training college in Bearsden, which was apparently going well. Internally, the number of e-journals was up to 1,500, but large publishers were finding it difficult to agree terms for site licences. The end of the decade saw the first e-book subscriptions. Students were queuing to use computer terminals. The new store at Spencer Street, replacing Thurso Street, was in use, with its own online catalogue.

Andrew Wale now retired. He had served the Library for twenty years, a period which saw changes in information technology inconceivable in the late 1970s. But print culture was not dead. By 1999 Library volumes issued totalled 808,393. Wale issued this prediction to his successors: 'Constant development at a very fast rate of change will dominate the environment and determine the agenda' – a fitting way to end this chapter.

* The foundation for this chapter was provided by Glasgow University Archives, whose collection of the papers of the University Library Committee spanned the whole period surveyed here. Study of these papers has been supplemented with reference to published histories of the University and its buildings as a whole and to other publications, notably the Festschrift for R. O. MacKenna, published as a special issue of the *Library Review* in 1991.

Social studying.

A Personal Memoir

I went to Glasgow University in September 1957 for the first of two years spent there as part of my degree course in Applied Chemistry (the other two years were at the Royal College of Science and Technology, now part of the University of Strathclyde). My first contact with the University Library was through the Student Reading Room, which I used regularly between classes. At that time the male students sat to the left of the issue desk, and the women on the right. A few bold souls mingled at the far end with members of the opposite sex. Later in my career I came to know the delights of the rather claustrophobic steel stacks in the main library, and the intriguing upper hall, with Victorian engineering publications in the gallery; my abiding memory of that place is the distinctive smell of decaying leather bindings. When I moved to the 'Tech' I found the library equally seductive, interspersing my reading of course books with delving into vintage engineering periodicals and publications on the history of technology.

The availability of these publications on the shelves of academic libraries had a profound influence on my career path. I came to terms with the systematic use of publications in foreign languages as well as in English, and began to see where gaps in published knowledge could be the basis for constructive research. In my subsequent career I have made much use of Glasgow University Library, especially the Geographical collections, including the large-scale Ordnance Survey maps. With the use – and the fascination – of academic libraries in my bones, as it were, I was very pleased to be approached by the Friends of Glasgow University Library to contribute to 'Friendly Shelves'.

Professor John Hume - immediate past Chairman of the Royal Commission on the Ancient and Historical Monuments of Scotland.

Chapter 5

The Twenty-first Century –
New Horizons

Exterior of University Library. [GUPU 14-048-131].

Helen Durndell
University of Glasgow

Overview

The compelling focus in the first decades of this century has been upon laying strong foundations for a real integration of print and digital resources within a major research library, opening up the riches held in the collections to scholars and the public worldwide and reconfiguring the physical library into a welcoming space that facilitates the exchange of ideas and engagement.

Context

Despite dire predictions for libraries, when people believed emerging technologies would make them irrelevant, university libraries have continued to function as catalysts for discovery, learning, research and collaboration. Today's students use smart phones in addition to laptops and tablets, and libraries offer learning opportunities across multiple media enabling students to access, create and share knowledge across local and global networks. The twenty-first-century university library has to be a curator of new knowledge, an innovator in developing collaboratively built and collectively held digital collections.

Glasgow University Library continues to evolve, anticipating emerging needs of students and staff as changes in technology bring opportunities and challenges. The aim is to offer comprehensive access to contemporary research literature and an excellent gateway to historical sources, held locally and globally. After much forward planning so as to minimise disruption to normal library operations and to maintain a safe and secure working environment throughout the refurbishment, the physical building has been

Café study. Photographic Unit [GUPU 14-083].

transformed from a warehouse for books into a beacon for interactive learning and knowledge creation across both the physical and digital realms, enabling discovery and learning in the context of a dynamic academic framework. Since the new millennium, our specialist collections and archives have moved centre stage both as physical settings facilitating student engagement with rare/unique items and advanced graduate research, especially across the humanities, and as digital gateways available locally and to scholars worldwide. The use of social media has been a continuing theme in achieving high levels of engagement.

From 2001 library membership overall has increased by 35% to 54,500, outstripping the 26% growth in the number of annual full-time equivalent students (22,954) in the

The new High Demand shelves.
Photographic Unit [GUPU 14-398-3062].

Busy study spaces.
Photographic Unit [GUPU 14-398-3028].

first fifteen years of this century. The actual headcount figure has almost trebled to 24,920 individuals; library usage measured by entries to the main Library building has increased by 77% to 1,955,000, and the use of print and digital information resources has quadrupled from around 200,000 transactions a year to around 900,000 transactions. There are now 1,347,000 catalogued print books, outnumbered by access to 1,853,000 e-books, and journal titles amount to 53,300, of which 51,900 are electronic journals.

Digital Services

The role of the library as a physical repository of knowledge has been transformed as virtually all knowledge can readily be accessed digitally by anyone, anywhere. The role of librarians is now to facilitate access to what individuals or organisations really need to find and know in this ocean of distributed information.

As barriers of space and time are eliminated, users expect increasingly more direct and immediate access to scholarly materials, to the world's rarest historical artefacts, to visual art, to recorded music, and to broadcast archives.

Library staff have been developed in parallel skill sets to serve users of both physical and virtual collections, integrating these resources seamlessly, thus expediting access and supporting the full gamut of research and scholarly exchange. Rather than choose one world over another, the University of Glasgow Library has a foot in each, steering equally well through the traditional and the digital library landscape.

The first-class digital services created by the Library include: ReadingLists@Glasgow, an online reading list service that is integrated with the Library catalogue and electronic resources; LibraryTree, which turns Library activity into a game and enables students to rate, review and recommend Library content; and a choice of Resource Discovery Tools within the catalogue, supplemented by entry points to the collections via Flickr, YouTube, Facebook, Twitter,

Instagram, Eventbrite, HistoryPin, Wikis and outward-looking Blog posts.

Another significant growing area of activity involves the custodial management of the research outputs of staff and students. Following an early research project (Daedalus, originating in 2004), the Library now offers a suite of repositories (covering publications, PhD theses, and research data) in which the output of University staff and students is catalogued and, where possible, the full text of publications made available. This suite of services called Enlighten is available to all at **www.gla.ac.uk/services/enlighten**.

The process of discovering scholarly materials has evolved significantly over the past decade. Yet, although many users begin their search outside the library space using a diverse range of tools and workflows, the Library is well placed within this new information landscape as described above.

E-everything

The early twenty-first century has seen a complete transformation from print first to digital first.

The University has been visionary in supporting the early adoption of digital within the Library by ensuring sufficient budgets to cope with the costs of transition; specifically, in responding positively to requests from the Library to fund the purchase of digital back files of journals. This process was made more straightforward by the establishment in 2002 of the Library Research Annexe located at Hamiltonhill, around four miles from the main campus. This store offers excellent environmental conditions with twenty linear kilometres of high-density shelving for low-use print

research materials. As well as responding to the assimilation of St Andrew's College of Education by the University, it has been an essential element in relocating stock from each floor of the main Library building to allow a more effective use of space. Another essential element was active early participation in the UK Research Reserve – a collaborative distributed national research collection managed by a partnership between UK Higher Education organisations and the British Library. This allows de-duplication of low-use print materials and the consequent release of space. The University of Glasgow was a partner in the first phase of this project, and it was crucial to allowing significant progress in a move to digital collections while revitalising scarce space at the centre of the campus.

University of Glasgow Library staff were early leaders of national coordinated purchasing of information literature, as serials and books. In 2007 this led to a study to advise on the potential for a Scottish Digital Library jointly funded by the Universities of Glasgow and Edinburgh. The resultant Scottish Higher Education Digital Library was established in 2009 as a joint collaboration involving all members of the Scottish Confederation of University and Research Libraries. Such partnerships are essential to provide equal access to a wide range of current research literature, digitised primary sources, e-learning materials and data. Where possible, national and global collaboration achieves the best value for budgets and most effective use of staff resources.

Of annual budgets currently standing at just over £5m for materials, from 2015 onwards some 87% is reserved for digital resources and only some 13% for print and other media.

Space and services

As collections and services become increasingly networked, the physical Library continues to offer a neutral space, neither home nor office, with a range of environments to support research and learning, from social gathering space to individual study carrels.

The University's investment in electronic journals has allowed significant redevelopment of space, together with improved access to the content held in the journals.

In response to changes in teaching methods, learning patterns, increased student numbers and the move to digital, the redesign has focused on the internal ambiance of the Library, aiming to remodel it to modern contemporary standards; to provide high quality, adaptable and technology-rich learning spaces throughout with a broad availability of printed material and Wi-Fi connection; and to improve comfort conditions by enhancing lighting, and temperature and humidity controls.

The study spaces now range from casual seating to silent study carrels and allow the maximum benefit of daylight with appropriate glare control, while illumination in book stacks is also uniform.

Presence-detection lighting control and high-efficiency light sources ensure energy reductions, while Thyristor-drive technology permits close control of air delivery to match ambient temperature and humidity demands which

can vary significantly. The floors are coupled together through four atria-style spaces which allow extensive introduction of daylight into reading areas. Together with the height of the building these features also offer a stimulating backdrop to intensive study.

Opening hours have increased by 37% to meet student need and because the internal environment can now sustain greater usage. The Library remains a beacon of learning and a hive of activity in the centre of campus. Currently, it is open from 7.15 a.m. to 2.00 a.m., seven days per week, and 361 days per year.

A particular highlight was achieved in 2009 with the opening of the remodelled Level 3 Annexe, refurbished to the designs of architects William Nimmo & Partners, and turning a dingy hall housing a variety of outdated current periodical shelving, old desking and a poor staff area into a bright, fit-for-purpose collaborative learning zone with a café/social learning area, six group-working booths with screens, three large circular group pods with acoustic/visual screening and a variety of other study desks, complete with networked PCs. The whole area was redesigned for group working and has been very popular with students.

Work began in January 2012 to re-clad the Library building. Many of the original concrete cladding panels, installed between 1965 and 1968, had deteriorated over time. The main building was re-clad with a watertight aluminium rain-screen system to provide a 'total envelope solution' extending the life of the building by another fifty years and updating its external appeal. This huge project, a £4.5m investment by the University, was completed on schedule in summer 2013

A study booth. Photographic Unit [GUPU11-72-06996].

Lesley Richmond amongst the Archives.
Photographic Unit [GUPU08-257].

A variety of study spaces.
Photographic Unit [14-2398-3037].

Helen Durndell with Princess Royal on the official opening
of the Textile Conservation Centre, 2011. Photographic
Unit [GUPU11-023-TCC147].

Library in the sunshine. Photographic Unit
[GUPU14-048-28].

Announcing the University Library with a new neon sign, 2013. Photographic Unit [GUPU 13-024 -8].

The new Postgraduate Study space, opened in 2013. Photographic Unit [GUPU 13-092-83].

Concentration [GUPU 11-040-6806].

despite the many challenges in achieving such a complex project across a twelve-storey building which was open throughout the period and delivering full services. The opportunity was taken to provide some external lighting and the addition of the words 'University Library' at the top of the building.

January 2013 saw the opening of a stylish new postgraduate study space offering 150 individual study places and five bookable group-study rooms, all with plasma screens and data connections. In addition, lockers and couches are provided and the whole space is Wi-Fi enabled. Card access on the doors allows entry for postgraduate students of the University. A display on one wall provides inspiring quotes from notable alumni of the University. Representing a £2m capital investment from the University, this refurbishment required the prior clearance of all library material from the Level 5 Annexe.

Summer 2014 saw the opening of the revitalised Level 3, now open plan, with an extension of the same welcoming design template from the café/social learning area. It offers study booths with screens, a beautiful glass-walled central area containing high-demand print material but not restricting views across the whole space thanks to the lower height shelving. There are also individual study desks with networked PCs, and a variety of alternative study spaces. In addition, three more new spaces have also been created – the LearnLab offers teaching space for digital skills training; the TalkLab is a meeting room which can be used for small conferences, talks and presentations; and the LoungeLab, which can also be used for events, is a comfortable relaxed seating area with a bright open outlook towards the main University buildings.

Throughout all the building projects, environmental improvements have been made with reductions in carbon and toxic emissions. All the lifts have now been fully replaced and conform to current safety and accessibility legislation.

In 2015, again to the architectural designs of William Nimmo & Partners, a £3m project started on refreshing the Level 2 public entrance to the main Library, last redeveloped in the mid-1990s, totally clearing the Level 2 area, and converting Level 1 (the old Sub-Basement storage area) into a more traditional study area with some 155 places. Now on Level 2 there is a versatile open-plan active learning zone where students can configure and use the space to best meet their needs. A flexible service point, enhanced self-service options, exhibition space, upgraded entrance hall and extended lobby space for holding additional public exhibitions/events complete the remodelled facilities. The new exhibition space enables the Library to display unique and distinctive collections, both physically and digitally, ranging from traditional wall-mounted frames to multi-touch interactive screens. Students, staff and visitors are able to explore the collections and view exhibitions or displays themed to conferences and other events.

Finally, the conservation and digitisation suites at the back of the area have been comprehensively

The Library Today

Library Height	90m
Library floor area	25,831m²
Number of floors	12
Number of lifts	5
Library staff and support staff (equivalent of 218 full time)	334
Study spaces	2,337
Meeting rooms	17
Postgraduate area	150 spaces
Conservation studio	122m²
Digitisation unit	91m²

Other main study spaces	
Round Reading Room	135
James Ireland Memorial (Library Dentistry)	80
James Herriot Library (Veterinary Medicine)	130
Chemistry Branch Library	70
Adam Smith Library (Social Sciences)	58

refurbished. The conservation studio is in an area which has hitherto not been upgraded since the Library was built in 1968. Restrictions on space, access and facilities mean that staff have been unable to carry out the full range of conservation interventions required given the importance of the renowned University collections and archives. New equipment such as inbuilt light boxes extend conservators' options and also enhance the learning and teaching experience, allowing space for volunteers, students, interns and other conservators to work in a modern, flexible environment. Once again, the University is delighted that the Friends of the Library have stepped forward with a major contribution to allow the Exhibition Space and the Conservation Studio to be properly equipped.

Reflecting recent general changes in library use, the University of Glasgow expects its Library to offer the best possible service in a modern, welcoming environment, providing a balance of flexible and special-use spaces to spur dialogue and engagement, through events, displays, meetings, presentations, and informal collaboration. The rejuvenated Library building not only enriches the campus experience but importantly also aids student recruitment and retention.

Engagement

The Archives Department merged with the Library in 2008, and in 2011 the University Archivist also took responsibility for the Special Collections department, with a full integration of services from 2016. The extent of archival material has greatly risen from 1,844 metres of manuscripts to 6,225 metres of manuscripts following the merger.

Staff within these departments have embraced social media to highlight the wonderful heritage collections held by the University, internally and globally. Where possible, external funding has been sought to fully exploit the collections, either in collaboration with academic colleagues or in response to particular funding streams. The Friends of the Library have been stalwarts across this period in funding a variety of projects from the provision of specialist equipment, conservation activity, new acquisitions and

cataloguing. One recent stellar example has been their support for the *Ingenious Impressions* Exhibition, held in the Hunterian Art Gallery in 2015. This event, curated by Julie Gardham, Head of Special Collections, provided a very public stage for the Glasgow Incunabula Project, which over many years has seen the former Keeper of Special Collections, Jack Baldwin, examine every one of the Library's 1,060 incunabula (pre-1500 printed items).

A web catalogue of these rarities **www.gla.ac.uk/ services/incunabula** has been skilfully created, contributing to global scholarship in this area.

The University Photographic and Print Unit is also integrated within the Library. An example of its activity is a project to digitise the pre-1914 records of the Royal Crichton Hospital, Dumfries, and the Gartnavel Royal Hospital, Glasgow, funded by a grant from the Wellcome Trust. This is enabling researchers from around the world to access an important resource for the study of mental healthcare. Further details of this important activity are provided within the Chapter on Unique and Distinctive Collections.

View from Level 11. Photographic Unit.

Librarians this Century

Andrew Wale succeeded Henry Heaney in 1998, having been Deputy Librarian from 1980. Prior to his time at Glasgow he had been Joint Deputy Librarian at Manchester Polytechnic and previously worked at York University Library. He remained in post until 2001.

Chris Bailey, educated in Merseyside, a Dundee University graduate, undertook a one-year library traineeship at Ninewells Hospital before studying for a postgraduate diploma in Librarianship at the University of Strathclyde. After a time at a college of further education in Oxford, she returned to work at Strathclyde, moving to the University of Glasgow in 1991. For three years Chris was Executive Secretary to the Consortium of University Research Libraries (now Research Libraries UK), before returning to the University of Glasgow Library and becoming University Librarian in 2001. Chris oversaw the incorporation of the St Andrews College Library on a newly refurbished level in the Library.

Helen Durndell, born in London, Aberdeenshire-educated and a graduate of the University of Aberdeen, took up the post of graduate trainee at Strathclyde University, where she acquired a postgraduate diploma in Librarianship before working at the Glasgow School of Art, and then at the Western School of Nursing. Helen joined Glasgow University Library in 1979 as a Subject Librarian for Engineering, moving to Circulation and then Enquiries in the mid-1980s and becoming a Principal Assistant Librarian in 1989. She was Deputy Librarian from 2001 and Librarian from 2006. Helen continued to extend the opening hours of the Library and oversaw the e-revolution and the introduction of the café and social learning areas. Helen has taken a leadership role in the library world, chairing SCURL (Scottish Consortium of University & Research Libraries) and acting as a Board Member of SLIC (Scottish Library & Information Council), SCONUL (Society of College, National and University Librarians) and the National Library of Scotland.

Susan Ashworth was appointed University Librarian from August 2015. Born in Scotland and educated in Rochdale, Susan graduated from the University of Glasgow with a degree in English and History and then gained a Master's degree in Librarianship at the University of Sheffield. Susan's career started in Manchester City Public Libraries running two branch libraries in the inner city; then she returned to Glasgow and the University Library as Head of the Issue Desk, before becoming a Subject Librarian in Science and Engineering plus Medical and Life Sciences and then a Deputy Director with particular responsibility for the Library's support for research.

The Café Area. Photographic Unit.

Chapter 6

Illustrated books in the Library – More than just words can say…

Roundel featuring the zodiacal sign Aquarius in the calendar for January. From the Hunterian Psalter, England, c. 1170. Archives & Special Collections, MS Hunter 229 (U/3/20), detail from folio 1r° [H229_0001rwf].

Laurence Grove
University of Glasgow

Illustrated Books as a Glasgow Speciality

If we were to ask people around the world where Glasgow beats the rest of the planet, some of the answers might be more expected than others. Perhaps football fever would feature, given that the first international was played here, and that the (religious) fervour that accompanies the Old Firm and the national team does justice to the fact that Glasgow has the highest number of UEFA elite stadia. Alternatively it could just be the friendliness of the place, a feeling reflected in modern marketing slogans such as the internationally acclaimed 'Glasgow's Miles Better' and the current 'People Make Glasgow' motto, and confirmed by the *Rough Guide's* 'World's Friendliest City' award. More traditional is innovation in architecture, ranging from the Victorian splendour of Buchanan Street to the riverside additions of Foster and Hadid, but overshadowed maybe by the Art Nouveau 'wow' factor brought by Mackintosh. In recent years the focus of Glasgow's contribution to the creative arts has arguably shifted somewhat. The hipsters and a UNESCO City of Music status tell us that the Fourth Art is nowadays up there, represented by the Celtic Connections festival, but also by the emergence of groups such as Belle & Sebastian, Franz Ferdinand and Texas. Yet the fact that since 2006 Glasgow has dominated the Turner prize with 30% of nominees suggests that the city's world-beater status continues to lie in the field of the plastic arts alongside architecture. The list goes on, and all are represented in the Library's collections: yes, even football (see, for example, *Free Kicks at Football* of 1882, Spec. Coll. Mu2-i.38).

Among the pioneering ventures that the city has witnessed and which are documented in the University Library holdings are the invention of television, the development of photography, and the launch of the first ever comic (more on the latter two below), but we also have arguably the world's best collection of illustrated books. Indeed, largely owing to the illuminated manuscripts from the collections of Dr William Hunter, the holdings of the University Library chart the history of illustrated texts that in the western world dates back to the illuminated manuscripts of late Antiquity.

Text/Image Specialities and the Stirling Maxwell Centre

The mainstay of Glasgow University Library's outstanding text/image speciality is the Stirling Maxwell Collection of emblem books and related literature. From 1843 onwards Sir William Stirling Maxwell (1818-1878), the University's Dean of Faculties (1857-59) and Chancellor (1875-78), amassed emblem books – see our top ten *Amorum emblemata* below for a precise explanation of what emblem books are – and went on to acquire several important Victorian collections that were to form the library at Keir House, near Stirling. This library was transferred upon his death, first, to Pollok House, in the park where the Burrell Collection now stands, and then in 1958, after a two-year delay, to the University of Glasgow – at least for all emblem-related material – via the will of Sir John, Sir William's son.

The collection consists of some 2,000 volumes, including emblem books, but also fête books, and other illustrated publications. Further Glasgow University Library collections supplement these holdings in related fields, for example via the

Ferguson Collection of alchemical literature, or the Gemmell Collection of Dance of Death material.[1] Most of the Stirling Maxwell works hail from the Renaissance or seventeenth century, but Sir William additionally included some Victorian volumes reflecting the contemporary revival of interest in romanticised medievalism. Overall of particular note are the ninety-plus editions of Alciato's *Emblematum liber*, the book from which the form takes its name, and the range of virtually all French emblem books, including related versions, such as the unique copy of Thomas Combe's translation of Guillaume de La Perrière.

Sir William did not stop there. Indeed, if anything he is best known for his love of Spanish paintings, of which his collection, mainly still kept at Pollok House, is one of the best outside Iberia. This love was to be joined with another as Sir William ensured that his book on the subject, *Annals of the Artists of Spain* (1848), was to be the first work on art illustrated by the photographic printing process, in this case using sensitised paper to produce Talbotypes. We will see more on Sir William Henry Fox Talbot's invention below, and on the Library's outstanding collections of early photography.

Other nineteenth-century illustrated texts of note in the Library holdings include Talbot's *Pencil of Nature* featuring high-tech images (for 1844), the thirteen boxes of nineteenth-century French political caricatures (Spec. Coll. HX 133), and the world's first comic, *The Glasgow Looking Glass* of 1825, part of the Murray Collection of local materials. Yet while Sir William's collection anchors our flagship text/image specialisation, this interest has extended beyond its base by the acknowledgement and exploration of related riches throughout the Library. As such, many of the collections offer research material for study in the Stirling Maxwell Centre for the Study of Text/Image Cultures, which owes its name and original existence to the collection of emblem books, but which has also, since 2011, gone on to emphasise text/image forms across genres and centuries. Alongside a digitisation programme, sponsorship of exhibitions, conferences and publications, teaching at undergraduate and postgraduate levels, the Centre has attracted to Glasgow scholars from the USA, Canada, Brazil, Spain, France, Russia, Romania, Italy, Ireland, Wales, England and so on…[2]

Spoilt for Choice

The growing recognition of the Stirling Maxwell Centre as the world leader in its field is due to, and in direct acknowledgement of, this unique specialisation permitted by the Glasgow holdings. Why this should happen here will be the question for our conclusion, but before then the abundance of riches creates a delightful dilemma: how do we convey in a necessarily limited number of words and illustrations something of the splendour of a phenomenon that seems all-encompassing and endlessly fascinating? How do we do justice to collections that all combine text and image, but which represent the full spectrum of media, styles, genres, countries and chronology?

The answer represents the popular vogue for everyday instruction in condensed form, bringing together text and image so as to provide a snappy memorable message. Individual emblems are discrete, but, when assembled as in a book, the collection as a whole can often build up to convey a bigger picture. My response, therefore, is to create ten Friendly Shelves emblems, each with a title – that of the book –, an image, and a *subscriptio*, i.e. my commentary, which when put together produce a snapshot of something special within our collections. And collectively they offer an appetizing glimpse into collections that. when taken together, are very special indeed.

Just as Gilles Corrozet in 1540 produced his emblem book entitled *Hecatomgraphie* or 'One Hundred Images', I am producing a *Decagraphie*, or 'Ten Images'. The choice is personal, but then so is the model of Corrozet: the acquisition of SMAdd.385, the 1540 edition of the *Hecatomgraphie*, in 1995 coincided, more or less, with my arrival in Glasgow. My *Decagraphie* of picture books will unashamedly have omissions and angles that might infuriate some previously friendly readers. Above all, the vagaries and shortcomings of my own cultural upbringing mean that my selection is, I am afraid, western-based and male-dominated.

The good that can come of this is that a top ten, like an emblem, is reader-focused, encouraging the recipient to rethink, explore, and respond with his or her own version. It is a starting point, not a *terminus ad quem*. My selection may be infuriating and limited, but it is above all challenging. One of the main omissions from my choice is that of any work from the current century, a gap squarely emphasised by the use of a chronological listing, from 1170 onwards, when so many other ways of organising the selection – by genre, by collection, by geography – would have been possible. Why? Because it is the format itself that is the twenty-first-century choice. The technology of today – the internet pages to be clicked with likes, and the vox-pop domination

of TV – is home to the top ten listing. How else, therefore, could we end a selection other than by asking the reader to explore the collections and reselect the past, and, so as to fill the gaps, to embark on the future choice, just as the University Library of the twenty-first century embraces the text/image world of online catalogues and the head-spinning resources of the web.

1. The Hunterian Psalter
MS Hunter 229 (U.3.20)
England, c. 1170

Anyone who has been lucky enough to have seen the Hunterian Psalter on display or, if very fortunate and privileged, to have consulted it, will know that it is a 'wow'-inducing treasure that opens our selection of ten. A 'wow' not just because of its (understandably) restricted access, the bomb-proof box in which it comes to the reader, or its reported multi-million insurance value, but above all, for me personally at least, for the experience of travelling though time and coming eye to eye with the past, whilst glimpsing a vision of eternity. Time is transcended when staring at the figure of Christ, but also through our encounter with the illustration for Aquarius, the everyday water-carrier, permanently struggling under the load and spilling the contents of his jar as portrayed in the zodiacal roundel for January in the opening calendar.

With its 210 leaves of carefully selected calf vellum and historiated initials, the beautifully written Hunterian Psalter is generally considered to be the world's masterpiece of English Romanesque book art. In particular, thirteen full-page miniatures illustrate scenes from the scriptures in vivid colours. Some portray a chronological progression in two 'frames' – the

1. King David from the Hunterian Psalter, England, c. 1170. Archives & Special Collections MS Hunter 229 (U.3.20) [H229_0021vwf].

can date it to just before 1173 (the year of his canonisation), and reference to several northern saints suggests it possibly would not have been composed for use in the south, a conjecture which explains its previous title of the York Psalter, although it might have been intended for use anywhere within that ecclesiastical province such as in the diocese of Lincoln.[3] To judge by the three commemorations of St Augustine, Bishop of Hippo, together with the cycle of Marian illuminations with Augustinian associations and the absence of the translation of St Benedict, this splendid manuscript seems to have been commissioned for use either in a house of Augustinian canons or by an individual connected with that order.

To repeat, the Psalter is a masterpiece of visual art, one which draws in the reader – today, but undoubtedly also 800 years ago – through the very beauty of the object and its pages. Yet at its base is a biblical text – a Psalter is a Book of Psalms –, although it is the portrait of King David that inspires us as we contemplate the psalms he was supposed to have created. A quick comparison can be made with the University's (and Scotland's) oldest complete western manuscript, MS Hunter 96 (T.4.13), a book of medical writings produced either in Northern Italy or Southern France and dating from the late eighth or early ninth century. Here the arches of the pre-Caroline script invite us in to a new beginning matching the one provided by the text's medical remedies despite their grounding in the Hippocratic and Galenic traditions. This manuscript and the Hunterian Psalter – not as old but more stunning in its artistry – remind us that, via the illuminations that underpin the birth of our medieval book culture, text and image work together to draw us in.

creation of Adam and Eve, and then the fruit of temptation, for example – others are single images, such as King David tuning his harp or the Assumption of Mary. The style is Byzantine with its gold backcloth, but the typically English elongated 'characters' are brought to life by their thin poise and piercing eyes.

William Hunter acquired the volume in 1769 at the Gaignat sale in Paris. From the lack of any allusion to Thomas à Becket's murder we

2. *Les Cent Nouvelles Nouvelles*
MS Hunter 252 (U.4.10)
France, c. 1470-1490

The same is true of MS Hunter 252, although the context and subject matter could not be more different and the manuscript is written in several hands. And as in the Hunterian Psalter the multiple frames of the images create a comic-strip narrative, although here virgins receive a far bawdier adoration.

2. Les Cent Nouvelles Nouvelles, France, c. 1470-1490. Archives & Special Collections MS Hunter 252 (U.4.10) [H252_0172vwf].

MS Hunter 252, also acquired by Hunter from the Gaignat sale, is the world's only surviving manuscript of the fifteenth-century collection of racy tales, *Les Cent Nouvelles Nouvelles* or 'One Hundred New Stories'. Presented to Philip Duke of Burgundy and modelled on Boccaccio's *Decameron* and Poggio's *Facetiae*, the tales largely fell out of favour between the sixteenth and nineteenth centuries – arguably less because of their saucy nature than owing to the early modern preference for identifiable authors over any anonymous supposed compiler –, but following Pierre Champion's 1928 edition (Paris: Droz) the collection has seen a number of translations and editions. To give an idea of the tone, tale LXXIX is the story of an over-enthusiastic doctor who administers clysters liberally. When he mistakes a passer-by seeking his lost donkey for a patient, he dishes out the treatment, causing the man to bray. When the nearby donkey reacts and is thus found, the treatment is admired for its efficacy! Elsewhere we enjoy a colourful cast of cuckolds, naïve young ladies and bed-hopping nuns and monks.

Each story opens with a vignette illustration of admittedly average stylistic quality displaying an often lively key scene from the story. Not only do these transport us to the people, decors and domestic interiors of the extensive fifteenth-century Duchy of Burgundy (including the Burgundian Low Countries), they also display incredible innovation with visual narrative techniques. Some have separate compartments providing frames, others play with 'continuous narrative' by showing the 'before' and 'after' actions side by side. Five centuries later Winsor McCay, Hergé or Dave McLean would be considered masters of the graphic novel for using such devices.

Nonetheless all the twentieth-century printed editions of the tales, despite being based on the Glasgow manuscript, went to press without the images, and with a few honourable exceptions most academic studies ignored them. Things are due to change with forthcoming scholarship, but this in itself can tell us something about the way we have viewed culture over the years. Previously pictures accompanying text were largely seen as an unnecessary or disturbing addition. Now, as comics gain cult status, we return to the mindset of the central and late Middle Ages as the picture interacts with the text to produce a 'double whammy' for the overall effect.

3. *Hypnerotomachia Poliphili,*
variously attributed
Hunter Bh.2.14
Venice: Aldus Manutius, 1499

The modernity of our third choice is attested by its starring role in the 2004 thriller *The Rule of Four* (New York: Dial) by Ian Caldwell and Dustin Thomason, in which Princeton students and their entourage delve into esoteric mysteries at the heart of which lies the *Hypnerotomachia Poliphili* or *The Strife of Love in a Dream* (the title given by Joscelyn Godwin to his 1999 translation). Thumbing through the volume in question it is easy to appreciate how it has the makings of an adventure worthy of Dan Brown. Indeed Dan Brown also name-checks it in *The Da Vinci Code*, as does Johnny Depp when playing rare book dealer Dean Corso in Roman Polanski's *The Ninth Gate* (1999). Here picture books produced by Lucifer himself hold the key to life's mysteries, along with a few naked romps with Emmanuelle Seigner. To allow a quick aside, Johnny himself is known to be a fan of old

3. *Hypnerotomachia Poliphili*, variously attributed, Venice: Aldus Manutius, 1499. Archives & Special Collections Hunterian Bh.2.14 [Bh.2.14 B2v].

books and is reported to have visited Glasgow University Library's Special Collections, as has Patricia Cornwell.

The *Hypnerotomachia Poliphili* is therefore modern in its appeal, but it also remains a masterpiece of the early art of printing, with its elegant layout and custom-made font. Bh 2.14 is a much-prized copy of the 1499 first edition, acquired by Hunter at the John Baber sale in

1766, but the Library also holds the 1545, 1554, c. 1600, 1883 and 1890 French and English editions and versions.

When we open the *Hypnerotomachia Poliphili*, its images draw us in with their bustling processions, exotic animals or extravagant costumes, but enigmas abound as we try to decipher who the characters are and what they are doing – why the dismembered bodies or the chained-up ladies pulling chariots? – or how the inscriptions and rebuses relate to the pictures. The dream-based interchange that is central to the overall narrative adds a further layer of esotericism, one that echoes the very naming of the author, to be found only in an acrostic formed from the opening letter of each chapter. This reads POLIAM FRATER FRANCISCVS COLVMNA PERAMAVIT, 'Brother Francesco Colonna has dearly loved Polia', indicating that the work is by someone called Francesco Colonna who was either a Venetian Dominican priest (1433/34-1527) or a wealthier namesake Roman governor. That said, it has also been ascribed to the Italian humanist Leon Battista Alberti (1404-1472) and, more speculatively, to the mighty Florentine ruler Lorenzo de Medici (1449-1492).

It is a work in which the two parts – the first from Poliphilus's viewpoint, the second from that of his allegorical beloved Polia (meaning literally 'many things') – overlap, creating the sort of self-referential narrative favoured in cinema productions such as *Trois couleurs*, *Momento*, or famously *Pulp Fiction*. The visual appeal is enhanced by the fact that images become sequential text, and the text becomes image through the use of print layout. Juxtaposed processional vignettes give the notion of

movement, as in a comic strip. If this is a graphic novel – as indeed suggested by the inclusion of the *Hypnerotomachia Poliphili* in the 2016 Hunterian exhibition *Comic Invention* –, then it is the top-of-the-scale luxury production for intellectuals and inquisitives.

4. Anonymous manuscript copy of Clément Marot's twelve stanzas titled *Visions de Pétrarque* (illustrated with watercolours)
S.M.M 2
France, c. 1534

Another example of an 'early comic' is S.M.M. 2, the manuscript *Visions de Pétrarque*, acquired with Sir William Stirling Maxwell's bequest, but with little known of its prior provenance. It is a 'comic' in that each scene is a depiction

4. Anonymous manuscript copy of Clément Marot's twelve stanzas titled *Visions de Pétrarque* (illustrated with watercolours). Archives & Special Collections S.M.M.2, France, c. 1534 [S.M.M.2-0023wf].

'before and after' consisting of a six-line verse and a facing illustration over two pages, thereby forming a picture narrative. We see a doe brought down by hounds, a sea-bound ship that then founders, a tree uprooted by lightning, a fresh spring consumed by an earthquake, a Phoenix self-inflicting a blood wound, and, finally, a woman's beauty that is then lost. The overall theme is that of transience, i.e. the inevitability of earthly decay with the passing of time.

Notwithstanding the elegance of this rendition of Petrarch's poetic *Visions*, it is the images that steal the show. The woman's swirling dress and flowing blonde hair have the delicate Renaissance beauty we might associate with Botticelli, and the sinking ship conveys the violence of the high seas. This immediacy compares with that of the trenchant work by DC superstar Frank Quitely in the *Comic Invention* display, a tribute to both artists for the way in which they leave a marking stamp on the imagination of the viewer. Such a comparison spanning five centuries is fitting for the a-temporal quality of S.M.M. 2: its central depiction of the passing of time is all the more striking for the antiquarian beauty of a manuscript on vellum, but a manuscript produced after the invention of printing, and thus a harbinger of the retro splendour of the Pre-Raphaelites, the Arts and Crafts movement, or discs on vinyl in the twenty-first century.

This is not the only peculiarity of S.M.M. 2. The text itself now appears in current editions of the complete works of the canonical Renaissance poet Clément Marot (1496-1544) as it is the base (and only) manuscript of his rendition of Petrarch's *Visions*. Our manuscript also has an interesting history in that the watercolours are now known to be the inspiration for the woodcuts that illustrate Jan Van der Noot's *Theatre of Worldlings* (first edition 1568). A further quirk from three centuries later is the addition of a nineteenth-century frontispiece entitling the volume *Emblems* [*sic*] *en rime françoise*. The fake historical spelling underlines the Victorian attraction to the past, as well as the (re)discovery of the fashion for emblem books, to which this addition is thus retrospectively attributed. Overall therefore S.M.M. 2 is a stunning mixture of a one-off cultural artefact and an object of outstanding artistic beauty.

5. Maurice Scève,
Délie: Objet de plus haulte vertu
S.M. Add.467
Paris: Nicolas du Chemin, 1564

Despite the caveats expressed in my introduction, another masterpiece of emblem literature does lead us into the twenty-first century in that it was acquired during the summer of 2014, but more on that below… Like the *Visions*, the *Délie* is a product of sixteenth-century France, and is now part of the Stirling Maxwell Collection. Unlike our previous offerings it does have a named author, Maurice Scève, although in this edition the initials 'M.S.' and his portrait suffice. Scève, born around 1501 and living until some time after 1560, is recognised as the main figure in the Lyon school of Renaissance poetry, although his fame is also associated with his supposed discovery in Avignon of the tomb of Laura, Petrarch's love inspiration. Here then is a further link with S.M.M. 2, as the *Délie*, like the *Visions*, is largely modelled on the *Canzionere*.

5. Maurice Scève, *Délie: Objet de plus haulte vertu*, Paris: Nicolas du Chemin, 1564, Archives & Special Collections S.M. Add.467 [SMAdd.467_titlepage].

Though the *Délie* does not label itself as an emblem book, the 449 *dizains* (poems of ten lines with ten syllables) are interspersed with fifty emblems that pick up on the general themes of the text, and whose motto generally echoes the final words of the *dizain* it directly accompanies. So in the case of *dizain* 150, the poem tells of the lover's inability to resist the loved one as being his undoing. The final verse, 'Son amytié, peu à peu, me ruyne' ('her friendship, little by little, ruins me') reiterates the words of the emblem's frame, 'Pour aymer souffre ruyne' ('to love suffer ruin').

The accompanying image is of ivy climbing a wall, with its structure thus to be undermined. Ivy is not mentioned in the *dizain*, but by association we refer to its emblematic resonances of fidelity but also betrayal, adding a further, but ambiguous, layer of meaning. Who is doing the ruining? If it is the lady, how does this fit with her 'vertu'? Is it the ruin of unannounced love or unrequited love? Or is it a love-hate clingy relationship?[4]

Ambiguity, both visual and textual, is the key to the *Délie*, which could be described as the best-ever collection of poetry that nobody understands. The arcane verses are peppered with text/image riddles that present picture puzzles to tease the reader seeking final meaning: a maiden stroking a unicorn, the Tower of Babel, the rising dead, Actaeon chased by his stags, a moth to the candle... The only message that seems to make sense at the end of it is that love, here for the eponymous Délie, conquers all, but that there is a good chance that the adorable Délie, an anagram of l'Idée, is in fact not human but rather the beauty that is Art.

Our edition is that of 1564, the second of two – the first being dated 1544 – but possibly the rarer one. Only a handful of copies are in public collections, and when this one came under auction at Christie's as part of the Yates, Thomson and Bright sale,[5] it was the first to have been placed on offer for decades, with no foreseeable second chance. The fact that Glasgow University Library, with help from the Friends, was able and willing to invest considerable sums in a book of this calibre – and to win it when the hammer came down – is tribute to its enduring appeal, but also to foresight and commitment worthy of Hunter and Stirling Maxwell to whom we owe our previous choices.

6. Otto Van Veen, *Amorum emblemata*, with manuscript additions by François Tristan L'Hermite

S.M. Add. 392

Antwerp: Hieronymus Verdussen, 1608

Another emblematic S.M. Add. item acquired with acumen and with its own unique story to tell is this copy of the major collection of love emblems by the humanist draughtsman and painter Otto Van Veen (1556-1629), published in three polyglot versions – Latin, French and Dutch – and continuing the seventeenth-century tradition begun in Amsterdam, 1601, by the artist Jacques de Gheyn illustrating Dutch poems on love by Daniel Heinsius. When in 1997 Maggs Bros of London contacted the Library for a possible sale of an emblem book, we were delighted to inspect it, but knew that we already had a 1608 *Amorum emblemata* (S.M. 1050). The book itself proved to be an interleaved copy – a common practice of the day enabling owners to personalise it with additions by themselves

and friends. It was the additional annotations that caught our attention, and then drove us to excitement as we realised many of them to be verses by François Tristan L'Hermite (1601-1655), one of the leading poets and dramatists of the Louis XIII era. The excitement grew as it became clear that the poems, whose references to a restless sleep, the flame of love, or the watering of flowers previously had remained enigmatic, were playing upon and interacting with the cupids of the facing emblems. Thirteen further poems were not known from print sources, but were undoubtedly lost works by Tristan, perhaps forming part of certain works of youth to which the poet refers in a published letter.

One of these thirteen is opposite the emblem which shows Cupid holding aloft the number 1, encouraging us to decipher the meaning that love, like the stream in the background, is less strong if it is shared, a theme picked up by the facing poem as shown here. (For a quick aside, this same Cupid also appears in Vermeer's *Lady Standing at a Virginal*.) Throughout the volume, Otto Van Veen (1556-1629), often best known as the master of Rubens, worked with engraver Cornelis Boel (1576-1621) to create and embellish this whimsical Cupid character who flies through the air, breaks across metal and fights off monsters, and whose adventures must have drawn in readers much as those of Superman do today.

Emblems function through a layering of text and image whereby the individual parts are superseded by the combined result. In the case of S.M. Add. 392 a further palimpsestic layer comes from the addition of the Tristan poems, as well as that of further verses by others yet to be fully explored.

6. Otto Van Veen, *Amorum emblemata*, with manuscript additions by François Tristan L'Hermite, Antwerp: Hieronymus Verdussen, 1608. Archives & Special Collections S.M. Add. 392 [S.M. Add. 392-page 65.wf].

Where Tristan is concerned, printed image also joins with time-machine access to the creative process: certain of the manuscripts have scribbled corrections, as we imagine Tristan refining his art directly onto the page, in what is now, we believe, the only literary manuscript in his own hand. S.M. Add. 392 exemplifies, if any document can, the thrill of historical detective work.

7. Papers relating to the case of Mary Toft
Hunter Aa.7.20
England, 1726

Our seventh choice is not a single document but several, all concerning a curious event. Having given birth on 27th September 1726 to what appeared to be the body of a cat, Mary Toft (c. 1701-1763), a servant from Godalming, called upon John Howard, a leading Guildford obstetrician, who then attended and presided over the subsequent 'births' of a variety of animal parts as well as nine dead rabbits.[6] Howard's reaction was to seek publicity, sending letters to the country's leading surgeons as well as to the secretary of King George I. Mary Toft's renown increased, aided by a statement from Nathaniel St André (c. 1680-1776), surgeon to the King, that he believed the phenomenon to be genuine – an opinion shared by the young Scottish physician John Maubray (1700-1732), who likewise subscribed to the theory of 'maternal impression' and the existence of 'sooterkins' (fabled small creatures born to susceptible women influenced during pregnancy by the presence of animals or household pets). Toft finally confessed to staging a hoax on 7th December 1726: at the instigation of Howard, and others, and with the help of a porter to smuggle rabbits, she had inserted the bodies herself before acting out the births. The publicity continued as Toft

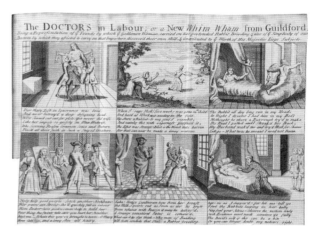

7. *Papers relating to the case of Mary Toft*, England, 1726. Archives & Special Collections Hunterian Aa.7.20 [Aa.7.20 _plate14f].

became a prison celebrity, while St André in particular, and the medical profession in general, were now disgraced. Numerous pamphlets followed, generally mocking in tone, as well as satirical prints, and a play, *The Surrey-Wonder: An Anatomical Farce*, produced, according to a contemporary print, at London's Theatre Royal.

Papers relating to the Mary Toft affair have been brought together in the Hunterian collection, in particular for volume Aa 7.20, via James Douglas, a doctor on the periphery of the case. Alongside various pamphlets, of particular interest are two visual depictions: *The Doctors in Labour; or a New Whim Wham from Guildford* (anonymous, 1726) and William Hogarth's *Cunicularii or the Wise Men of Godliman in Consultation* (1726). The former consists of four rows of three images, each accompanied by a six-line verse telling the story, initially in accordance with Mary Toft's account, whilst portraying St André as a court jester. The Hogarth print, which would have appeared in the run-up to Christmas, parodies the episode via reference to the visit of the Wise Men, who in this case are un-wise establishment figures. Hogarth adds touches of bawdy humour through the dumb-struck husband (character E), Samuel Molyneux (character B), the Prince of Wales's secretary, as philosopher 'Searching into the depth of things', and Howard (character D), here implied as being in collusion with the hoax, telling the rabbit-bringing porter 'It's too big'.

These pieces are also examples of Early Modern image narrative, essentially pre-industrial comics. Hogarth is also a key figure in the search for an inventor of the comic strip, with his candidacy supported by the use of speech bubbles, his grotesque caricatures and their biting satire, and the portrayal of narrative through images. This is despite Hogarth being active some one hundred years prior to Rodolphe Töpffer (1799-1846), the Swiss schoolmaster whom French-language critics have crowned the 'inventeur de la bande dessinée' by dint of the adventures of M. Pencil, M. Cryptogame and others penned for the amusement of his pupils. The prints from the Mary Toft case are therefore interesting in that they predate the most commonly cited Hogarth pieces, such as *The Rake's Progress* (1735 for the prints), by half a decade, and those by Töpffer by over a century.

From an analytical viewpoint Mary Toft is interesting in that she promotes, literally but also metaphorically, a 'bottom up' approach to culture. Her tale [*sic*] presents history through the deeds and doings of the everyday, a method developed critically by the likes of Michel de Certeau in his *L'Invention du quotidien* and Michel Foucault in *Histoire de la folie à l'âge classique* or *Surveiller et punir*, to be followed,

in the twenty-first century, by a methodology labelled as 'Everyday Studies'. Books may recount the deeds of Kings and Gods, but in cases such as this they also portray the follies and tribulations of common folk, the 'Man bites dog' of their day, depictions that are rendered striking in satirical images, and to be appreciated centuries on by those willing to look beyond the writings of canonised authors.

8. *The Glasgow Looking Glass*
Bh14-x.8.
Scotland, 1825-1826

The contest for the title of world's first comic becomes central with our next publication, the centrepiece of the 2016 Hunterian exhibition *Comic Invention*. This volume is a luxury coloured gathering of all issues of the *Glasgow Looking Glass* bequeathed in 1921, but the Library also has single numbers, black and white bound volumes, and the 1906 facsimile reprint.[7] Produced by the ex-London satirical cartoonist William Heath (c. 1795-1840) with John Watson and Thomas Hopkirk, the *Glasgow Looking Glass* first appeared on 11th June 1825 and ran for 19 issues until June 1826, changing title to the broader *Northern Looking Glass* from issue 6 (18th August 1825). The sharp increase in its selling outlets between issues 1 and 16 points to a soaring success, and the publication's notoriety is to be gauged by references in contemporary accounts of Glasgow life, such as John Strang's *Glasgow and its Clubs: Or Glimpses of the Condition, Manners, Characters, and Oddities of the City, During the Past and Present Centuries* (London: Richard Griffin, 1856). Indeed it seems that the *Looking Glass*'s undoing was in fact its celebrity, with its biting satire making

8. *The Glasgow Looking Glass*, Scotland, 1825-1826. Archives & Special Collections SP Coll Bh14-x.8. [Bh14-x.8_vol1_page1].

not having been publicised as a process before 1818. Its four-page (originally three, but always one folded sheet) content was a mixture of local and international satire, touching upon politics, character types and fashions. Many of these were single frame gags or spoofs of journalistic habits, such as the 'Advertisements' section in which 'well aired furnished rooms' for 'Board & Lodging' accompany an image of the Duke Street prison (issue 1), or the 'Public Library' which is pictured at 75 Hutcheson Street, in fact the address of the publisher (issue 2)! The words 'To be continued', implying narrative continuation, feature from the first page of issue 2, here for a 'Series of Occasional Essays: No 1 On Taste', although the first picture narratives are the *Voyage of a Steam Boat from Glasgow to Liverpool*, for which one or two images were published in issues 2 to 6 depicting the various stages of the journey, or, starting in issue 4, *History of a Coat*.

The first episode of *History of a Coat* gives four rows in two columns advancing from a bored shepherd boy, to the shearing of a sheep, the fabrication of the coat, its dandy owner, and his renouncing of the coat after it gets damaged in a fight. Subsequent instalments, with the conclusion in issue 6, show the coat's fortunes as it flits from owner to owner, and so doing provides a chronicle of the various strata of society, an 'object narrative' on a par with Balzac's *La Peau de chagrin* (1831), or even the building that is the central character of Chris Ware's *Building Stories* (2012). The creation of narrative through image, with an overlap of text – some of the frames are labelled – would make this the first comic strip within the first 'comic'. Elsewhere the *Glasgow Looking Glass* also provides speech bubbles, or narratives with

enemies for Heath, who, also spurred on by drinking debts, fled back to London at the height of its popularity.

From first glance onwards the *Glasgow Looking Glass* was striking as a publication dominated by images, and one can but imagine how original it must have appeared to its tentative 1825 readership, and how high-tech, coming from the lithographic presses of John Watson, lithography text beyond simple labelling, as in the seven-frame story of Scottish Hogmanay revelries and the subsequent price paid on New Year's Day, as told in issue 14 'more for the information of our English, than our Scottish Readers'.

The *Glasgow Looking Glass* therefore fills all the criteria necessary to qualify as the world's first comic, and within its pages carries the first comic strip. Why then did it go undiscovered and unnoticed for so long despite being locally reprinted in 1906? One can only assume that in pre-internet and online catalogue days scholars would not have thought to look amongst the shelves of a medieval Scottish University for the precursor to *Beano* and Batman.

9. Sir William Henry Fox Talbot, *The Pencil of Nature*
Photo A18
London: Longman, Brown, Green, and Longmans, 1844

Whereas the *Glasgow Looking Glass* pounced upon visual technology developed elsewhere – lithography is generally credited to Alois Senefelder in Munich in 1796 before the published announcement and distribution of the process in 1818 –, Sir William Henry Fox Talbot (1800-1877) personally created the technology upon which others were to pounce. Although the methods used for his Talbotypes, as he was to name them, were surpassed within a few years, he nonetheless provided the essentials for what we now know as photography and photo-mechanical printing, and *The Pencil of Nature* is the volume that started it all off.

Talbot's correspondence shows that he spent considerable time following Louis Daguerre's progress towards the invention of the photographic Daguerrotype, improving on the Frenchman's methods by dint of the fact that his Calotype process, which he unveiled in 1841, used negatives, thereby allowing multiple copies to be made of a given image. In 1844 Talbot published *The Pencil of Nature* through Longman, Brown, Green, and Longmans of London. The work was originally published over two years and in six fascicules, although our copy (Photo A18) is in a single volume.[8] This was the first published collection of photographic images.

The Pencil of Nature consists of 24 well composed photographic illustrations, each with a title and short, perceptive or occasionally Romantic commentary on the facing page, plus an introduction outlining the methods and importance of the new process. The attractive

9. Sir William Henry Fox Talbot, *The Pencil of Nature*, London: Longman, Brown, Green, and Longmans, 1844. Sp Coll Photo A18 [PhotoA18_plateVI].

variety of the images chosen underlines the broad scope of the new process, taking examples from interior objects such as china dishes or a bust of Patroclus, outdoor scenes from the farms and countryside, or city-based architectural motifs, and copies of artworks, including a lithograph of caricatures and a facsimile of a 1484 manuscript.

As well as combining a technological breakthrough with a work of aesthetic beauty, *The Pencil of Nature* is of interest to us for the insight it gives into the assumptions underpinning the culture of the image at the time. On an immediate level it is significant that Talbot felt the need to publish his showpiece collection of photos with one or two sides of accompanying complementary text. This could be explanation of technical matters associated with the new process, both as used in the plate in question and with respect to further possibilities, but it could also contextualise in a wider cultural sense, outlining the broad possibilities offered by the new photographic art, as compared with the subtleties of a master painter.

Talbot is at pains to give his achievement as artistic a presentation as possible, as he makes clear in the text that accompanies Plate VI, 'The Open Door', referring to his work as 'the early beginnings of a new art', and so making the image not just a representation but also a metaphor for the process. Similarly in the case of the ladder image (Plate XIV), we can see that what may appear to be a rustic arrangement of randomly chosen objects is in fact laden with symbolic significance, as humankind progresses upwards.

The Pencil of Nature represents a milestone in the journey of the modern image, one that is supplemented by the Dougan and the Hill & Adamson Collections, treasuries of early photography that make this a key strength of the University Library with its special isolated low-temperature conservation facilities offering amongst the best such material resources in Europe.

10. The Edwin Morgan Scrapbooks
MS Morgan C/1-16
Scotland, c. 1931 – c. 1966

Mass photography combined with text creates our final choice, perhaps the most eclectic of the ten, but also another unique strength of Glasgow University Library. The Edwin Morgan scrapbooks were compiled by the future first Scots Makar (Scottish national poet) from childhood, around the age of 11, until the late 1960s, when Morgan was in his forties. As such they are a Glaswegian work in progress, an artistic creation, and a chronicle of one man's times. The scrapbooks were purchased by the University from Morgan himself in 1981, and form part of the unique broader collection of over 1,500 manuscripts relating to his life and works.[9]

Physically, the scrapbooks started as compilations of newspaper and magazine cut-outs in ledger books, with Morgan later reworking these into larger albums, and adding marginal comments and drawings. Later volumes increasingly include typescript and handwritten comments from the poet, as well as drawings, photos, postcards, stamps and memorabilia in various formats. The subjects are as eclectic as Morgan himself, reflecting his intellectual curiosity and

10. The Edwin Morgan Scrapbooks, c. 1931 – c. 1966. MS Morgan C/1-16. Archives & Special Collections [MS Morgan C4_525-6]. The inside cover of Morgan Scrapbook no. 11 (covering 1953-55) shows a fantasising young boy, symbolising himself, facing the No. 18 tram that linked his Burnside home with central Glasgow and could represent life's journey. Just as the Scrapbooks offer an enhanced reflection of his mundane daily life, so he writes his name in reverse, associating himself with northern European shamans, who used mirrors in their magic rituals and reputedly exploited their reindeer's ability to fly. Hence the central declaration 'Morgan himself is a shaman' and the self-referential nickname 'Eddie Reindeer'. Time-travel is also implicit in the pasted extract from 'childhood memories' by Soviet writer Konstantin Pantovksy (1893-1968).

current trends in the arts and architecture, political and social happenings, world news and *faits divers*, fashion and stars in vogue. Text supplements or nuances the images, or sometimes provides an ironic contrast. Above all juxtapositions can surprise and amuse, with poems next to politicians, and, particularly in later albums, a liberal splattering of sparsely-clad young men.

To take one example from album 12 (pages 2240-2559, covering 1954-1960), on pages 2317-2320 Morgan provides 1954 newspaper cuttings, including some from the *Sunday Post* and *Sunday Mail*, outlining the 'Gorbals Vampire' scandal: several sightings by children of a vampire in Glasgow's Southern Necropolis were, according to authorities, to be blamed on the nefarious influence of popular horror comics. To contextualise the debate, Morgan provides a mosaic of excerpts from such comics in their full gory splendour, overshadowing the original articles and the comments from disgruntled authoritarians, including a planned meeting with local dignitaries to discuss the influence of this popular literature. The effect is to draw the reader in – just as horror comics do – whilst giving us a glimpse of popular Glasgow culture in the 1950s in the context of the worldwide debate sparked off by Frederik Wertham's study *The Seduction of the Innocent* (New York: Rinehart, 1954) that had publicised the 'harm' done by comics and led to the US Comics Code. Nonetheless, faced with Morgan's montage we cannot help but find the comics more enticing than the staid finger-wagging. Without comment Morgan creates an aesthetic arrangement that sparks the anti-establishment sentiment in us and reinforces the poet's motto, 'Change Rules!'.

Overall then the Morgan scrapbooks provide a mixture of the intriguing and the titillating, a chronicle of twentieth-century society, but above all they exude a poetic, enigmatic quality. They clearly bear the stamp of Surrealism, but also that of modernism and the push for progress. It is interesting to note the inclusion on the inside back cover of album 12 the *Paris Match* cover featuring a black soldier that Roland Barthes made central to his iconoclastic *Mythologies*. Like the emblem books central to the text/image strength of the University Library, the scrapbooks exhibit the phenomenon whereby the overall creation transcends the sum of its individual parts. The same is true of Edwin Morgan's poetry in general, and indeed true of the Library as a whole.

Conclusion: Why Glasgow?

Hopefully this hit parade of aesthetic treasures has provided a taster delicious enough to persuade even the most fastidious of text gourmets that Glasgow University Library offers an unparalleled menu for the image feaster. But as promised in our introductory starter, we should perhaps ask why Glasgow? Why is Glasgow a depository for such delights in the twentieth-first century, but also why has Glasgow served as text/image cook down the ages?

Of course, the two questions are linked. As this volume shows, Glasgow's outstanding collections have been built up over many years, and are indebted largely to those who had foresight and broad interests. It is no coincidence that both William Hunter and Sir William Stirling Maxwell, two of the principal names in our list of benefactors, explored culture in its widest sense: anatomy,

'History of a Coat', from *The Glasgow Looking Glass*, Scotland, 1825-1826. Archives & Special Collections Sp Coll Bh14-x.8 [Bh14-x.8_vil.1_no.4_page 4].

numismatics, mineralogy, literature and art for the former; heraldry, politics, printing, Iberiana and photography for the latter. With the interchange, mixing and *bricolage* of interests comes an inevitable amalgam of genres as text and image intertwine.

But why Glasgow as producer of the world's first comic, home to the montage mind of Edwin Morgan, and now mecca for Turner Prize winning cross-genre compositions and the to-be place for *Comic Invention*? My personal answer would be that, as an international trading port since the late seventeenth century, Glasgow is a montage city, a cosmopolitan hybrid, full of contrasts that come together to create an imaginative whole that is often beyond imagination. It is a city with a working-class industrial base, but also with a mercantile, professional and cultural elite supporting national opera, ballet and theatre, and a world-class ancient University. It thrives on every kind of low culture that Bourdieu could imagine – football, pubs, heavy music and banter (the patter) – yet nurtures a broad-based education system admired worldwide, and produces exquisite art from Mackintosh to Morrison. It is a place that has the vibrant narrative of the Second City of the Empire, yet also the picturesque stand-still imagery of surrounding lochs, islands and mountains, some of which can be surveyed from the twelfth-floor Reading Room of Special Collections. In practical terms, for the birth of comics in 1825 Glasgow's status as a blossoming industrial centre with its associated social trappings made it an obvious location for popular satire that used the latest know-how. Following on from there, the University Library, supplemented of course by the city's other libraries, remains elitist yet accessible in keeping with the University's policy of outreach, a hybrid contradiction worthy of the mosaic of text/image gems that decorate them.

1   For more information on these and indeed on the Stirling Maxwell Collection, see the website of Glasgow University Library's Special Collections Department: www.gla.ac.uk/services/specialcollections. This site includes links to pages specifically on the Stirling Maxwell Collection, as well as to David Weston's 2011 paper 'A Brief Introduction to the Stirling Maxwell Collection of Emblem Books at the University of Glasgow': www.gla.ac.uk/media/media_197709_en.pdf. I am indebted to this document for much of this current overview, which also formed the basis of a presentation, 'Emblems and Impact', given at the Society for Emblem Studies Tenth International Conference at Christian-Albrechts-Universität, Kiel, in August 2014.

2   For an introduction to the Stirling Maxwell Centre's activities, see its website at: www.gla.ac.uk/schools/mlc/research/stirlingmaxwellcentre.

3   Full details of the manuscript, including an extensive bibliography, are to be found via its catalogue entry: http://special.lib.gla.ac.uk/manuscripts/search/detail_c.cfm?ID=34725.

4   For full analysis of this *dizain* in its broader context, see Laurence Grove, 1992. This reference adds a further personal note to my exploration of the University Library holdings as the article was my first in print, and was published shortly before my arrival in Glasgow (despite the given dating of the volume).

5   For a journalistic account of the unique nature and importance of this sale, see www.telegraph.co.uk/culture/art/artsales/10946649/For-sale-the-3m-library-that-time-forgot.html.

6   For an overview of events, illustrations of documents, and extensive secondary bibliography, see Special Collections August 2009 Book of the Month page, composed by Niki Pollock: http://special.lib.gla.ac.uk/exhibns/month/aug2009.html. See also Laurence Grove, 2011. Much of the material for this section is based on this analysis, a version of which also appeared on the *Comics Forum* (www.comicsforum.org/?s=Rabbits).

7   Much of this section draws upon material for the exhibition's catalogue, *Comic Invention* (by Laurence Grove and Peter Black, published by BHP Comics), where further details of the *Looking Glass's* fortunes can be found, as well as an edited facsimile of the first issue. Otherwise T*he Looking Glass* is absent from virtually all histories of comics. The only secondary sources dedicated to it are John McShane, 'Through a Glass Darkly – The Revisionist History of Comics', *The Drouth*, 23 (2007), 62-70, and the Special Collections June 2005 Book of the Month page by Julie Gardham at http://special.lib.gla.ac.uk/exhibns/month/june2005.html.

8   A facsimile edition edited by Larry J. Schaaf. 1989, is also available. On Talbot, see Harry J. P Arnold, 1977; Mike Weaver, 1992; and the Special Collections February 2007 Book of the Month page by Sonny Maley at http://special.lib.gla.ac.uk/exhibns/month/feb2007.html. This current text also draws upon chapter 5, 'The Nineteenth Century: Photos, Funnies and Film' (pp. 93-116) of Grove, 2010 and 2013.

9   For full details of the holdings, see the University Library catalogue at http://special.lib.gla.ac.uk/manuscripts/search/detail_c.cfm?ID=5. For an overview, illustrations, and further bibliography, see in particular the Special Collections virtual exhibition on the Scrapbooks: www.gla.ac.uk/services/specialcollections/virtual exhibitions/edwinmorganscrapbooks/.

Chapter 7

Unique and Distinctive Collections

A man feasts, from the historiated 'K' from the calendar for January in The Hunterian Psalter, England: c. 1170. Archives & Special Collections, MS Hunter 229 (U.3.20), detail from folio 1r° [H229_0001rwf].

John Moore & Lesley Richmond
University of Glasgow

As in the past, the Library of today continues to provide support to the University community in its teaching, learning and research needs. Our collections reflect an ever-widening and dynamic range of topics but, more significantly, access to information (in a variety of formats) today is as important as the acquisition of material. This is reflected in the holdings, which are held in our various collections. While not comprehensive, this chapter seeks to give a sense of the range and diversity of these holdings, concentrating on those which are recognised as particularly 'unique and distinctive'. However, those collections held within the James Ireland Memorial Library (covering Dentistry), the James Herriot Library (covering Veterinary Medicine) and the Chemistry Branch Library are equally unique in their own way.

Special Collections
The Scottish Theatre Archive
Early Photographs
The University Archives
The Scottish Business Archive
Children's Literature
Central and East European Studies
Map Collection
Travel, Topography and Exploration
Botany Collection
Medicine Collection

A sixteenth-century galleon sets out across the sea. This watercolour is from the manuscript *Visions de Pétrarque*, France, c. 1534, acquired with Sir William Stirling Maxwell's bequest. Archives & Special Collections, S.M.M.2 [S.M.M.2_0007wf].

A multi-coloured peacock surrounded by flowers is a common motif in United Turkey Red textiles. This is one of thousands of designs contained in sample books for the group of Vale of Leven dyeworks, which constituted United Turkey Red Co. Ltd. of Alexandria, West Dunbartonshire, Dyers and Calico printers, the largest bleaching, finishing, dyeing and printing firm in Scotland. Archives & Special Collections [01_UGD013-8-1_detail].

Special Collections

Acquired since the University's foundation in 1451, the material held within the contemporary Special Collections today reflects over 500 years of scholarship and spans 2,000 years of human activity across the world from a papyrus fragment recording sale of property in first-century Greece to letters written in his Glasgow flat by Scotland's former national poet, Edwin Morgan (1920-2010). Consisting of over 200,000 manuscript items and around 200,000 printed works, it is one of the foremost resources in Scotland for academic research and teaching. Subject strengths include the arts, social sciences and the history of law, science and medicine, while holdings of medieval and Renaissance manuscripts, alchemical works and emblem literature are of international importance.

Special Collections holds around 300 medieval and Renaissance manuscripts, many of which are decorated and illuminated. Although found across a number of collections, the most significant derive from the Hunterian Library.

The jewel in the crown is undoubtedly the **Hunterian Psalter** (MS Hunter 229). One of a small group of twelfth-century elaborately illuminated English psalters, it is a splendid example of Romanesque book art. Apart from a fragmentary palimpsest in the National Library of Scotland, Hunter's library also contains the earliest western manuscript in Scotland. This is an eighth- or

An intricately decorated initial 'B' inhabited by nude figures and grotesques, with medallions representing angels at the corners. This marks the start of the text of the psalms *BEATVS UIR* (Blessed is the man) in the Hunterian Psalter, England, c. 1170. Archives & Special Collections, MS Hunter 229 [H229_0022rwf].

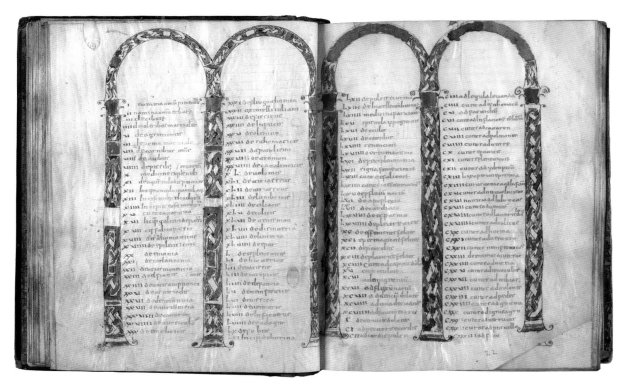

Scotland's oldest complete western manuscript, a collection of medical texts by Hippocrates, Galen and others compiled somewhere with Visigothic connections in Northern Italy or, more probably, Southern France in the late eighth or early ninth century. Special Collections, MS Hunter 96 (T.4.13), folios 21v - 22r [MS Hunter 96 21v 22r].

ninth-century compilation of various medical texts (MS Hunter 96), incorporating works by Galen and Hippocrates. Other important early manuscripts include a Byzantine copy of the **Greek Gospels** (MS Hunter 475) and a twelfth-century **Boethius** (MS Hunter 279) that has recently been reassessed as having possibly been produced in Kelso. Otherwise, the strength of Hunter's manuscript collection lies in later fifteenth-century volumes, including two literary manuscripts which are unique survivors: the *Cent Nouvelles Nouvelles* (MS Hunter 252) – a collection of licentious tales in French – and Chaucer's allegorical love poem, the *Romaunt of the Rose* (MS Hunter 409).

Notable medieval manuscripts from other collections include an early fifteenth-century copy of the *Legenda Aurea* from Bruges (MS Gen 1111) – exceptionally important both for its augmented content and its remarkably rich decoration; a small number of illuminated continental **Books of Hours** (MS Euing 3 & 4, and MS Gen 288); and a workaday copy of **Euclid's Geometry** (MS Gen 1115) that may have been used in early teaching at the University. Later manuscripts of interest in Hunter's library include Diego Muñoz Camargo's *Historia de Tlaxcala*, a sixteenth-century manuscript originating in post-Spanish conquest Mexico (MS Hunter 242).

This copy of the Greek Gospels from the later twelfth century is an important early manuscript on parchment and a superb example of Byzantine art. Archives & Special Collections, MS Hunter 475 [H475_0110v_111rwf].

Compartmentalised miniature from *Les Cent Nouvelles Nouvelles* (One Hundred New Stories), a unique collection of licentious tales in French from the Duchy of Burgundy. France, c. 1470-1490. Archives & Special Collections, MS Hunter 252 [MS Hunter 252 70r].

Romaunt of the Rose. The only surviving manuscript copy of Chaucer's French-inspired allegorical poem on the art of love, dating from the second half of the fifteenth century. Archives & Special Collections, MS Hunter 409 [H409_0057vwf].

In addition to the manuscripts and archive material found within our named collections, there are over 1,700 collections in a general sequence (MS Gen). The material in this 'collection of collections' ranges widely in date, format and extent, from individual items through to extensive archive collections comprising hundreds, sometimes thousands, of documents. Examples include the correspondence of philosopher and political

economist Adam Smith (MS Gen 1035) and the papers of John, William and Allen Thomson regarding eighteenth- and nineteenth-century medical education and practice (MS Gen 1476).

Other significant medical collections include the papers of Hunter's mentor, the physician and professor William Cullen (1710-1790), and the controversial twentieth-century psychiatrist and author, R. D. Laing.

Art and literature are also well represented among our more recently acquired collections: these include the papers of artists James McNeil Whistler and Bet Low and the writers Jane Duncan, Alasdair Gray and Edwin Morgan.

There are 1,060 fifteenth-century printed books in Special Collections – the largest collection of **incunabula** in Scotland, and one of the most important in the United Kingdom. Of these, twelve are unique. Survivors of the first print revolution, many of these fascinating books are beautifully decorated and contain the traces of over 500 years of ownership history. Highlights from our collection include: ten books printed by William Caxton; a richly illuminated **Breviary** on parchment, produced as an important gift (Hunterian Bf.1.18); the ***Rudimentum novitorium*** with its hand coloured maps (Hunterian By.1.12); Erhard Ratdolt's edition of ***Regiomontanus*** containing working scientific instruments (BD7-f.13); and a copy of the ***Hypnerotomachia Poliphili***, the most beautiful book of the Venetian Renaissance (Hunterian Bh.2.14). Scattered across a number of collections, these books have recently been catalogued in great

St. Alban from an early fifteenth-century copy of the *Legenda Aurea* (*Golden Legend*) from the city of Bruges and significant for its augmented content and remarkably rich decoration. It is a collection of saints' lives by Jacobus de Voragine, Archbishop of Genoa, which became a late medieval bestseller. Archives & Special Collections, MS Gen 1111 [G1111_0295v.df].

A Book of Hours, a private Christian devotional book of texts, prayers and psalms. This manuscript's scheme of illustration incorporates a beautiful sequence of illuminated miniatures portraying scenes from the Christmas story. It was produced in the Netherlands in about 1460 and is one of the 3,000 volumes of devotional texts in the Euing Collection. Archives & Special Collections, MS Euing 3 [MS Euing 3 double page opening 48v 49r].

atlpopocayan

Guerra de Atlpopocayan ques en los bolcanes de Maçaya

Diego Muñoz Camargo's *Historia de Tlaxcala*, a manuscript of 1581-85, originates from the post-Spanish conquest of Mexico and is a beautiful and historically important description of the social, political, religious and cultural history of the area. It was written in both Spanish and native Nahuatl by Camargo, an educated mestizo, and describes an area that was not part of the Aztec empire. Archives 8 Special Collections, MS Hunter 242 [H242_0307v.wf].

Glasgow holds the largest single collection of the correspondence and papers of the artist James McNeill Whistler (1834-1903), who received an honorary Glasgow doctorate shortly before his death and whose mother was of Scottish descent. Over a third of the 7,000 letters are written by him. An extensive reference library of over 1,000 volumes on Whistler includes some 200 books from the artist's library, a nearly complete collection of his own publications and exhibition catalogues, thousands of his press-cuttings and hundreds of photographs. The major part of the collection was donated and bequeathed by Miss Rosalind Birnie Philip (1873-1958), Whistler's sister-in-law, who inherited his estate. Archives & Special Collections, Whistler 160-165 [Sp Coll Whistler PH1_98].

detail and virtually brought together: see the Glasgow Incunabula Project website for more information (**www.gla.ac.uk/services/incunabula**).

Over half of our incunabula are to be found in the library of William Hunter. One of the finest eighteenth-century libraries to remain intact, it contains many early printed treasures and ground-breaking texts. Comprising some 10,000 volumes, about a third of the books are medical-related. Otherwise, Hunter's wide ranging interests are reflected in his library, with books on fine topography, botany, zoology, astronomy, numismatics, fine art, exploration and travel (including Americana) and certain aspects of vernacular literature. Hunter also incorporated the collection of Theophilus Siegfried Bayer (1694-1738) into his library, and subsequently it also contains an important subset of 200 Chinese and other oriental books and manuscripts. The Hunterian collection was bequeathed to the University and arrived in Glasgow in 1807. It should be noted that the collection as it is found today may more

A pencil draft with colour pen scribbles for 'Mutation', a colour poem written by renowned Scottish poet Edwin Morgan in 1969, printed at Glasgow Print Studio and published by the Third Eye Centre in 1978. Edwin Morgan (1920-2010) was a titular Professor of English at the University of Glasgow from 1975 to 1980. His extensive collection of papers held by the University includes biographical material, scrapbooks, papers relating to his academic career, drafts of poems and translations, correspondence, reviews, essays, talks and subject files relating to radio and television, theatre projects, poetry readings and tours. Archives & Special Collections MS Morgan P/1/445 [MS Morgan P_1_445].

properly be known as the Hunterian *Museum* Library, since throughout the nineteenth century it attracted many further donations and additions that were not distinguished in any way from the core collection of Hunter's original bequest.

Another 'star attraction' is the nineteenth-century collection of Glasgow insurance broker William Euing (1788-1874). Containing some 12,000 books in total, it may be divided into three parts: a general collection of 7,000 volumes that is especially strong in seventeenth- and eighteenth-century English literature (including a copy of **Shakespeare's First Folio** edition of 1623), illustrated works and fine bindings, and books on travel and exploration, art, architecture, design, marine biology and Scottish history; a collection of bibles, psalters, books of prayers and hymns amounting to 3,000 volumes; and a collection of 2,500 volumes of early printed music, including rare theoretical works and numerous scores and part-books. Amongst its manuscript treasures is an early seventeenth-century lute book (MS Euing 25).

The library of John Ferguson (1838-1916), bibliographer and Regius Professor of Chemistry at the University of Glasgow from 1874 to 1915, is another collection of international importance. Its main strengths lie in alchemy, chemistry and related topics such as books of secrets, metallurgy and mineralogy, with important offshoots into the occult sciences and witchcraft, the Rosicrucians, Paracelsus and the Romani language. It contains some 7,500 volumes, many of which are extremely rare.

Sir William Stirling Maxwell's collection of emblem books, originally formed in the nineteenth century, is now recognised as an internationally important research resource. It comprises over 2,000 works on emblem and device literature, ranging in date from the first edition of Alciati's *Emblematum Liber* (1531) to the nineteenth century. They are supported by

Printed on vellum in Paris in 1519, this beautiful copy of the *Argonautica* is richly decorated, emulating a manuscript in its production. The text by Gaius Valerius Flaccus, originaly written in the latter part of 1 AD, recounts the adventures of Jason and the Argonauts in their quest to retrieve the Golden Fleece. This version was produced by Josse Bade, one of the great scholar printers of the early sixteenth century. Archives & Special Collections, Hunterian Bq.2.11 [bq.2.11_book3illustr.wf].

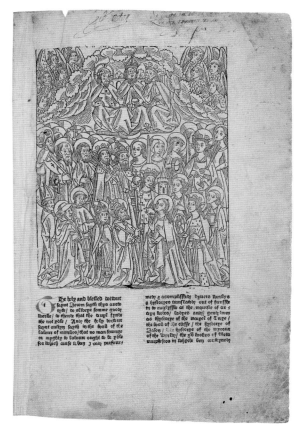

A page from *The Golden Legend*, Westminster, c. 1483-84, a collection of saints' lives (Compare the earlier Bruges manuscript on p. 175.). It is one of ten incunabula produced by William Caxton, England's first printer, which were collected by William Hunter (1718-1783). Archives & Special Collections, Hunterian Bg.1.1 [Bg_1_1_1R].

This exceptional hand-illustrated copy of the *Breviarum Romanum*, the liturgy of daily prayers for the Roman Catholic Church, was produced on vellum in Venice in 1478 by the celebrated French printer Nicholas Jenson; skilfully illuminated by Petrus V, it is the most extensively decorated Italian copy known. Folio 14r is a page of the Psalter decorated with a fool in a medallion and others in a landscape. Archives & Special Collections, Hunterian Bf.1.18 [Bf_1_18_b4R].

a strong collection of books on allied subjects, such as fête books and ceremonial albums, medal books and books of allegorical figures.

Interestingly, the University's Old Library is now regarded as a special collection in its own right. Consisting of the 20,000 or so books acquired by the Library by the end of the eighteenth century, it covers a wide range of topics that reflect the curriculum of the University, including theology, philosophy, classics, history, law, mathematics, geography and medicine. Highlights include copies of first editions of Diderot's *Encyclopédie* and the first modern *Dictionary of the English Language* by Samuel Johnson.

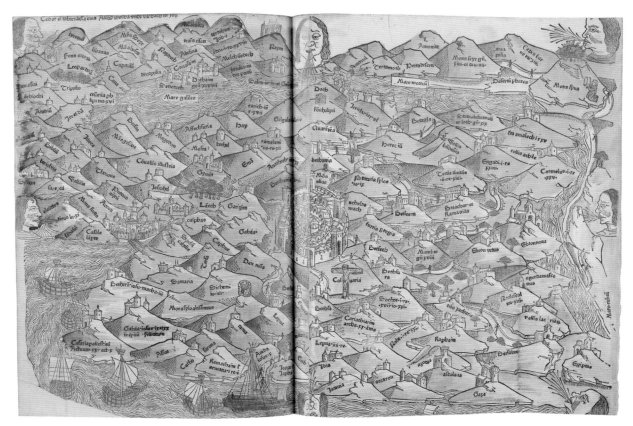

This striking work from the *Rudimentum Novitiorum*, published in 1475 by Lucas Brandis of Lübeck, is characteristic of its period in depicting the geography of the Holy Land in an allegorical fashion. Based on an east-west orientation, with the Mediterranean port of Jaffa at the bottom, it is centred on Jerusalem. More significantly, it is inscribed with Biblical narratives, such as Moses receiving the Ten Commandments on Mount Sinai, as a way of articulating and inculcating religious belief. Archives & Special Collections, Hunterian By.1.12 [By_1_12_174V_175R].

As the Library's general collections are assessed for their uniqueness or significance, material is transferred to the care of the Special Collections Department. One example of such material is that of novels. Amounting to just under 1,800 titles, this represents a resource of major importance for late eighteenth- and nineteenth-century literary scholars. Its primary focus is on the fiction of the nineteenth century, with many works outside the boundaries of the mainstream areas of interest or research.

Meanwhile, many other books that are not found in named collections (single donations, or transfers from main library stock, for instance) are placed in the general Rare Books sequence. As can be understood, a miscellany of subject areas is represented here, although literature and natural history are particularly well represented. Examples of outstanding books include Thornton's *Temple of Flora*, early editions of Robert Burns' *Poems, chiefly in the Scottish Dialect*, and William Blake's masterpiece, *Europe: A Prophecy*.

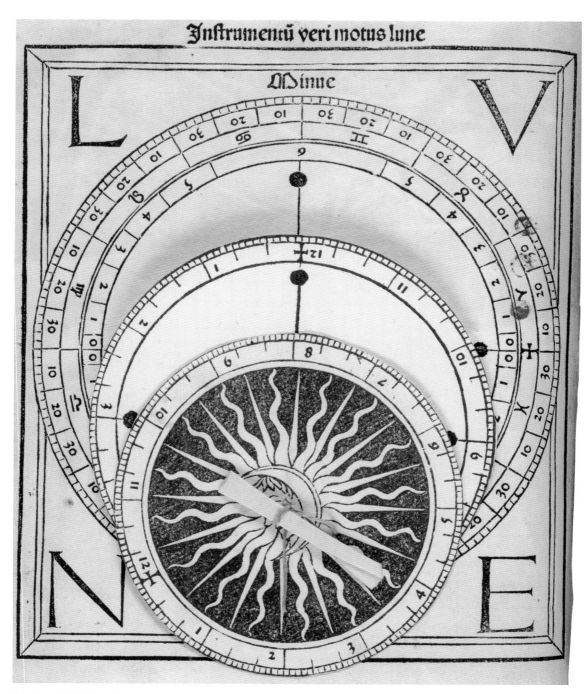

Produced in Venice in 1482 by the early German printer, Erhard Ratdolt, this edition of Joannes Regiomontanus's *Kalendarium* (Calendar book) contains working instruments such as paper wheels to tell the hour and show the motion of the moon. Archives & Special Collections, BD7-f.13 [BD7_f13_29v].

Divinity, religion and theology form the basis of a major collection that was deposited in 1974 from Trinity College (founded in 1856 as a theological college for the ministry of the then Free Church of Scotland). Some 2,000 early printed items, which were acquired over its existence, were selected from its general book stock for preservation, including items from the personal libraries of such scholars as John Eadie (1810-1876), theologian and biblical critic, James Mearns (1855-1927), reviser of Julian's *Dictionary of Hymnology*, and Constantin

von Tischendorf (1815-1874), celebrated as the man who first discovered and published the fourth-century *Codex Sinaiticus*, the oldest complete manuscript of the New Testament. The Tischendorf material is also notable for its wide range of eastern travelogues.

The personal library of David Murray (1842-1928), a Glasgow lawyer, antiquary and bibliographer consists of 15,000 printed volumes (containing over 23,000 items) and some 200 manuscripts. This constitutes a superb regional

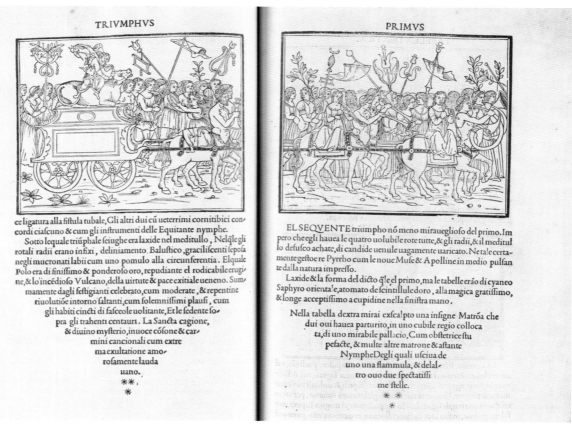

The *Hypnerotomachia Poliphili*, arguably the most beautiful book of the Venetian Renaissance, was published at the very end of the fifteenth century by Aldus Manutius, the Italian humanist printer who founded the Aldine Press. It tells the story of a quest for lost love and is illustrated with more than 170 woodcuts. Archives & Special Collections, Hunterian Bh.2.14 [Bh_2_14_K6V_K7R].

history collection with a wealth of seventeenth- and eighteenth-century Glasgow imprints, especially those printed by Robert Sanders, the Foulis brothers and Robert Urie. Nineteenth-century strengths include material on the economic and social development of the west of Scotland, publications relating to Glasgow and its University, engraved topographical works, maps, Scottish newspapers, directories and periodicals. There is a particular abundance of printed ephemera: broadsides, street literature, chapbooks, advertisements and files of newspaper cuttings. This collection is complemented by that of Robert Wylie (d. 1921), with 1,000 volumes relating to the history and topography of Glasgow, including unique material relating to the successful Glasgow International Exhibitions of 1888 and 1901, many early Glasgow directories and periodicals, in particular *The Glasgow/ Northern Looking Glass*.

Finally, perhaps some less well known collections are worthy of a mention to demonstrate the further riches of Special Collections. Left-wing publications are well represented in the Broady (socialist pamphlets) and Left Book Club collections. Collections adding another seam of European literature are those named Scarfe-La Trobe (Spanish *sueltas*, short plays published from the late seventeenth century to the nineteenth century in small pamphlet format), Hepburn (first editions of nineteenth-century English novelists and poets) and Scottish poetry (predominantly the publications of Edwin Morgan and Ian Hamilton Finlay).

The library of Sir William Hamilton (1788-1856), the Scottish metaphysician and advocate

born in the College of Glasgow, consists of nearly 8,000 volumes, with an emphasis largely on works on aesthetics, logic and the history of philosophy. Classical texts are strongly represented, including 150 editions of Aristotle alone. In addition, thirty-two editions of the work of George Buchanan, the Scottish humanist and tutor to King James VI, form part of this particular collection. Through the efforts of Professor John Veitch (1829-1894), among others, Hamilton's library was purchased for the University in 1878. On his death, Veitch's own collection of more than 400 volumes, mostly of early printed editions of medieval philosophers, including Peter Lombard (c. 1096-1160), William of Ockham (c. 1287-1347) and John Duns Scotus (c. 1266-1308) was presented to the Library by his widow. Supporting these are some 180 volumes from the library of the Greek scholar, Richard Claverhouse Jebb (1841-1905), at one time Professor of Greek at the University. This relatively small group of books comprises mainly Sophoclean literature, but several volumes bear important manuscript annotations.

Preserved in the Blau Collection are nearly 200 Hebrew books, over half of which date from the sixteenth century. Over a period of more than thirty years, Henry George Farmer (1882-1965), the British musicologist and orientalist, donated a collection of books and papers relating to military and oriental (especially Arabic) music and musical instruments, Scottish music, concerts and variety theatre in Glasgow, as well as correspondence with contemporary composers, such as Hamish MacCunn. One notable collection of particular relevance to Scottish history is that gathered by John James Spencer of documents relating to the ill-fated

Darien Scheme, Scotland's disastrous attempt to found a trading colony on the Isthmus of Panama at the end of the seventeenth century. Finally, in this selection, a wealth of early printed mathematical and astronomical material (including an important annotated copy of Newton's *Principia*) is found in the library of Robert Simson (1687-1768), who was Professor of Mathematics at the University from 1711 until 1761.

More information on all these collections in this chapter (and more) is detailed on these websites **www.gla.ac.uk/services/specialcollections** and **www.gla.ac.uk/services/archives**

| **Julie Gardham**

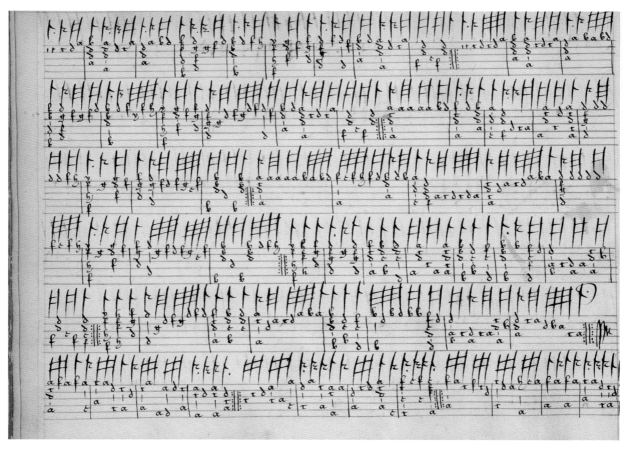

Only a small amount of English lute music of the late sixteenth and early seventeenth centuries was published, and therefore surviving manuscripts are the principal sources of the repertoire. This important manuscript is dated to sometime in the 1620s and contains seventy-two dances for the lute written in tablature. Included are some unique items, as well as works by Dowland, Holborne and Cutting. Archives & Special Collections, MS Euing 25 [MS Euing 25_25].

Cantiones quae ab argumento sacrae vocantur...., London, 1575. Thomas Tallis (c. 1505-1585) spanned the period between the early Tudor composers and the late Elizabethans. William Byrd (1543-1623) was probably his pupil and became one of the greatest English composers of all time. They shared a joint appointment as organists of the Chapel Royal. In 1575 they were granted a licence which gave them sole right to print music in England. In this year they published the *Cantiones sacrae*, which contains sixteen items by Tallis and eight by Byrd. The only other works by Tallis to be published during his lifetime were five anthems set to English words. Archives & Special Collections, Sp Coll R.b.47 [R.b.47_Vol2_Page 4].

This original elephant folio edition of Robert Thornton's sumptuous work *Temple of Flora* (London, 1799-1807) is probably the most renowned of all great flower books. Containing thirty-one plates, it was produced by a variety of techniques, with the impressions being finished by hand. This mezzotint depiction of tulips is one of the most justly famous plates. Archives & Special Collections, e23 [e.23_Plate25Tulips.wf].

The emblem is a woodcut or engraving representing pictorially a moral lesson, accompanied by a motto, epigram, verse or prose explanation. The *Emblematum liber* is the first edition of the first emblem book, compiled by the Italian lawyer Andrea Alciati and published in Augsburg in 1531 by Heinrich Steyner. This volume is from Sir William Stirling Maxwell's unrivalled collection of emblem and device literature which he assembled over a period of forty years. Archives & Special Collections, SM 18 [SM18_A7v-A8rwf].

The outstanding literary enterprise of the eighteenth century, the *Encyclopédie* expressed the philosophic spirit of the age. Mainly the work of Diderot and d'Alembert, other contributors included Voltaire, Montesquieu, Turgot, Rousseau and Buffon. Each volume caused a sensation throughout Europe as it appeared. Adam Smith was responsible for ordering the first seven volumes for Glasgow University Library during his term as Quaestor (1758-1764). Shown here is the famous plate of 'épinglier' (pin maker) from volume 21, said to have influenced Smith in his ideas on the division of labour when writing *The Wealth of Nations*. Archives & Special Collections, Bn5-a.1 [Bn5_1.1_PlateIII_Epinglier.wf].

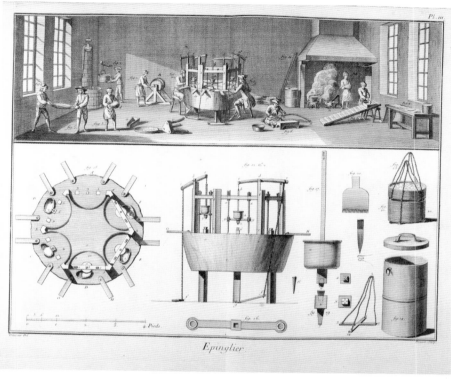

Epinglier.

This rare first Edinburgh edition of Robert Burns, *Poems, chiefly in the Scottish dialect*, 1787, is embellished with manuscript notes and poems in Scotland's national bard's own hand. The first Edinburgh edition was virtually a collected works of Burns' poetry, containing all his poems from his first publication, in Kilmarnock, plus twenty-two new poems. Archives & Special Collections, RB 2521 [RB2521_Hermitage].

The illuminated book *Europe: A Prophecy* (Lambeth, 1784) is unquestionably one of the University of Glasgow Library's greatest treasures. It is the second of William Blake's *Continental Prophecies* and is one of his most complex, obscure and elusive works. William Blake (1757-1827), English poet, painter, and printmaker, was one of the most significant and celebrated figures in western art and poetry. Archives & Special Collections, Sp Coll RX132 [RX132_pl.1.wf].

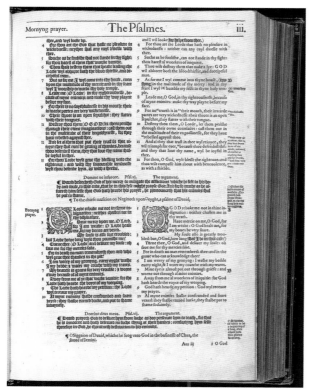

Designed by the Japanese artist Ryukei (1874-1944), this woodblock print (February 1904) comes from a collection of fifty-seven Japanese prints dating from the period of the Russo-Japanese War which depict significant elements of the conflict from the Japanese point of view. They were donated to the University in 1935 by Percy Hillhouse, Professor of Naval Architecture from 1921 until 1942, who had been the first professor in this subject at Tokyo Imperial University before returning to his native city. Archives & Special Collections, e159 [e159_plate06].

Several thousand early printed volumes from Trinity College, the Glasgow-based theological college, were placed on permanent deposit in the University of Glasgow Library by the General Assembly of the Church of Scotland in 1974. The deposit included the personal library of the biblical scholar John Eadie (1810-1876), whose collection includes several rare Bibles and other theological works. Shown here is his 1568 edition of the *Bishop's Bible*. Archives & Special Collections, Eadie e101 [Eadie 101_folioiiir_Psalm6-7_wf].

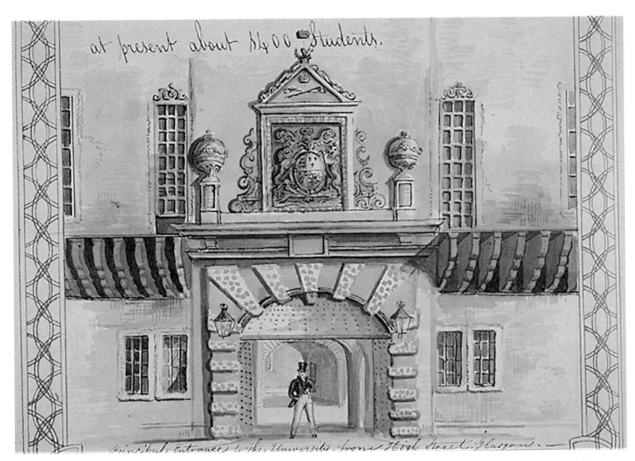

Among the Murray printed books and manuscripts is an early nineteenth-century account of the Barony Parish of Glasgow, compiled by a wealthy Glasgow merchant James Hopkirk; it contains an important collection of ink drawings of Glasgow buildings by an unidentified artist, possibly his botanist son Thomas, including this depiction of the University's 'Old College' on the High Street. David Murray (1842-1928), the Glasgow lawyer, antiquary and bibliographer, gave the University Library his superb collection of antiquarian books and manuscripts, including student notes, local histories, museum studies and legal texts. Archives & Special Collections, MS Murray 636 [Mu0636_0052dwf].

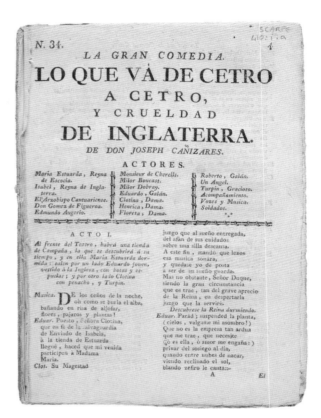

Comedias sueltas (or simply *sueltas*) were short plays published in pamphlet format in Spain from the early sixteenth to the nineteenth century. The Scarfe-La Trobe collection covers a wide range of dramatic genres and comprises nearly 2,000 items consisting of 1,068 plays. This is a *suelta* written by De Don Joseph de Canizares (1676-1750). Archives & Special Collections Scarfe 410.11.a [Scarfe_410.001].

Taken from a set of five volumes of watercolour drawings depicting the ordinary people of Glasgow, these illustrations are often the only known record of various costumes and uniforms of the city, offering a rare glimpse into the past. This image is a copy of one hanging in the Merchants' House of Glasgow and is of Robert Sanders of Auldhouse, one of the city's leading businessmen and an early Glasgow printer, who died in 1730. Archives & Special Collections, Ms Murray 592 [Mu0592_0019wf].

John Duns Scotus's commentary on the *Sentences of Peter Lombard*, was a popular medieval scholastic text. This copy, produced in Venice in 1477, is decorated by Matteo Felice, one of the leading Neapolitan artists of the day. Like many of the books which were produced in the early years of printing, this work has been illustrated in the style of an illuminated manuscript, and includes the coat of arms of Cardinal Giovanni of Aragon (1456-1485), its original owner. Subsequently, the book was confiscated by King Charles VIII of France after his invasion of Naples and later passed into the personal collection of Jean-Baptiste Colbert, Comptroller-General of Finance under Louis XIV. Archives & Special Collections, Hunterian By.2.3. [By.2.3_folioA2r.wf].

The Workes of William Shakespeare,

containing all his Comedies, Histories, and
Tragedies: Truely set forth, according to their first
ORIGINALL.

The Names of the Principall Actors
in all these Playes.

William Shakespeare.
Richard Burbadge.

John Hemmings.

Augustine Phillips.

William Kempt.

Thomas Poope.

George Bryan.

Henry Condell.

William Slye.

Richard Cowly.

John Lowine.

Samuell Crosse.

Alexander Cooke.

Samuel Gilburne.

Robert Armin.

William Ostler.

Nathan Field.

John Underwood.

Nicholas Tooley.

William Ecclestone.

Joseph Taylor.

Robert Benfield.

Robert Goughe.

Richard Robinson.

Iohn Shancke.

Iohn Rice.

The names of the principal actors in Shakespeare's plays from the 'First Folio'. Only eighteen of Shakespeare's plays appeared in print during his lifetime but the collection (now known as the 'First Folio') containing thirty-six of his works was published in 1623, some seven years after the bard's death. This copy in the University of Glasgow Library is extremely important for its contemporary annotations. Here the annotator has recorded his personal experience of the actors, purporting to 'know' Joseph Taylor and Robert Benfield and to have seen John Lowine 'by eyewittnesse'. Archives & Special Collections, BD8-b.1 [BD8-b.1_Name of the Principall Actors pc].

The Scottish Theatre Archive

Some of the most recent acquisitions to the Library's unique and distinctive collections are to be found in the Scottish Theatre Archive. It was founded in 1982 with funding from the Scottish Arts Council but since 1985, the University Library alone has been responsible for its funding and staffing.

The role of this Archive is to preserve and promote interest in Scotland's theatrical heritage – personal, political, corporate and national. It is open to anyone with an interest in Scottish theatre and provides a resource for undergraduate and postgraduate study, particularly in the area of Theatre Studies, at the University. The Archive is an invaluable research tool and reference centre for theatre practitioners, historians and members of the public from across the world.

Since 1982 the Archive has grown significantly, and continues to expand rapidly. The coverage is very broad, from the late eighteenth to the twenty-first centuries, and includes traditional and contemporary theatre, music hall and pantomime as well as straight drama. The Archive has an essential role in preserving the history of drama companies and theatre buildings which no longer survive, but also in managing the archives of a number of major active companies, notably the National Theatre of Scotland, Scottish Ballet and the Citizens Theatre, Glasgow. These are three of the largest collections within the Archive, which also includes the BBC Radio Scotland script collection and the Jimmy Logan collection of music-hall material. Other material relates to the Scottish Repertory Theatre, the Scottish National Players and the Royal Lyceum Theatre, Edinburgh, Glasgow Unity, Molly Urquhart and her theatre, and the Scottish Theatre Company, in addition to the Dundee Repertory Theatre, the Wilson Barrett Company, Mayfest and the Edinburgh Festival Fringe.

There are interesting links with material elsewhere in the Library; for example, a Shakespeare First Folio in the Euing Collection gives readers an insight into the original dramatic performance. The papers of the twentieth-century Scottish poet Edwin Morgan emphasise his collaborations with TAG Theatre and other stage companies.

The contents of the different STA collections vary, but they generally include programmes, scripts, production notes, photographs, posters, and press cuttings. Some of the collections also include business papers and correspondence. The Archive has extensive holdings of play-scripts, totalling over 7,000 titles, and continues to acquire new material, including one-off donations from people who have worked in the theatre or who have collected material relating to their own theatre–going activity.

| **Sarah Hepworth**

A poster for Gregory Burke's 2006 *Black Watch*, a play of verbatim accounts from former soldiers with black humour and ambitious theatricality. The play brought the new National Theatre of Scotland to the attention of the public and critics alike. Archives & Special Collections, STA NTS [STA NTS 1_2].

A poster for a variety show at the Britannia Music Hall, Trongate, Glasgow, 16th January, 1905. The Britannia opened as Campbell's Music Saloon in 1857 and changed its name several times during its lifetime. It became the Tron Cinema from 1923-27 and then reverted to one of its former names, the Panopticon, until its closure in 1938. Archives & Special Collections, STA Bx.6 [B.x.6].

The *Taming of the Shrew* presented at the Royal Lyceum Theatre, Edinburgh, in November 1946, by the Wilson Barrett Company, starring Richard Matthews and Ann Brooke. Scotland`s largest repertory company, the Wilson Barrett Company, presented over 400 plays and some revues over 15 years until 1954 in the Alhambra Theatre Glasgow, Royal Lyceum Edinburgh, and for a time in Aberdeen. Presenting a play every week in each season and rehearsing in that week for the next week`s play, it operated profitably and received no subsidy. Archives & Special Collections STA Inglis 300 [STA inglis 300 p.17].

A poster for Clydebuilt: a season of Scottish popular theatre from the '20s, '30s and '40s, featuring the plays *Gold in his Boots*, *In Time of Strife*, *Johnny Noble*, and *Men Should Weep*. John McGrath, playwright and director, founded the 7:84 Theatre Company in 1971 and toured in Scotland, England and Wales until 2008. The aims of 7:84 were to present the realities of working-class life and history to working-class audiences in venues often shunned by established national companies. Archives & Special Collections, STA Cv 2/18 [STA Cv 2_18 (Clydebuilt)].

A poster for *Five Past Eight* at the Alhambra Theatre, Glasgow on 19th May, 1958. The renowned Alhambra Theatre in Glasgow's Wellington Street opened in 1910 and operated until 1969. One of the largest and best equipped theatres in Britain, it became famous for high-quality pantomime, musicals, drama and revues, including the summer spectaculars known as the Five Past Eight shows, which could run for over five months each year. Archives & Special Collections, STA WAT 25/36 [STA WAT 25_36].

Early Photographs

The Library also holds outstanding collections of photographs and early books about or including photography, which illustrate developments from the first 'sun pictures' of the 1830s through to the early twentieth century.

Among the earliest material is a copy of William Henry Fox Talbot's ground-breaking publication *The Pencil of Nature*, issued in parts from 1844 and the first publication to be illustrated with photographic prints, using Talbot's calotype process which drastically cut lengthy exposure times. With the acquisition of the Dougan Collection in 1953, the Library is also fortunate to have over 450 salted paper prints and nearly 500 calotype negatives produced in the 1840s by the pioneering and prolific Scottish photographic partnership of David Octavius Hill (1802-1870) and Robert Adamson (1821-1848). This collection is second in size and significance only to the holdings of their work in the Scottish National Portrait Gallery. (There is some overlap but much that is unique in both collections.) In addition, Robert O. Dougan (then Deputy Librarian of Trinity College, Dublin) acquired over a hundred volumes and albums of photographs. These include early illustrated publications on photography and prints by local and international professionals such as Robert Macpherson (1811-1872), Samuel Bourne (1834-1912) and Thomas Annan (1829-1887). This material also contains interesting and unique examples of amateur work, including an album of experimental photographs of people and places attributed to a Northumbrian middle-class girl, Fanny Pickard (1847-1901).

Over 450 salted paper prints and nearly 500 calotype negatives were produced in the 1840s by the pioneering and prolific Scottish photographic partnership of David Octavius Hill (1802-1870) and Robert Adamson (1821-1848). The photograph here shows Robert Adamson and his family c. 1844. Archives & Special Collections, [HA0336].

Dougan's background was in book collecting and among the publications is one of the first scientific works to use photographic illustrations, *The Expression of the Emotions in Man and Animals* (1872), by Charles Darwin. By the second half of the nineteenth century photography had become the dominant medium of visual record, presenting public buildings and infrastructure projects in stunning large format images. An interesting example of this is the collection of Thomas Annan's remarkable images of *The Old Closes and Streets of Glasgow* created between 1868 and 1871. Commissioned by the City of Glasgow Improvements Trust as a record of the notorious slum dwellings prior to their destruction, they are also beautiful demonstrations of the photographer's skilful use of light and composition. The use of photography to record civic achievements is evident elsewhere, including an album of images taken in Australia in the 1870s at a time of rapid economic and population growth.

Early photographs are also an integral part of some of the Library's other significant collections, including those of the artists James McNeill Whistler (1834-1903), James Paterson (1854-1932) and Jessie M. King (1875-1949), complementing correspondence, biographical material and other records of their work.

Sarah Hepworth

Close No. 46 in the Saltmarket, photographed by Thomas Annan (1829-1887) for *Photographs of old closes, streets, etc., taken 1868-1877*, commissioned by the City of Glasgow Improvements Trust as a record of the notorious slum dwellings prior to their destruction. Annan's remarkable images provide an immediate impression of the conditions within the working-class areas of old Glasgow. Archives & Special Collections, Dougan 64 [Dougan64_plate22_no.46 Saltmarket].

A photograph of the Lahori Gate of the Red Fort in Delhi, India, taken in the 1850s by Samuel Bourne (1834-1912), a travel photographer, renowned for his landscape and architectural images of India. He formed the oldest surviving photographic studio in the world, Bourne & Shepherd, which still operates in Calcutta. Archives & Special Collections, Dougan 96/97 [Dehli_Dougan_96_67].

Cloisters under Bute Hall

A photogravure of the undercroft under the Bute Hall on the University of Glasgow's Gilmorehill campus, published in reproduced in *University of Glasgow Old and New*, ed. William Stewart, 1891. James Craig Annan (1864–1946), the son of Thomas Annan, worked in the family business T. & R. Annan and was a master photogravure printer and a leading pictorialist photographer. Photogravure is a photo-mechanical process whereby a copper plate is coated with a light-sensitive gelatine tissue which has been exposed to a film positive, and then etched. Archives & Special Collections, Mu21-x.2, plate 30 [Old & New No.30].

A Japanese temple from an album of photographs of romanticised scenes of Japan, dating from around 1880. The images are monochrome with heavy hand tints of mostly rural scenes, temples, palaces, forts, gardens and fishermen. Locations include Kobe, Yuoshima, Kanasawa, Nagasaki, Kyoto, Arima, Osaka, Tokyo, Fujiyama, Yamato, Biwalake. Archives & Special Collections, DC 90/4/2/4 [SCH-2548].

The photographer's wife and friends paddling in the sea at Gullane, East Lothian, featuring Miss M. F. Cameron, Miss E. McGhie, Mrs W. F. Jackson and Miss J. I. Cameron, 9th August, 1912. A photograph from the W. F. Jackson collection of photographs. Archives & Special Collection, DC111/1/02159 [DC111-1-02159].

The University Archive

Since 1955, when David Wilson Reid (1928-1973) was appointed as the first professional archivist, the Archive collections have become the official centralised memory of the University. The oldest records are charters, dating back to 1304, conveying land and privileges to the Blackfriars in Glasgow that eventually came into University hands. It also has comprehensive records of the University's management, administration, staff and students dating from its fifteenth-century foundation to the present day. Such documents provide an insight into the history of the University itself as well as the inspirational people who have been part of our community down the centuries. Collecting the records of alumni, staff and student groups continues to be an important part of the archival work of its staff. In addition to recording the corporate functions of a place of learning, there is a commitment to collecting the details and background of the people who have chosen the University of Glasgow as their place of study.

The first known mention of cataloguing the University records dates from 1490, when it was noted in the *Annales Universitatis Glasguensis 1451–1558* that 'in accordance with a proposition of the Lord Rector, a parchment book is ordered to be procured, in which important writs, statutes, and lists of the University, are to be engrossed: and also a paper book, for recording judicial proceedings' (GUAS, Clerk's Press 26613). The Clerk to the Faculty, and subsequently the Clerk of Senate, maintained the records of the University to ensure that the privileges, rights, policies and finances of the University were kept in good order. The acquisition of books and the functioning of the Library is a feature of the records from earliest times.

Throughout the centuries the University has prioritised the care of its most important records. Some of the early decisions taken to protect valuable documents were not entirely successful. In 1560, during the political unrest accompanying the Scottish Reformation, the then Chancellor, Archbishop James Beaton, a supporter of the

Inventor of Television. The matriculation slip of John Logie Baird, who attended the University of Glasgow from October 1914 to March 1915. He took classes in Electricity (Pure and Applied), Engineering and Natural Philosophy with a view to sitting the examinations for a BSc degree. On 26th January, 1926, he gave the world's first demonstration of a practical TV system in front of members of the Royal Institution in London. Archives & Special Collections, R8/5/35 [R8/5/35/.1 John Logie Baird].

Two covers from the *Glasgow University Magazine* from 1953 and 1987. Known as *GUM*, the *Magazine* was founded in 1889 and published by the Students' Representatives Council. It is the oldest student publication in Scotland. Today *GUM* continues to be a stylish and cutting-edge, culturally aware magazine that covers a wide range of topics from fashion to art to politics and beyond. Archives & Special Collections DC198 [dc198_1_94] and [dc198_1_53].

Marian cause, fled to France taking with him for safe-keeping many of the vital property records and valuables of the Cathedral and the University, including the mace and the founding papal bull. Although the mace was sent back in 1590, the archives were not. Principal Dr James Fall told the Parliamentary Commissioners of Visitation on the 28th of August, 1690, that he had seen the bull at the Scots College in Paris, together with the many charters granted to the University by the kings and queens of Scotland from James II to Queen Mary. Fifty years later the documents could not be found.

Student records are among the largest accumulations and are the most widely consulted materials in the collection. They show how the student population has changed with the times. In the seventeenth century, many students stated that they were the younger sons of earls, lords and lairds. In the ten years after 1675, three sons of the Duke of Argyll and four of the Duke of Hamilton attended Glasgow.

By the eighteenth century most students at Glasgow were the sons of ministers, merchants, professional men or farmers. The records show that while most at that time still came from the west and south-west of Scotland, significant numbers were coming from Presbyterian Ireland. Those that came from England and Wales had an important reason to travel north as they were dissenters and those of other faiths who were deterred by the religious tests of English and Irish universities. Links were formed early with the colonies, initially North America but, later, further afield. Such connections often resulted in interesting acquisitions. For example, David Campbell, a bookseller of Boston, sent two books on Native American languages to the Library in 1693. Over the course of the nineteenth and twentieth centuries, the student population became increasingly international and by 2015-16 the University was welcoming students from over 140 countries.

Given its remit, the Archive has a large collection of photographs of the University campuses, premises and people, as well as the architectural plans of University buildings in the High Street, Garscube and Gilmorehill.

Closely linked to the material relating to the University itself are the collections of predecessor and affiliated bodies, such as Anderson's College of Medicine, Glasgow Veterinary College, Glasgow Dental Hospital & School, Queen Margaret College, St Andrew's College of Education, St Mungo's College of Medicine, and Trinity College. The archives of student organisations include the Students Representative Council, the University Union, the Queen Margaret Union and many other societies and clubs. The personal papers of inspirational figures connected to the University can also be found. These include the pioneer surgeon, Professor Sir William Macewen (1848-1924), who was also appointed Honorary Surgeon to Edward VII, University Rector and political icon Jimmy Reid (1932-2010) and alumnus and inventor of television John Logie Baird (1888-1946).

The University Archive is essential to the current business of the University but it is also a primary resource for Scotland's educational, intellectual and cultural history from 1451 to the present day.

| **Moira Rankin**

Left: The original design for the clock tower for the new University of Glasgow building, 1866. The spire and clock show great similarity to the Grand Hotel, St Pancras, London, which George Gilbert Scott (1811-1878), the University's architect, also designed. When building work on the new campus stopped in 1871, the tower was only built to the turret stage. John Oldrid Scott (1841-1913), George's son, redesigned the spire with the now familiar lattice stone work. Archives & Special Collections, GUA12464 [GUA1264_Clock Tower].

Above: Letter from Adam Smith (1723-1790), accepting the office of Rector of the University of Glasgow, 16th November, 1787. He remembers his days as a student and professor at the University 'as by far the happiest and most honourable period of my life'. Archives & Special Collections, GUA32202 [GUA32202pgs 1-3].

The Scottish Business Archive

Bringing together the records of many of Scotland's businesses, industries and industrialists, the Scottish Business Archive is an internationally significant collection for the study of Scotland's impact on the world economy. The Archive has over 500 business collections, containing the records of over 1,200 companies, and covers nearly every aspect of industrial and commercial activity in Scotland, offering a unique insight into Scotland's economic and industrial heritage from the eighteenth century onwards. Its collection of shipbuilding records is unrivalled and includes those of John Brown, builders of the *Queen Elizabeths* and *Queen Mary*. It is very strong in heavy engineering records, reflecting the industrial heritage of the west of Scotland, and these include the records of the North British Locomotive Co., which in 1903 operated the largest locomotive factory in the world, Mirrlees Watson & Co., sugar machinery manufacturers, and Babcock & Wilcox Ltd, boilermakers. It also holds the records of: the House of Fraser Group, files which include material from department stores located throughout the United Kingdom; James Finlay & Sons, East India merchants; the Gourock Ropework Co. (including the records of the New Lanark Mills, Robert Owen's utopian industrial concern of the late eighteenth century); J. & P. Coats, thread manufacturers to the world; Anchor Line and Ellerman Line, ship owners; Harper Collins Publishers; brewers such as Tennents and Youngers; whisky companies who are the producers of such brands as Laphroaig, Teachers and Long John; confectioners; investment trusts; paint manufacturers; agricultural merchants; racecourse owners; furniture manufacturers; salvagers; insurance companies; and many, many more.

The Archive has its roots in the work of the University's first professor of Economic History, Sydney Checkland. The first appointment to the Chair of Economic History in 1957, he built up a department carrying out excellent research in the fields of business, banking and urban history. Instrumental in the foundation of the Business Archives Council of Scotland in 1960, he also set in train the development of a research resource which would become the Scottish Business Archive. As economic decline took its toll on many of Scotland's biggest industrial names, the Department of Economic History made arrangements to take in the records of these industries and make them available for academic research. In 1975 the management of these records was transferred to the University Archive, and work continued to establish partnerships with the Scottish business community to manage their historical records. For the past forty years Archive Services have welcomed many researchers from all parts of the globe who have travelled to Glasgow to research the worldwide impact of Scotland's industry and commerce.

Drinks

Whilst whisky first comes to mind when mentioning the Scottish drinks industry, the importance of beer to the national economy should not be underestimated. Both are represented in the Scottish Business Archive, with the brewing-related collections being particularly extensive and representative of the market.

Whisky is a market which trades on its rich heritage. Visitor attractions at distilleries, linked together by whisky trails, can be found

The pier and distillery at Bunnahabhain, Islay. The Bunnahabhain Distillery was opened in 1882 by the Islay Distillery Co. Ltd, which merged with William Grant & Co. to form the Highland Distilleries Co. Ltd. The distillery produced whisky for blending, mainly in the Famous Grouse and Black Bottle blends, until the late 1970s when the 12-year-old single malt whisky was launched under the Bunnahabhain brand. Archives & Special Collections, UGD217/19/27a [ugd217-19-27a].

across the whisky-producing areas of Scotland. This relatively recent phenomenon celebrates the heritage of individual brands and draws on the records which document production methods, the distillery premises and staff, and the marketing of the whisky itself. A treasure in the archives of Laphroaig (D. Johnston & Co. Ltd) is a glimpse into the story of Bessie Williamson. Bessie, who studied at the University of Glasgow with plans of becoming a teacher, was first appointed to the position of temporary shorthand typist at the distillery in 1934. By the 1940s she had risen to the position of manager and then became the major shareholder in the owning company in 1954. She was the only woman to manage and own a Scotch whisky distillery in the twentieth century.

With records dating from the mid-eighteenth century, the story of Scotland's brewing heritage can be traced through the archives of over a hundred companies involved in this trade; information on dates for the development and first production of beers and lagers or on the exploration of export markets can be discovered, and the marketing campaigns of the past enjoyed again.

Textiles

Cloth and ropes for ships and railway rolling stock, thread for embroidery and clothing, dyes

Adding a barrel in the Ardmore Distillery maturation warehouse, 1970s. Ardmore Distillery, Kennethmont, Aberdeenshire, was built by Adam Teacher of William Teacher & Sons Ltd in 1897-98. Adam Teacher died in 1898 just when the finishing touches were being made to his distillery. Ardmore Distillery was created to guarantee supplies of malt whisky for blending, primarily for Teacher's Highland Cream. Archives & Special Collections UGD306/2/2/4/3(46), [UGD306_2_2_4_3-46].

for cotton and carpets, cotton, calico, leather and muslin for clothing, carpets for coronations and lounges, and ready-to-wear clothing of every sort - all can be found in the archives which document the Scottish textile industry. Across the nineteenth and twentieth centuries, Scottish firms secured a worldwide foothold, with such celebrated names as J. & P. Coats, United Turkey Red, and James Templeton trading on their reputation for quality thread, vibrant cloth and sumptuous carpets.

The archives of design and manufacturing processes can be particularly striking, varying from designs for intricately woven patterns to images which demonstrate the size and scale of the industrial processes. The Stoddard-Templeton Design Archive demonstrates the wide range of artistic styles favoured over 150 years of carpet manufacturing. Images from the Paisley mills of Coats and Clark provide a sense of the thunderous clatter of the workplace.

Retail

The House of Fraser Archive offers a fascinating glimpse into the history of one of Britain's leading department stores. Founded in 1849 as a small drapery shop on the corner of Argyle Street and Buchanan Street in Glasgow, it expanded rapidly, acquiring some 200 different stores, including Harrods in 1959, and opening branches in many parts of the world. The House of Fraser Archive provides a wealth of information on the company's history. The archive is an outstanding source for the history of British design, fashion, tastes, lifestyles, consumerism and consumption from the early nineteenth to the end of the twentieth century.

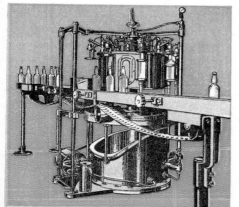

The Teacher bottling plant with the Lowvac filling machine illustrated on a blotting pad. William Teacher entered the grocery and spirits business in 1830 and acquired his first licence for premises at 50 Cheapside St, Glasgow, in 1836. By 1864 the company was in the wholesale business with headquarters in St Enoch Square, Glasgow. By 1937 they were the market leaders in the USA. Archives & Special Collections, UGD306/2/1/18/9b [UGD306-2-1-18-9b].

Shipping

The sea, the original motor of globalisation and the great transporter of goods, plays a vital, if often unrecognised role in the economic health of the world. Scotland's involvement in the world's shipping lanes continues as Glasgow continues to dominate as a major world ship management cluster. The photographs, advertising literature, details of captains and crews, freight and resorts visited by some of the great shipping companies such as Anchor Line, Clyde Shipping, Currie Line, and Ellerman reveal a great deal of life earned and enjoyed at sea. From the 1850s Anchor Line ran services to America, extending its Mediterranean service to India once the Suez Canal was opened. From 1865 to 1939 the company ran a weekly passenger and cargo service from Glasgow to New York, carrying many continental as well as British emigrants. In the early 1900s, three large liners left the Clyde every Saturday for America, carrying some 4,500 people.

Shipbuilding and Engineering

From the mid-eighteenth century Scottish engineers transformed the world. In the nineteenth and twentieth centuries, Scotland's heavy engineering industry produced ships, locomotives and rolling stock for export. It contributed significantly to Britain's reputation as the workshop of the world, and provided employment and a way of life for successive generations of families within their local communities. From the ships sent from William Simon's Greenock yard to run the Union blockade during the American Civil War through to the launch of the *QE2*, the west of Scotland's shipbuilding heritage is preserved in the archives of various Clyde-based shipbuilders. Through

Bessie Williamson at work in Laphroaig Distillery, Islay, 1970. Bessie Williamson, the manager of Laphroaigh Distillery and a University of Glasgow graduate, is credited as the creator of the distinctive phenolic, peaty character of Laphroaig that is today revered by malt whisky enthusiasts from all over the world. Archives & Special Collections, UGD306/1/34/17/19/10 [UGD306-1-34-17-19-10].

the company order books of Glasgow's North British Locomotive and of Kilmarnock's Andrew Barclay, the construction of railway engines for passenger and freight services within the United Kingdom and across the British Empire can be discovered.

The voluminous archives which survive for these ship and locomotive yards testify not only to the multitude of skills enjoyed by a large and varied labour force but to the works they produced and their purchasers. Order books and contracts detail customer requirements. Plans and specification books demonstrate how these demands were met, and photographs show the assembling of ships and locomotives in the yards ready for their launch into the sea or onto the tracks.

| **Clare Paterson**

Left: A promotional blotter for George Younger & Son Ltd of Alloa, 1939. George Younger, a member of a family of saltpan owners in Culross, Fife, was brewing beer in Alloa, Clackmannanshire, from 1745. George Younger & Son Ltd was incorporated in 1897 and traded across the world. It became part of the combined Scottish interests of Caledonian Breweries Ltd, which merged with J. & R. Tennent Ltd, Glasgow, in 1966 to form Tennent Caledonian Breweries Ltd. Archives & Special Collections, SBA GY11/12/1.

The Empire Exhibition, 1938, in Bellahouston Park, Glasgow. A Tennent's Lager promotional showcard. The Tennent family have been associated with brewing in Glasgow since the mid-sixteenth century, brewing on the Wellpark site since 1740. A new purpose-built German Lager Brewery was built at Wellpark between 1889 and 1891. Archives & Special Collections, SBA T11/7/11 [T11-7-11].

An artist's impression of the design concept for the first-class main lounge of RMS *Queen Mary* with carpet by designer Agnes Pinder Davis, 1936. This lounge was the social centre of first-class life on board, morning to night, and echoed to the sounds of concerts, teas, films, dancing and other entertainments. James Templeton & Co. Ltd. made the carpets for all the luxury liners of the Cunard fleet. Archives & Special Collections, STOD201/1/2/2 [STOD-201-1-2-2].

70

James Templeton's carpet factory on Glasgow Green, designed after the Loggia Doge`s Palace in Venice from *Scotland's Industrial Souvenir*, Bemrose & Sons Ltd, Derby & London, 1905. The catalogue contained advertisements from the best of Scottish industry and was sent to Chambers of Commerce, British Embassies and Boards of Trade in every part of the world. Copies could also be found on UK railway carriages and Cunard passenger ships sailing the oceans. This copy was issued by James Templeton & Co. Ltd. Archives & Special Collections, fBh2.57 [Templeton advert - fBh2.57].

A Tree of Life Persian carpet design with weaving instructions from the Stoddard-Templeton Design Archive. The Tree of Life is a popular motif in oriental carpets, pottery and other decorative items. It is thought to have originated in ancient Mesopotamia. Archives & Special Collections, STOD/DES/26/3 [STOD_DES_26_3].

A design sketch for the lounge carpet of the Cunard Atlantic liner RMS *Aquitania* from the Stoddard-Templeton Design Archive. The colour scheme for the lounge was wine red and grey. The *Aquitania*, nicknamed 'ship beautiful', was built by John Brown of Clydebank and launched on 21st April, 1913. Archives & Special Collections, STOD/DES/133/27 [Aquitania lounge].

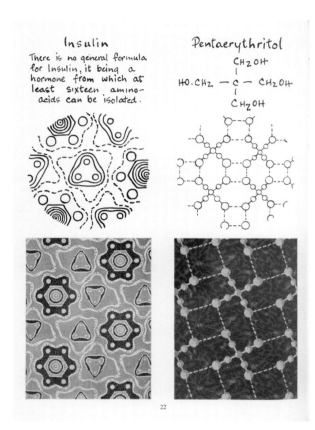

James Templeton & Co. Ltd's 1951 Festival of Britain carpet designs based on the crystal structures of insulin and pentaerythritol. The carpets featured in the Regatta Restaurant at the South Bank Exhibition in London, the principal showcase for the Festival Pattern Group, a unique project involving X-ray crystallographers, designers and manufacturers. Archives & Special Collections, STOD 201/2/15/1 [Stod 201_2_15_1].

A stylised Far East design (no. 646) on paper with two borders (nos. 647 and 645) for printed cotton textiles from the Milton of Colquhoun pattern book, 1790s. The 'Milltoun of Colquhoun' had established bleach-fields in the eighteenth century, soon giving rise to calico printing and weaving. By 1794 Milton is claimed to have had Scotland's first powered looms, forty of which were supposedly installed under the supervision of the renowned inventor and engineer, James Watt. Archives & Special Collections, DC90/7/3/3 [dc90_7_3_3_nos646-648].

Making cotton sewing thread reels in the old turning shop at the Paisley factory of J. & P. Coats, c. 1887. In 1802, James Coats (1774-1857), a weaver from Paisley, Renfrewshire, Scotland, set up in business, laying the foundation of the business that was to become J. & P. Coats Ltd, thread manufacturers, Paisley. 'Coats Land' in Antarctica is named after James Coats Jnr and his brother Andrew, who backed the Scottish Antarctic expedition of Dr William Bruce. Archives & Special Collections, UGD 199 Photographic Album [UGD199/Old Turning Shop].

A mouse and a frog went a-walking. A ticket label for a bale of cotton textiles sent by the Alexandria Turkey Red dyeworks to Adamson, Gilfillan & Co. Ltd, Singapore and Penang, 1900s. United Turkey Red Co. Ltd, bleachers, finishers and dyers of Alexandria, was formed in 1898 through the amalgamation of John Orr Ewing & Co., Archibald Orr Ewing and William Stirling & Sons. All textile bales featured distinguishing marks and illustration for ease of transport and security of recognition in overseas countries with myriad languages. Archives & Special Collections, UGD13/7/4 [UGD013/7/4 label 2889].

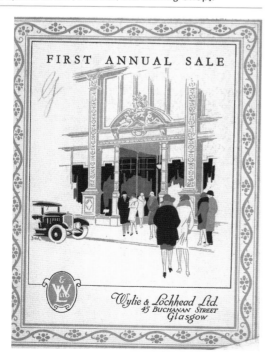

The front cover of the first annual sale catalogue of Wylie & Lochhead, January 1930. The catalogue features furniture, furnishings, floor coverings, leather goods, fancy goods, ironmongery, electrical goods, china and sports equipment. Archives & Special Collections, FRAS272/8 [FRAS272-8].

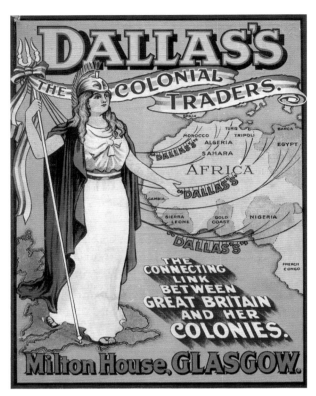

The autumn women's clothing catalogue from John Falconer & Co. Ltd, Aberdeen, 1932. Founded in 1828, the company was acquired by the Scottish Drapery Corporation Ltd in 1939 and by House of Fraser Ltd in 1952. The store thereafter operated as the Aberdeen branch of House of Fraser Ltd. Archives & Special Collections, HF34/7/1/1 [Hf034-7-1-1].

The front cover of Dallas's colonial export price list, c. 1915. Dallas & Co. was established in 1865 as a drapery store, operating from Milton House, 166-170 Cowcaddens, Glasgow. By the early twentieth century it also had an extensive mail-order business in West Africa. It was acquired by Fraser Sons & Co. Ltd in November 1942. Archives & Special Collections, FRAS 799/3 [hf015_7_1_22(2)].

The Robin Hood stained green bedroom suite from a Wylie & Lochhead general catalogue of furniture, furnishings, mantelpieces, floor coverings and ironmongery, 1910s. Wylie & Lochhead of Buchanan Street, Glasgow, were originally cabinet makers and funeral undertakers, developing into house furnishers and a department store, latterly acquired by House of Fraser. Archives & Special Collections, FRAS272/4. [fras272--p73].

Going Up! One of the attended lifts in Dickins & Jones, 1930. Dickins & Jones, the London department store, began as a linen drapery in Oxford Street moving into their impressive premises in Regent Street, which were to remain their flagship store until its closure in 2006. The business was acquired by Harrods in 1914 and then by House of Fraser in 1959 [FRAS1104/4].

An Anchor Line poster for its transatlantic and Mediterranean service. The Anchor Line Ltd had its beginnings in 1838 when two brothers, Nicol and Robert Handyside, established themselves in Glasgow, as shipbrokers and merchants. In 1856 it ran its first transatlantic crossing and by the twentieth century it also offered Mediterranean cruises and passenger sailings to India and Pakistan. The company had distinctive Scottish roots and was famous for its sleek ships and for the comfort it offered its passengers at a very affordable cost. The company employed some of the finest marine artists of the day to create its stunning posters. Archives & Special Collections, UGD255/1/40/33 [ugd255_1_40_33].

An Anchor Line poster for its 1939 Cruises. Archives & Special Collections, UGD255/1/40/28 [ugd255_1_40_28].

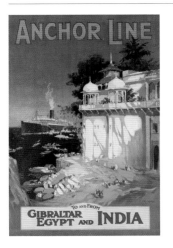

An Anchor Line poster for sailings to and from Gibraltar, Egypt, and India. W. Welsh, the artist has signed his work. William Welsh (1889-1984) was an American muralist, illustrator and portraitist who was very successful in the commercial world. Archives & Special Collections, UGD255/1/40/9 [ugd255_1_40_9].

An Anchor Line poster for the Glasgow and New York via Londonderry service. This poster's artist has signed his work. Kenneth Denton Shoesmith (1890-1939) was a member of the Royal Institute of Painters in Water Colours and of the British Society of Poster Designers. Archives & Special Collections, UGD255/1/40/16 [ugd255_1_40_16].

An Anchor-Donaldson Line poster advertising voyages to Canada, 1928. The passengers in the foreground may be emigrants embarking on a new life across the Atlantic, or simply tourists. The Glasgow shipping companies Anchor Line (Henderson Brothers) and the Donaldson Line both operated services to Canada. In 1916 they agreed to share these routes and form a joint company, Anchor-Donaldson, to operate the services. Archives & Special Collections, UGD255/1/40/21 [udg255-1-40-21].

Three Harland & Wolff shipyards on the Clyde in the 1930s: Harland & Wolff came to the Clyde in 1912, acquiring the sites of three adjacent shipyards at Govan (foreground), including that of Robert Napier and the London & Glasgow Shipbuilding Company. From 1913 onwards, the entire site was reconstructed by structural engineers Sir William Arrol & Co. into one modern shipbuilding yard with seven berths and lofty tower cranes. The yard closed in 1963 after building nearly 300 ships. Across the river at the confluence of the Kelvin are: (top right) the group's A. & J. Inglis's Pointhouse shipyard with the tripod crane; and D. & W. Henderson's Meadowside shipyard, on the west bank of the Kelvin. Archives & Special Collections, UGD241/2/1 [ugd241/2/1 pg.5].

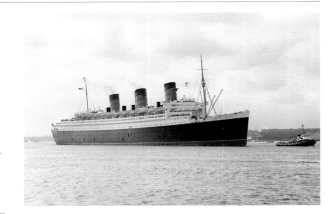

The RMS *Queen Mary* approaching harbour with tug, 1930s. Built by John Brown & Co. Ltd. in Clydebank, as the world's largest liner, the *Queen Mary*, along with her younger sister RMS *Queen Elizabeth*, were built as part of Cunard's planned two-ship weekly express service between Southampton, Cherbourg, and New York. *Queen Mary* sailed on her maiden voyage on 27th May, 1936, and captured the Blue Riband in August of that year. After distinguished service in peace and war she is now docked and open to the public in Long Beach, California. Archives & Special Collections, DC113/2565/6 [dc113-2565-6_queen_mary].

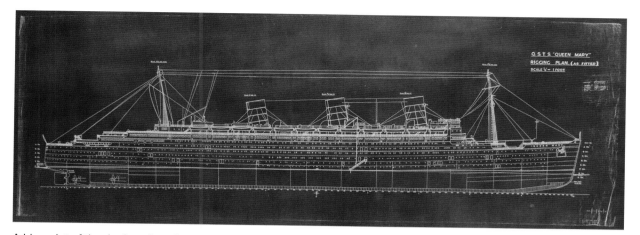

A blueprint of the rigging plan of the RMS *Queen Mary*, c. 1933, John Brown & Co. Ltd. Negative cyanotype blueprint from original drawing UCS 1/110/534/2. Printed by Roger Farnham and Harry Magee. [C7 T103- Queen Mary].

The cover of the invitation to the launch of Cunard's RMS *Lusitania*, on 7th June, 1906, from the builders, John Brown & Co. Ltd of Clydebank. Launched by Mary, Lady Inverclyde, the passenger liner set new standards for speed, size, and luxury on the Atlantic winning the coveted Blue Riband. The ship was torpedoed and sunk by a German U-boat on 7th May, 1915, causing the deaths of 1,198 passengers and crew. Archives & Special Collections, UCS GUAS Ref: UCS 1/113/1 [Lusitania Invite].

A photograph of the R34 airship at Inchinnan, Renfrewshire, where it was produced by the industrial conglomerate William Beardmore & Co. Ltd, early in 1919. The R33 and R34 British rigid airships were designed and built for the Royal Naval Air Service towards the end of the First World War. The R34 became the first aircraft to make an east to west transatlantic flight in July 1919 and by the return flight it successfully completed the first two-way crossing. This airship was decommissioned two years later after being damaged during a storm in January, 1921. Archives & Special Collections, UGD100/1/11/3/69 [UGD100-1-11-3-69_airship_r34].

NORTH BRITISH LOCOMOTIVE CO LTD, GLASGOW

SAN PAULO RAILWAY (BRAZIL).
PASSENGER LOCOMOTIVE WITH TENDER. Four Cylinder "Simple."
Reference No. L581.   4-6-0 Type.   5-ft. 3-in. Gauge.

The 4-6-0 type San Paulo Railway passenger locomotive built by the North British Locomotive Co. Ltd, 1914-1918, reproduced from *An Account of the Manufacture of the North British Locomotive Co. Ltd, during the period of the War, 1914-1918, with a short History of the Firms which constituted the Company when formed in 1903*, published by the North British Locomotive Co. Ltd in 1918. Archives & Special Collections, UGD11/12/1 [UGD11-12-1-L581].

A promotional advertisement for the innovative Bennie Railplane, which was a form of rail transport invented by George Bennie (1891–1957), and which moved along an overhead rail by way of propellers. Bennie began work on the railplane in 1921, and in 1929-1930 he built a prototype on a trial stretch of track at Milngavie, Glasgow, with one railplane car to demonstrate the system to potential clients. Despite international interest Bennie could not obtain the financial backing he required to develop his revolutionary transport system and by 1937 he was bankrupt. Archives & Special Collections, DC85/3/4 [Dc085-3-4_bennie_railplane_ad].

The Clyde Villa 60-ton capacity crane at berth 81 on Plantation Quay (now Pacific Quay) loading North British locomotives onto a freighter for the export trade, 1920s. The crane was the first heavy lift crane to be installed in Glasgow Harbour and remained in service after the completion of the 130-ton crane at Stobcross Quay, Finnieston Street, (in 1893) and also at Princes Dock (in 1895). Archives & Special Collections, GD329 [dockrail].

Children's Literature

The disseminated children's literature collection has its origin in the inherited material which came from St Andrew's College, Glasgow, a local teacher training college which merged with the University in 1999. The original collection was, therefore, designed to support the work of student teachers on school placement and reflected those authors and themes which had been popular in Scottish schools. As such, it was not at that point a comprehensive collection of children's fiction – in general, public libraries would have had larger and more varied holdings. However, in succeeding years, stock selection for this collection has broadened considerably. This reflects the wider needs of the university community, the increasing interest in the genre as a field of research in its own right and the addition of several new programmes dealing specifically with children's literature, for example the Masters degree in Children's Literature run by the School of Education.

Contained within the collection there are, as one might expect, a considerable number of novels which are often referred to as standard children's classics – *Alice in Wonderland, Tom Sawyer, Black Beauty, The Secret Garden, Treasure Island, and Little Women*. More modern titles which have subsequently become so well known that they could also be said to fall into this category are also represented – **Roald Dahl's** *Charlie and the Chocolate Factory*, **Katherine Paterson's** *Bridge to Terabithia* or **J. K. Rowling's** *Harry Potter* series.

Picture books also feature in this list of classics – for example, **Pat Hutchins'** *Rosie's Walk*, **Maurice Sendak's** *Where the Wild Things Are* or **Eric Carle's** *The Very Hungry Caterpillar*. Indeed, picture books have formed an important part of the collection for many years, demonstrating

Toy books. This set of chapbooks well illustrates the type of children's literature available at the beginning of the nineteenth century. They were produced by the Glasgow publisher James Lumsden and include such popular tales as *Old Mother Hubbard* and her wonderful dog and the *History of Goody Two Shoes* and her brother Tommy. These works reflect the contemporary attitudes towards children and often have a didactic tone, frequently being abridgements of popular literature. Often accompanied by crudely hand-coloured illustrations, these small books were often more widely read than many of the more established works of their day. Archives & Special Collections, Bh13-c.28 [Bh13-c.28 group1].

THROUGH THE LOOKING-GLASS,

AND WHAT ALICE FOUND THERE.

BY

LEWIS CARROLL,

AUTHOR OF "ALICE'S ADVENTURES IN WONDERLAND."

WITH FIFTY ILLUSTRATIONS
BY JOHN TENNIEL.

London:
MACMILLAN AND CO.
1872.

[The Right of Translation and Reproduction is reserved.]

Examples of children's literature can also be found within the Hepburn Collection of first editions of nineteenth-century English literature. Unlike other children's books of the mid-Victorian era, which were frequently instructional or moral tales, the Alice books were a success enjoyed by both adults and children alike for their wit and satire. Charles Dodgson (1832-1898), whose pseudonym was Lewis Carroll, employed the *Punch* artist, Sir John Tenniel, to illustrate his much-loved work *Alice's Adventures in Wonderland* (1865) and *Through the Looking Glass* (1871), and these are the ones which still stick in most people's minds. Archives & Special Collections, Hepburn 99 [Hepburn 99 Title].

as they do the importance of not just text but illustration in developing children's imagination and visual literacy.

Throughout the 1990s, stock selection began to encompass the increasing publication output for young adults. Previously a somewhat neglected area, authors such as **Anne Fine, Jacqueline Wilson, Philip Pullman** and many others have contributed to the creation and success of this genre, and the library's collection has a significant number of titles designed for this specific age group.

The Library has been consistent in purchasing those titles which have been prize winners or which have featured in the shortlists of the major children's book prizes, such as the

Carnegie Medal for children's fiction, or the Kate Greenaway Award for children's book illustration. In addition, the collection reflects certain local book awards, sometimes run by public libraries, where children themselves are the judges. Children's book reviews, magazines and websites such as Book Trust, Carousel, and Books for Keeps, are important sources of evaluation and identification of quality titles. All these ensure that not only is there a representative sample of excellence in publishing for children in the Library holdings but also that stock is current, and that new authors, especially those who appeal to children, are featured.

A deliberate feature of stock selection policy was the purchase of fiction designed to support school curriculum topics. For example, children studying the Second World War may also have been encouraged to read the **Michelle Magorian** novel *Goodnight Mister Tom*, which deals with evacuees, and student teachers regularly use **Rosemary Sutcliff's** *The Eagle of the Ninth* when teaching the Roman history of Britain. A particular favourite is **Kathleen Fidler's** *The Desperate Journey* which deals with the Highland Clearances. Representing a further significant theme, those books dealing with particular events or issues in children's lives – family bereavement, divorce, disability – have also been identified and purchased.

Significant effort has gone into the creation and maintenance of a strong collection of titles with a Scottish dimension; this drive encompasses titles by Scottish authors, stories set in Scotland or those with a Scottish theme. The Scottish children's book scene is thriving and lively and such luminaries as **Therese Breslin, Mollie Hunter**

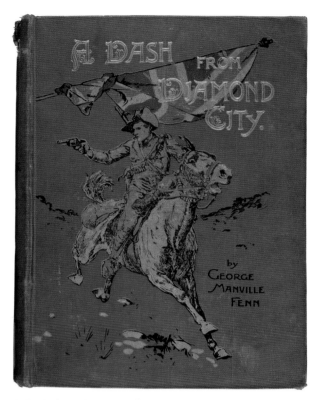

A Dash from Diamond City, written by George Manville Fenn, illustrated by F. A. Stewart, published by Ernest Nister, London, 1901. George Manville Fenn (1831-1909) was a writer of boys' books, amongst other work. Frank Algernon Stewart (1877-1945) was a war artist for the *Illustrated London News* and became particularly known for his paintings of hunting scenes. JF Historical FEN [A Dash from Diamond City].

and **Julia Donaldson** are all well represented in the Library. Past winners and shortlisted authors of the Kelpie Award, the annual prize for new Scottish writing for children run by publisher Floris Books, also feature heavily.

In addition to the selection and purchase of individual fiction titles, the Library has sought to acquire such material as encyclopaedias and dictionaries to support the research and teaching of children's literature. For this

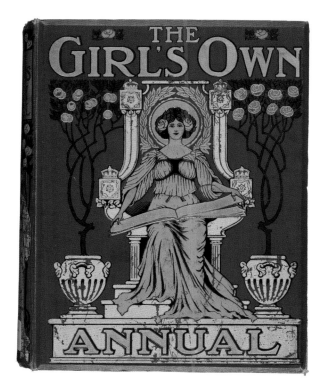

The Girl's Own Annual, 1898. A variety of magazines and annuals for children were published in Britain from the mid-nineteenth century onwards. Initially titled *The Girl's Own Paper*, the annual was published from 1880 to 1956. It provided a mix of stories and educational and improving articles, with 'Answers to Correspondents' and occasional coloured plates, poetry and music. JNF Hist052.083. [The Girl's Own Annual].

purpose, particular information on authors is especially relevant. A special effort has also been made to purchase bibliographies dealing with particular aspects, genres or themes in children's literature. These listings could include historical or fantasy fiction, for example, or children's fiction with multicultural themes, or stories written in serial form. Subscriptions to several noted journals such as *Children Literature in Education* or the *Journal of Children's Literature and Librarianship* further complement these materials, providing the necessary academic resources for the serious study and research of the genre.

As well as 'modern' titles, the Library is actively collecting historical children's literature. While there are excellent examples of such earlier writings among the holdings within our Special Collections, strong efforts have also been made to obtain items from the middle of the nineteen century up to the 1930s. This material is harder to obtain, but second-hand bookshops and specialist reprint publishers are able to supply a good selection. Nineteenth-century holdings include children's books published by Lumsden, and archive material of publishers Blackie & Son and William Collins. The collection now includes examples of all the popular genres, such as school stories, stories with a strong religious/moral element, and adventure stories. Many celebrated authors, such as **Angela Brazil** or **G. A. Henty**, are featured as well as examples of some of the most popular magazines of the time such as *Chums* and *The Girl's Own Annual*. Additional interest is provided by the many colour plates and illustrations within these items and by the fact that a number of them were 'presentation copies', i.e. prizes for school work or Sunday school attendance, and still have the original certificates pasted in. This collection appeals to a wide range of students and researchers. In addition, its attraction and impact extend beyond those interested in education or children's literature alone to include researchers in social and cultural history, art history and indeed any aspect of the Victorian era and the early twentieth century.

Honor Hania

Central and East European Studies

Glasgow's Central and East European Studies and Slavonic collections are among the best in the country and are comparable with larger and more specialised libraries within the United Kingdom. Relevant material is spread across various donations and sections of the Library, covering a wide range of topics and including unique items of national importance.

Two distinct collections held within the Department of Special Collections merit particular mention. The Trotsky Collection consists of an extensive assemblage of material written by, or relating to, Leon Trotsky (1879-1940), Communist revolutionary, founder of the Red Army and one of the leaders of the 1917 October Revolution. This large collection of Trotskiana was donated to the Library in 1983 by Trotsky's bibliographer, Louis Sinclair (1909-1990), and comprises some 1,800 editions of Trotsky's works in forty languages. Numerous secondary items and several hundred periodical and newspapers featuring articles on Trotsky supplement his own publications. This collection also includes papers and published material presented by the widow of Isaac Deutscher (1907-1967), another of Trotsky's biographers, for example, the first Russian edition of **Where is Britain Going?** (1925) and copies of two films of Trotsky in Mexico, purchased from the cameraman who shot them.

Additionally, material gathered by a local school teacher forms the Bissett Collection, which includes more than 1,500 pamphlets, including works by Lenin, Kropotkin and Tolstoy. It is characterised by a left-wing view of the Soviet Union and includes an almost complete set of Left

Cover of *One Year of Revolution: celebrating the first anniversary of the founding of the Russian Soviet Republic*, Socialist Publication Society, 1918. An extensive collection of Trotskiana was donated to the Library in 1983 by Trotsky's bibliographer, Louis Sinclair (1909-90). It comprises some 1,800 editions of Trotsky's works, together with numerous secondary items and several hundred periodical and newspapers featuring articles on Trotsky. Archives & Special Collections, U72.237 [U72.237].

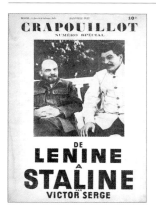

The cover of *De Lenine à Staline*, written by Victor Serge, a special edition of the French magazine *Crapouillot* ('the wee toad', as French soldiers affectionately called their mortars in WWI), January 1937. It was also published as a book in English by Pioneer Publishers, New York, in the same year. Archives & Special Collections, Trotsky 119 [TrotskyPersSerge].

Book Club editions, as well as a number of scarce local imprints, e.g. publications of the Bakunin Press and the Strickland Press in Glasgow.

The general Central and East European holdings include published collections of historical, statistical, legal, diplomatic and Communist Party documents, as well as literature produced by dissident groups. There is a substantial series of publications on the history and economic history of the relevant republics and regions, and a significant number of documents on the history of individual enterprises. The collection of Soviet era statistics and official publications for the entire USSR is of great historical value, as no single library in the United Kingdom or in the countries of origin has full sets of statistical publications. This multi-lingual corpus requires specialist skills in its acquisition, arrangement and cataloguing. In recent years the Library has concentrated on

This well-preserved phylactery dates from 1661 and was intended as an amulet to protect its owner. It is the only Armenian manuscript held in Glasgow and depicts St George. Archives & Special Collections, MS Gen 1498 [G1498_roundel].

Map of Muscovy from Sigismund von Herberstein's *Rerum Moscoviticarum commentarii*, Basle, 1556. This third edition of the first authentic account of Russia by a western traveller was based on the author's two visits to Russia during the first half of the sixteenth century. Between 1517 and 1518, Baron Sigismund von Herberstein (1486-1566) travelled as the diplomatic envoy of the Holy Roman Emperor, Maximilian I, in an attempt to arrange a truce between Russia and Lithuania. Nine years later, he returned to renew a treaty agreed in 1522. His own knowledge of Slovene allowed him to communicate freely with Russians, giving him an unique insight into the contemporary geography, politics and social conditions of sixteenth-century Russia. Archives & Special Collections, Bk4-d.10 [Bk4-d.10].

increasing its holdings of microfilm and digital collections of important archival material, which became only recently available for the first time. These include archives of the Soviet Communist Party, the Comintern Archive, papers of the Red and White armies, the Russian biographical archive and the Pravda and Izvestiia digital archives. Research on the Baltic States is supported by material within the John Hiden Baltic Research Archive, which contains Foreign Office documents from the inter-war period, in addition to material dealing with the early period of post-Soviet economic and political transformation.

The Library also has significant holdings of historical material relating to Slavonic Studies. The collections of Russian and Czech literature are particularly distinguished. A number of eighteenth-century Russian books are held within Special Collections, including items probably donated to the University by Semyon Efimovich Desnitsky, a former graduate of the University who subsequently became Professor of Russian Law at the University of Moscow. He has been recognised as 'the father of Russian jurisprudence' and, together with his colleague, Ivan Andreyevich Tretyakov, became the first Russian student to study in Britain at Glasgow under the sponsorship of the Empress Elizabeth II. More recently, acquisitions include an excellent set of Russian émigré literature, which, in addition to monographs, includes periodicals such as *Sovremennye Zapiski* (Contemporary Notes), published in Paris in seventy volumes from 1920 to 1940, and *Novyi Zhurnal* (New Journal), published in New York since the 1940s, as well as newspapers *Russkaia Mysl'* (Russian Thought), again published in Paris, and *Posev* (The Sowing), produced in Frankfurt am Main. To

The cover of *Fascism: its History and Significance*, by L. W., London: The Plebs, 1924, from the Plebs sixpenny series. Glasgow schoolteacher James Bissett 's collection of some 1,500 left-wing pamphlets (ranging in date from the late nineteenth century to the late twentieth century) was purchased by the University of Glasgow in 1981. It includes an almost complete set of Left Book Club editions and a number of rare local imprints. Archives & Special Collections, Bisset q62 [Bisset_q62_coverwf].

supplement these, the Library also has an almost complete set of the pre-revolutionary *Voprosy filosofii i psikhologii* (Questions of Philosophy and Psychology). A number of significant bibles are held within Special Collections. Many of these are part of the Euing Collection, and include an

Former United States Secretary of State, Madeleine Albright, and Dr Jan Culik viewing Václav Flajšhans' *Písemnictví české slovem i obrazem: od nejdávnějších dob až po naše časy* (An Illustrated History of Czech Literature from ancient times to the present day, 1901).

1822 copy of the New Testament in Slavonic and Russian, a number of early Polish examples and a Bohemian Bible from 1596.

Highlights of the Czech collections include Josef Jungmann's five-volume Czech-German dictionary from the 1830s. This had a significant impact in laying the foundations for modern Czech vocabulary. Also of importance are first editions of Karel Jaromír Erben's folklore collections from the middle of the nineteenth century and some beautifully produced works, such as Václav Flajšhans's history of Czech literature from the early twentieth century which contains inserted facsimile letters from a range of authors. This collection of Czech material is also renowned for an almost complete set of works of émigré publishing from the communist era (1948-1989), in particular the total output of Josef Škvorecký's Toronto-based '68 Publishers' – his close colleague Dr Igor Hájek was the Czech Senior Lecturer at Glasgow from 1983 until his death in 1995.

| **Morag Greig & Kay Munro**

Map Collection

Glasgow University has a long and distinguished tradition in topographic science and surveying. In 1954 a former Assistant Director of the Ordnance Survey, Lt.-Col. J. S. O. Jelly, was appointed lecturer in the Department of Geography and gave instruction in surveying. Encouraged by Professor Ronald Miller, then head of department, an innovative academic programme of survey and mapping sciences was developed, particularly under the guidance of John Keates, whose influential work on map design and production is still recognised as a standard reference work.

Inevitably, the University Library Map Collection has been influenced by the numbers of students studying this particular discipline. It has an extensive holding of contemporary national map series of European countries at scales varying between 1:50,000 and 1:200,000, which reflect the different mapping styles of the individual national mapping agencies. Combined with our sequence of national atlases, these holdings support research within the Geographical and Earth Sciences disciplines. Additionally, the Library holds a comprehensive collection of maps produced by former members of departmental staff, which includes a survey of the Breiðamerkurjökull Glacier in south-east Iceland and a visitors' map of Dar es Salaam in Tanzania.

The collection now consists of more than 60,000 sheets, with a worldwide coverage. It is one of the few academic map libraries in Scotland, supporting University research and teaching across the whole university calendar but also available for consultation by members of the general public. Supplementing the sheet map series is a considerable collection of over 400 topographic and thematic atlases, cartographic reference books and gazetteers. Maps and related material can be found elsewhere in the Library – most notably the historical holdings within the Special Collections Department – while certain specialist maps (e.g. ancient maps of the classical world, linguistic atlases) are located on the appropriate subject levels.

Particularly notable treasures within the Special Collections holdings include: the twenty-sheet 1739 plan of Paris by Louis Bretez (Hunterian Ax.1.5); Horwood's plan of the cities of London and Westminster (HX85), published between 1795 and 1799 in thirty-two sheets and, at that time, the largest map ever printed in Great Britain; an eighteenth-century manuscript Japanese map of the world (MS Hunter B/E2); and a copy of the first complete printed atlas of Russia, produced in St Petersburg in 1745 – *Atlas Russicus* (Ax.1.1).

Our general holdings are notably strong in coverage of the British Isles and Scotland in particular. Through the generosity of two extensive donations of Ordnance Survey material, from Edinburgh University Library and the Ordnance Survey Historical Archive itself, the Library has an excellent assemblage of maps of Glasgow and the west of Scotland. It contains an almost complete set of the first edition Ordnance Survey six-inch series for all Scottish counties, as well as considerable coverage of the various editions at the twenty-five inch scale, particularly for the counties of Lanarkshire, Renfrewshire, Stirlingshire, Dunbartonshire and Ayrshire. In addition, it

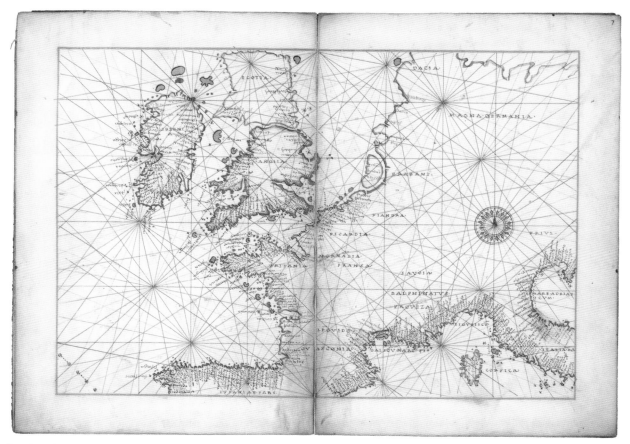

Baptista Agnese's depictions of *Northwest Europe*, Venice, c. 1542, show Scotland separated from England by a narrow strait, a common feature of sixteenth-century portolan charts and thought to be the result of unintelligent copying of earlier examples rather than of any real belief in Scotland's insularity. Agnese (c. 1500-1564) was a cartographer from the Republic of Genoa, who worked in the Venetian Republic. Archives & Special Collections, MS Hunter 492 (V.7.19) [MS Hunter 492_maps].

holds most of the sheets of the 1:500 town plans for burghs in the west of Scotland, dating from the mid-Victorian period. As these are the most detailed maps of the period, they are a superb resource for local researchers.

Among many unique maps of Glasgow can be highlighted a most attractive and detailed hand-coloured copy of Thomas Sulman's bird's-eye panorama of the city produced for the *Illustrated London News* in March 1864, an excellent copy of David Smith's six-sheet survey of the city of 1821, based on the earlier plates of Peter Fleming, and his one-sheet reduction of 1828.

Supplementing this topographical coverage, the Library also holds a large number of geological maps, again depicting many parts of the world. Overall, the present policy for the Collection

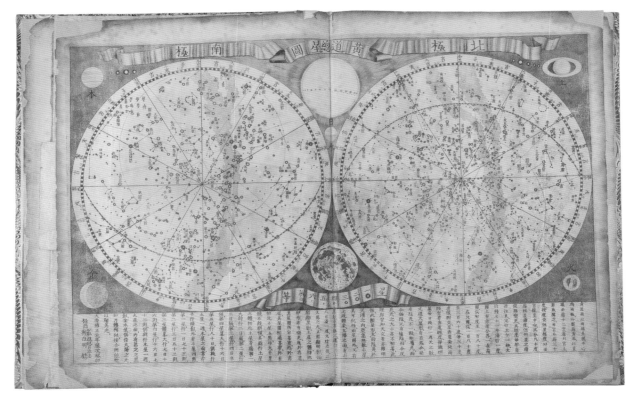

Dating from the eighteenth century, this engraved Chinese star map comes from the *Globus Coelestis Sinicus Explicatus* and exhibits both the Northern and Southern stellar hemispheres. In the border, the Sun is shown with its spots and certain other planets, while the lower margin contains a 53-column enumeration of those stars indicated on the map in Chinese characters. Archives & Special Collections, MS Hunter 10 (S.1.10) [H10_starmapwf].

is to focus on the British Isles in particular but also to retain unique historical maps from the world beyond. These include extensive coverage of various theatres of conflict produced by the military surveys of both Great Britain and the United States, much dating from the Second World War but also containing, for example, a map showing the movements of major units of the British Commando Units in the Falkland Islands in the summer of 1982 and a collection of sheets of battle plans from the Desert Campaign in Egypt and Palestine from the Great War.

Additionally, there is comprehensive coverage of many former British territories and colonies throughout the world, based on work prepared by the Directorate of Overseas Surveys. This results in the Library holding detailed maps for such diverse locations as Saint Helena, Mahé in the Seychelles, and Tarawa Atoll in Kiribati. One particularly noticeable strand of mapping within the Map Collection is a diverse holding of mountaineering and trekking maps for many of the major mountain areas in Europe, China and the Himalayas (e.g. a 1988 map of the Mount Ararat region in eastern Turkey and a trekking map of the Simien Mountains of Ethiopia).

Many of the unique early maps, mostly dating from the nineteenth century, are kept under supervised control and cover such diverse subjects as Charles Booth's descriptive map of London poverty (1889), Murdoch McKenzie's charts of the west coast of Scotland (1776), a map of Norway once owned by Edward Whymper, the first man to climb the Matterhorn, several works prepared for the Palestine Exploration Fund (including maps by H. H. Kitchener), Diakoff's colourful map of China dated 1931 and prepared for school use, sketches of parts of North America dating from the American Revolutionary War and James Cook's chart of New Zealand, explored in 1769 and 1770. Early atlases include a copy of John Thomson's 1832 *Atlas of Scotland* and a rare copy of the six-volume Belgian *Atlas universel de géographie* prepared by Phillippe Vandermaelen (1827) – an early example of lithographic printing.

Increasingly, maps are available online or in digital format and our paper map holdings are supplemented and enhanced by access to, among others, the **EDINA Digimap** service, which allows staff and students to view, annotate and print Ordnance Survey maps and data at all scales, as well as providing download functionality. The service also allows access to the British Geological Survey's on- and off-shore mapping, enhanced by detailed rock information and photographs, historical Ordnance Survey maps at a variety of scales dating from 1843 to 1996, marine charts and bathymetrical data for the UK coastal zone, and environmental land cover data from the Centre for Ecology and Hydrology.

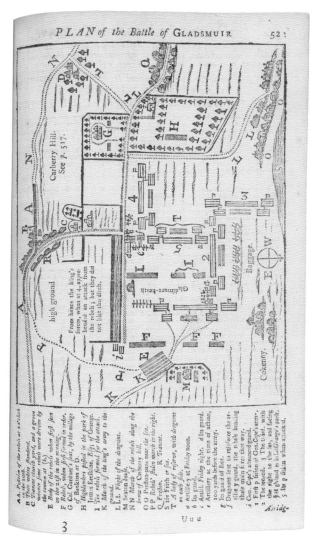

Plan of the Battle of Gladsmuir, reproduced In *The Gentleman's Magazine*, vol. 15 (1745). This is a diagrammatic sketch of the battle of Prestonpans on 21st September, 1745, when a renowned Highland charge scattered the inexperienced Hanoverian troops and dragoons under Sir John Cope in a matter of minutes. This map accompanies a published letter from one of Cope's officers and illustrates the troop dispositions and actions. Pm4642 [Stack Pers_p521].

As many earlier maps are also now available online through such sites as the National Library of Scotland's map images pages or the portal **OldMapsOnline**, the Collection has developed a growing gallery of images which promotes the unique items within its holdings. With a marked demand for the reproduction of images, the availability of a wide-format scanner and inkjet printer enables staff to offer high quality prints or digital files to Library users.

| **John Moore**

Map of Kanan Devan Hills Produce tea estates, c. 1950s. The Glasgow firm of James Finlay & Co., cotton manufacturers and East Indies merchants established in 1750, began to diversify into tea estate management around 1882 and by 1901 was managing extensive tea estates in India and Sri Lanka. The Assam, Sylhet, Cachar, Dooars, Darjeeling and Travancore estate covered over 270,000 acres, 77,000 acres of which were planted with tea. The expanded firm was by now the leading Indian tea supplier in the UK market with five main subsidiary companies to manage the tea-growing interests – including Kenan Devan Hills Produce Co. Ltd. The last tea estates in India were sold to the Tata Tea Co. of Bombay in 1982. Archives & Special Collections, UGD 91/16/6/1 [ugd091-16-6-1].

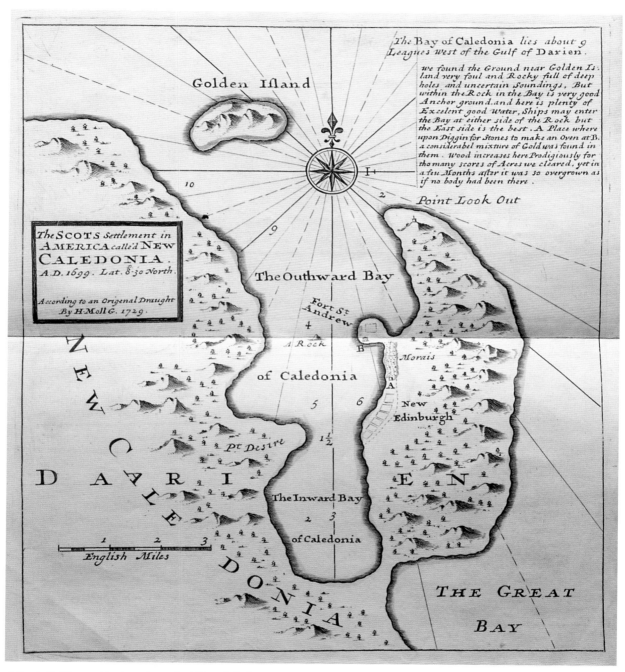

The Bay of Caledonia *lies about 9 Leagues West of the Gulf of Darien.*

we found the Ground near Golden Island very foul and Rocky full of deep holes and uncertain Soundings, But within the Rock in the Bay is very good Anchor ground, and here is plenty of Excelent good Water, Ships may enter the Bay at either side of the Rock but the East side is the best. A Place where upon Diggin for Stones to make an Oven at B. a considerabel mixture of Gold was found in them. Wood increases here Prodigiously for tho many scores of Acres we cleared, yet in a few Months after it was so overgrown as if no body had been there.

Golden Island

Point Look Out

The SCOTS *Settlement in* AMERICA *called* NEW CALEDONIA. A.D. 1699. Lat. 8.30 North.

According to an Origenal Draught By H. Moll G. 1729.

The Outward Bay

Fort St. Andrew

A Rock

of Caledonia

Morais

New Edinburgh

Pt. Desire

The Inward Bay

of Caledonia

NEW CALEDONIA

DARIEN

THE GREAT BAY

English Miles

A Scots Settlement in America called New Caledonia, 1699. Focusing on material relating to the Darien Scheme, the Spencer collection provides a wealth of rare primary and secondary sources on this disastrous attempt to found a Scottish trading colony in Central America at the end of the seventeenth century. Archives & Special Collections, Spencer f18 [Spencer f18.wf].

Travel, Topography and Exploration

The non-medical section of William Hunter's library reflects his deep and wide interests in an extensive range of subjects, which included topography and the expedition literature of his day. His library reflects a particularly strong selection of books on exploration and travel, with a wealth of Americana, as well as important materials on the East Indies and on contemporary voyages to the South Seas. Examples of these include copies of Daniel Denton's **Brief Description of New-York** (1670), the first English-language description of the area and perhaps most famous for its early statement of 'manifest destiny', the posthumous **Journal of a Voyage to the South Seas** (1773) by the Scottish Quaker, Sydney Parkinson (1745-1771), which records his collection of plants

Two boats on Loch Coruisk, from William Daniell & Richard Ayton, *A Voyage round Great Britain*, 1826. Loch Coruisk, In Gaelic *Coire Uisg*, the 'Cauldron of Waters,' is an inland fresh-water loch, lying at the foot of the Black Cuillin in the Isle of Skye. This celebration of the British coastline contains over 300 aquatint engravings of its most picturesque stretches. These were the work of William Daniell (1769-1837), one of the foremost landscape artists of his day, and they sought to illustrate the grandeur of our natural scenery. Accompanied by Richard Ayton, who was responsible for the text, the tour took twelve years to complete. Interestingly, Daniell passed through the Highlands of Scotland during the very years that the Highland Clearances were at their peak. He lauded the Duke of Sutherland, one of the primary offenders during the Clearances, for his extensive programme of road building yet fails to mention the mass forced evictions of thousands of crofters. Archives & Special Collections, f53-f56 [Loch Coruisk].

and animals in association with Joseph Banks on James Cook's first voyage to the Pacific in HMS *Endeavour* (Bk2-d.17 and K.2.13), and Herman Moll's *View of the Coasts, Countries and Islands [...] of the South-Sea-Company* (1711: K.6.28). Significant foreign topographical works include the four-volume *Description géographique, historique, chronologique, politique, et physique de l'Empire de la Chine et de la Tartarie chinoise*, written by the Jesuit French historian Jean du Halde in 1735, which sparked a European enthusiasm for China for several generations (Bo.1.9-12), the Huguenot Aubry de la Mottraye's travels in Europe, Asia and Africa (1727: K.1.1-2) and Linschoten's *Navigatio ac itinerarium Iohannis Hugonis [...] in Orientalem* (1599: K.2.14), which contributed to a wider knowledge of navigation

Fold-out engraving portraying the discovery of Niagara Falls from Louis Hennepin's *New Discovery of a Vast Country in America, extending above four thousand miles, between New France and New Mexico*, London, 1698. Hennepin, a Franciscan missionary and explorer accompanied the explorer La Salle to the Niagara River in 1678 and thence across the Great Lakes. Captured by Sioux Indians, Hennepin was rescued in 1681. After La Salle's death Hennepin published *Nouvelle Découverte d'un très grand pays situé dans l'Amérique*, Utrecht, 1697. His extravagant claims to have explored the Mississippi to its mouth (as did La Salle) have discredited his writings. He did, however, provide the first printed description of Niagara Falls, an illustration of which appears in both the French and English editions of his book. Archives & Special Collections, Bk3_h.15 [Bk3-h.15_0029.wf].

'Corean Chief and his Secretary,' from Basil Hall, *Account of a Voyage of Discovery to the West Coast of Corea and the Great Loochoo Island*, London: John Murray, 1818. Captain Basil Hall (1788-1844) was a British naval officer and author from Dunglass, East Lothian, whose account describes this commission, his explorations in the little known eastern seas, and his visit to Canton (Guangzhou). T13-y.1. [Korea Voyage of Discovery].

through the Malacca Strait and thereby broke the Portuguese monopoly of trade in the region. The three volumes detailing the travels of Paul Lucas, antiquarian to Louis XIV and published between 1704 and 1719, provide one of the earliest sources of information on Upper Egypt (K.7.17-23), while three works by Adam Olearius (1599-1671) narrating his travels with a German legation to the Shah of Safavid Persia in 1637 introduced Europe to Persian literature and culture (K.1.4-5 and K.5.16-17).

Nearer to home, Hunter's collection includes copies of the 1596 edition of Lambarde's *Perambulation of Kent* (Bv.3.31), the 1583 Paris edition of Nicolas de Nicolay's *La Navigation du Roy d'Escosse, Jacques Cinquiesme* and a collection of plans and views of the château of Versailles dating from about 1680 (Ce.1.9). In addition to works held within Hunter's library, other significant named collections of relevance to topography include those gathered by Alexander Bennett McGrigor, a member of the University Court between 1884 and 1887, and the German textual scholar, Constantin von Tischendorf, both of whose interests covered the topography of Palestine and the Near East. Library holdings of works on this region are also well supported by the many early publications of the Palestine Exploration Fund (founded in 1865) and benefit from the interest the Ordnance Survey took in mapping Jerusalem at this time. An entirely different but equally significant collection is that of more than a thousand glass photographic negatives made by William Spiers Bruce (1867-1921), the Scottish naturalist and polar scientist who organised the Scottish National Antarctic Expedition, 1902-04. These images cover locations in the Falkland Islands, the South

Orkneys and Spitzbergen. Additional material held elsewhere within Special Collections includes the journal written by Patrick Gass of the Lewis and Clark Expedition published seven years before the official report (Sp Coll d.7.3) and James Bruce's *Travels to Discover the Source of the Nile* published in five volumes in 1790 (BG52-b.6-10).

With the Library holding copyright deposit status between 1710 and 1836, much additional contemporary literature relating to what was, arguably, the high point of discovery and the expansion of the British Empire was added to the general collections. Throughout the nineteenth and twentieth centuries, the Library's holdings were enhanced by the reports of many major expeditions written by both British and foreign scientists. Notable examples of this literature include the writings of the French explorer, Jules Dumont d'Urville describing his exploration of the south and western Pacific in the *Astrolabe* (T9-c.1), David Livingstone's *Narrative of an Expedition to the Zambesi* (1865: HA08753), and the works of Alfred Russel Wallace, discussing his travels in both South America and the Malay Archipelago. In recent years, the growing interest in the history of geographical discovery has led to the Library collecting within the extensive genre of studies of earlier travel literature. Several of these are available as reprints or electronic editions of the original texts. Again, this material is supported by the many sketches, letters, narratives and diaries of individual tours through Europe, the Levant, North America and the Indian sub-continent held within the travel and topography sequences of the Library's press-mark holdings. These include the writings of Thor Heyerdahl, Freya

The magnificent lyre bird from John Gould's *The Birds of Australia*, London: 1848-1869. The work originally appeared in thirty-six parts between 1840 and 1848. Gould and his wife (and illustrator) Elizabeth had travelled to Australia from England in 1838 to prepare the book. It is a massive work comprising eight folio-sized volumes that depict and describe all of the 681 Australian bird varieties then known, many of them recorded by John Gould (1804-1881) himself for the first time. The birds are illustrated by beautiful hand-coloured lithographed plates. Archives & Special Collections, n1-a.1 [n1-a.1-Lyre Bird].

MENURA SUPERBA.

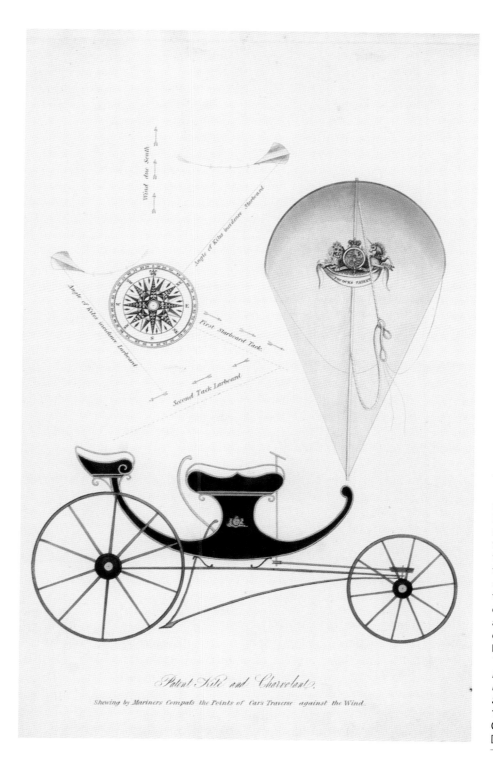

Patent Kite and Charvolant.

Shewing by Mariners Compass the Points of Cars Traverse against the Wind.

The Char-volant, a lightweight carriage that could be pulled along by two kites attached by controllable lines rather than horses. The name for this apparatus came from the French for kite, *cerf-volant*, and the French for carriage, *char*. This carriage, according to the author, could reach speeds of twenty miles per hour. From George Pocock, *The Aeropleustic Art or Navigation in the Air by the use of Kites, or Buoyant Sails*, London: W. Wilson, 1827. Archives & Special Collections, BG46-a.6 [BG46-a.6_fp26.wf].

Photographs from the Scotia Antarctic Expedition, 1902-1904. Two scientists are seen skiing on ice with their dog Russ, while Scotia is temporarily beset in the Weddell Sea, 70° 25' S, 22nd February, 1903. Although overshadowed by Scott's concurrent Discovery Expedition, the Scottish National Antarctic Expedition, which was led by William Spiers Bruce, completed a full programme of exploration and scientific research. This included the establishment of a weather station which has been in continuous operation since 1903. Subsequently described as 'by far the most cost-effective and carefully planned scientific expedition of the heroic age', it was backed and supported by members of the Coats family and the Royal Scottish Geographical Society. The Library holds a collection of nearly 1,000 stereographic glass plate negatives of photographs taken during the trip. Archives & Special Collections, WSB Photo C1/212 [WSB Photo C1/212].

Adélie penguin (*Pygoscelis adeliae*) rookery, Graptolite Isle, 15th October, 1903. Archives & Special Collections, WSB Photo C1/781 [WSB Photo C1/781].

Stark, Harry St John Philby, James Buckingham, Harry Franck, J. Fenimore Cooper, Richard Burton, Alexander von Humboldt, F.S. Smythe and Captain Charles Sturt.

Expedition literature ranges from the Scientific Reports of the British Trans-Antarctic Expedition (1955-58), led by Sir Vivian Fuchs, through those of the Dutch Siboga expedition to Indonesia (1899-1900), to the Challenger Expedition (1872-76), which laid much of the foundation of modern oceanography. There are several works relating to the various attempts to discover a North-West Passage through to the Pacific and, as a consequence, to the subsequent searches for the Franklin Expedition, including the writings of Admiral Sir John Ross. Equally significant are the volumes of the *Description de l'Égypte*, a collective work prepared during the French army's unsuccessful expedition in North Africa under Bonaparte. This had included more than 150 scientists and savants and resulted in a fascination with ancient Egyptian culture and the birth of Egyptology in Europe. More recently, reports of the University of Glasgow Exploration Society include coverage of visits to Iceland, Trinidad, Gambia, Ecuador, Spitsbergen and the Seychelles.

Apart from the many monographs, journals and reports written either by individual explorers or at the conclusion of major expeditions, this particularly distinctive but disparate collection is further supported by complete runs of such significant British journals as those of the Royal Geographical Society and the Royal Scottish Geographical Society, in addition to the publications of the Hakluyt Society, which produces scholarly editions of primary records of voyages, travels and other related geographical material, including, for example, a recent two-volume investigation of the Matthew Flinders circumnavigation of Australia conducted between 1801 and 1803. Combined with the holdings in the Library's Map Collection and the relevant expedition material relating to the history of botany, the Library can boast a markedly strong holding in this genre. It is the breadth and depth of coverage within this particular aspect of human endeavour which make the collection particularly valuable as

both a resource and an area of study for future generations. As the drivers of trade and empire are re-assessed, these works provide the material for any reconsideration of history, cultures and politics.

| **John Moore**

Botany Collection

The study of plants has long had an association with their medicinal properties. Medieval Scotland had monastic and other walled herb gardens in such locations as Soutra Aisle but the nation's first recognised physic garden was established by Robert Sibbald and Andrew Balfour in the grounds of Holyrood Park in 1670. As part of the effort to establish medical education in Glasgow, the University, at the beginning of the eighteenth century, laid out a similar garden in the College grounds to provide plant specimens for its students. In 1704 John Marshall, a local surgeon, was appointed Keeper of the Physic Garden. Additionally, a Regius Chair of Anatomy and Botany was established in 1718. However, through time, it became increasingly obvious that the High Street site provided a poor environment for plants and, in about 1813, plans to create a new garden at Blythswood were under way. In that year, Thomas Hopkirk of Dalbeth (1785-1841), a pioneer local botanist and Fellow of the Linnean Society, published *Flora Glottiana*, one of the earliest British regional floras, which catalogued more than a hundred plants indigenous to the Glasgow area (Sp Coll Bower 43, q26, q27).

Following this, Hopkirk was a key figure in founding a Botanic Garden in Glasgow, initially at Sandyford, to display plant specimens. Local and University support combined to raise sufficient funds, while Hopkirk provided the bulk of the plants. In 1818 a Royal Charter created the Royal Botanic Institution and King George III founded a new Regius Chair of Botany. From this date, Glasgow was to develop as a major centre for the study of plants. Robert Graham, the first Regius Professor, went on to establish

the new botanic garden at Inverleith. He was succeeded by William Jackson Hooker (1785-1865), later knighted for his services to botany in Glasgow and subsequently first Director of Kew Gardens. Under his guidance, Glasgow achieved an international stature in the development of Botany. He conducted several extensive botanical field trips in Scotland, publishing in 1821 his *Flora Scotica* (Bower 21-23) as a description of Scottish plants. His many students included David Douglas (1799-1834), one of the nation's most remarkable plant collectors and his own son, Joseph Dalton Hooker, who became one of the greatest British botanists of the nineteenth century. Subsequent professors included George Walker-Arnott (1799-1868), who worked with Hooker on the plants collected on Beechey's Pacific voyage to the Bering Strait (Arnot q8), and Frederick Orpen Bower (1855-1948), who held the chair in Botany for forty years and under whose leadership the department became a world leader in the study of morphological botany.

Both Walker-Arnott and Bower were significant collectors of botanical books. In particular, the Walker-Arnott Collection of 970 volumes includes some of the finest examples of eighteenth- and nineteenth-century illustrated flora, including William Curtis's three-volume *Flora Londinensis* (e122-124) and Peter Pallas's *Flora Rossica* (1788: e131). It also contains a significant number of works by Carl Linnaeus, the Swedish botanist and father of modern taxonomy, including *Flora Lapponica* (1737: Sp Coll 2022) and *Flora Zeylanica* (1748: Sp Coll 2011). In support of these, the Library has a considerable collection of other floras by a number of important authors, including *Flora Japonica* (1784: Sp Coll 2588) by Carl Thunberg, possibly the most

Justicia Carnea,
Fleshcoloured Justicia.
One of the most important
scientific journals of all
time, *Curtis's Botanical
Magazine* first appeared
in 1787 and is the oldest
periodical in existence
which features coloured
plates, representing the
work of many acclaimed
botanical illustrators and
an exceptional pictorial
record of floral fashions.
It was founded by William
Curtis (1746-1799), whose
first major publishing
venture was his *Flora
Londiniensis*, begun in
1774. The choice of plants
described was often
influenced by the public's
appetite for the uncommon.
In the nineteenth century,
the magazine increasingly
included plants gathered
from further afield by
intrepid plant collectors.
David Douglas (1799-
1834), one of Joseph
Hooker's students,
collected extensively in
America on behalf of
the Royal Horticultural
Society. Archives &
Special Collections, Sp Coll
Periodicals, Vol. 62, 1835,
Plate 3383. [curtis_3383wf].

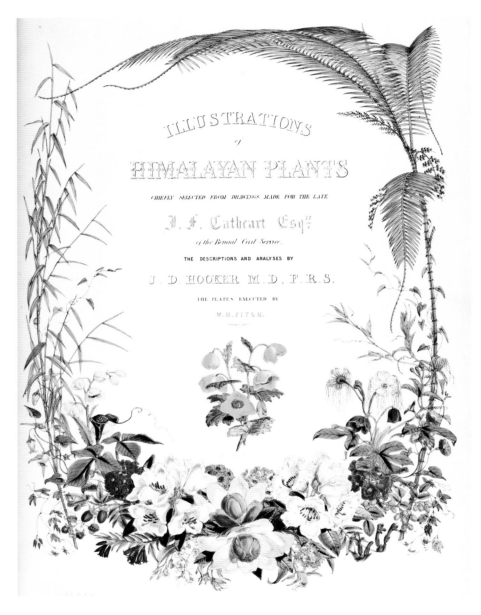

The frontispiece of J. D. Hooker, *Illustrations of Himalayan plants chiefly selected from drawings made for the late J.F. Cathcart*, London, 1855. Sir Joseph Hooker (1817-1911) and Thomas Thomson (1817-1878), both graduates of the University of Glasgow, spent much of their early careers travelling in India. They studied and recorded the natural flora, and in particular they identified many species of rhododendron previously unknown in the UK. Archives & Special Collections, Sp Coll RX 36 [2_india_title page].

successful of Linnaeus's students, Bentham's *Flora Australiensis* (1863-78: H22-c.10-16) and *Genera Floræ Americæ Boreali-Orientalis illustrate* (1848-49) by Asa Gray, the most important American botanist of the nineteenth century (H22-a.21-22). The earliest dated work in this collection is *Commentarii, in libros sex Pedacii Dioscoridis* by Pietro Mattioli, the Italian naturalist, and is a copy of the 1554 Venetian edition, which marks a transition from the study of plants as a field of medicine to that of a discipline in its own right (f313).

Rhododendron thomsonii, from J. D. Hooker, *Illustrations of Himalayan plants chiefly selected from drawings made for the late J.F. Cathcart*, London, 1855. Thomson and Hooker acquired an extensive collection of plant specimens between 1850 and 1851. Sir Joseph Hooker went on to succeed his father as Director of the Royal Botanic Gardens at Kew in 1865, but in 1854 Thomson returned to India where he was made Superintendent of the Royal Botanic Gardens in Kolkata and Professor of Botany at Kolkata Medical College. A bright red species of rhododendron was named *R. thomosonii* in commemoration of him. Archives & Special Collections, Sp Coll RX 36 [2_India_Rhododendron thomsonii].

The Bower Collection originally formed the University's Herbarium Library and includes a substantial number of illustrated volumes containing work by renowned botanical artists such as James Sowerby (1757-1822) including his *Coloured Figures of English Fungi or Mushrooms* (1797-1803: Bower f6-9). It also contains several important early works, including *The Anatomy of Plants* (1682: Bower f1) by Nehemiah Grew (1641-1712), the English plant physiologist. This work describes nearly all

the key differences of morphology in plant roots and stems. Bower also owned copies of the pioneering *Flora Scotica* (1777) by John Lightfoot, which studies both plants and fungi along Linnaean lines (Bower 9a/b), and *Anatome Plantarum* (1675-79) by Marcello Malpighi, possibly the first author to have made detailed drawings of the individual organs of flowers (Bower f10/ Hunterian Ab.1.19).

The Library has a wide range of botanical works by other significant authors. These include the British authors John Lindley (1799-1865), the leading British botanist, gardener and orchidologist – *Flora Medica* (1838: HA02733), *Pomologia Britannica* (1841: Sp Coll q95-97), *Sketch of the Vegetation of the Swan River Colony* (1840: H25-y.7) – and John Sibthorp (1758-1796) – *Flora Graeca* in 10 volumes (1806-40: Sp Coll e 170-179). Among the foreign botanical writers are Jan Commelin (1629-1692), author of *Horti Medici Amstelodamensis Rariorum tam Orientalis* (1697-1701: Sp Coll Hunterian X.1.6-7), and Albrecht von Haller (1708-1777), the pre-Linnean botanical taxonomist who wrote *Opuscula sua botanica* (1749: H25-f.29). Several of the works of major significance are based on expeditions, and these include *Flora Sibirica, sive, Historia plantarum Sibiriae* (1747-69: Sp Coll q374-378) by Johann Georg Gmelin (1709-1755), the German botanist and geographer whose studies were based on his participation in Vitus Bering's second Kamchatka expedition (1733-43). Jean Baptiste Aublet (1720-1778), founder of a botanical garden in Mauritius and creator of a vast herbarium which he bequeathed to Jean-Jacques Rousseau, drew on this collection

Detail of illustrators at work from Leonhart Fuchs, *De Historia Stirpium, Basel*, 1542. This massive folio volume is one of the library's grandest herbals, describing nearly 500 plants with superb woodcuts based on first-hand observation. It is the greatest work of the German humanist, Leonhart Fuchs (1501-1566), and is without equal among the books on herbs of its day which emphasise the value of these plants to physicians. Archives & Special Collections, Hunterian L.1.13 [L.1.13_page897.wf].

to prepare his *Histoire des plantes de la Guiane françoise* (1775), illustrated with almost 400 copperplate engravings (Sp Coll RQ313-316), while Charles Plumier (1646-1704), botanist to Louis XIV of France, published his massive *Nova Plantarum Americanarum Genera*

(1703: Sp Coll Bn1-g.19) following three plant expeditions to the West Indies.

Botanical illustration reflects not only ground-breaking advances in science but also charts the development in graphic art from manuscript illumination through to engraving, hand colouring and etching. Several of the books in William Hunter's library are concerned with plants. One of the earliest botanical works with woodcut illustrations which the Library holds is *De Historia Stirpium Commentarii Insignes* by Leonhart Fuchs, one of the founders of the study of Botany in Germany (Sp Coll Hunterian L.1.13). Printed in Basel in 1542, this landmark folio volume contained images of over a hundred species depicted for the first time, all based on first-hand observation. With the development of copperplate engraving as a means of illustrating texts, a more sophisticated and detailed image could be produced. In the early seventeenth century, the Dutch dominated the field and *Florilegium Amplissimum* by Emanuel Sweert, dating from 1614-1620, displays the innovative convention of portraying both the lower stems with bulbs and roots of plants alongside the upper stems and flowers (Hunterian X.1.12). Possibly the most celebrated of books illustrated with botanical drawings is Robert Thornton's *The Temple of Flora* (1807: Sp Coll e23). This elephant folio edition contains thirty-one plates produced by a range of techniques, often finished by hand colouring.

| **John Moore**

Varieties of Gladioli, from *The Flora of South Africa*, Capetown, 1913-32. The work, published in six volumes, was undertaken by Hermann Wilhelm Rudolf Marloth (1855-1931), a German-born South African botanist, pharmacist and analytical chemist. Archives & Special Collections, RQ 451, Vol. 6, plate 46 [RQ451].

Medicine Collection

In 1599 James VI granted a charter to Peter Lowe and Robert Hamilton which resulted in the creation of the Faculty (now Royal College) of Physicians and Surgeons of Glasgow. This body was to make the first attempts in the instruction of prospective medical practitioners and Lowe's surgical text, *A Discourse on the Whole Art of Chyrurgerie*, first published two years earlier (2nd edition, 1612 at Ferguson Af-c.11 or Hunterian Add. 297), became a standard work for surgeons of the time.

Glasgow University's association with the teaching of medicine goes back to the appointment of Robert Mayne as Professor of Medicine in 1637 but, in reality, the modern medical school only came into being when

John Banister delivering an anatomy lecture. From 'Anatomical Tables', compiled between 1499 and 1599. Banister (1533-1610) was an exceptional Elizabethan medical practitioner who qualified both as a surgeon and physician. He commissioned a set of anatomical tables, probably as visual teaching aids, and this painting, depicting his lecture at Barber-Surgeon's Hall in 1581, was the frontispiece of the work. Archives & Special Collections, MS Hunter 364 (V.1.1), frontispiece [H364_frontis.wf].

William Cullen became professor in 1751. Cullen had begun lecturing in late 1746 on the theory and practice of physic, to which he subsequently added materia medica, botany and chemistry. Many of his writings, such as *Synopsis Nosologiae Methodicae* (1769: Sp Coll Bo8-m.11), were based on his earlier lectures. More significantly, in 1736 Cullen offered the young William Hunter an apprenticeship in his Hamilton medical practice. Hunter is celebrated today as a renowned collector of books, coins, paintings and natural history specimens, assembled during his career as a highly successful teacher of medicine, anatomist and Physician Extraordinary to George III's consort, Queen Charlotte. His collection, which came to the University in 1807, is probably the best known of the Library's rare book collections and contains a considerable number of early medical texts. These include a fifteenth-century Syrian treatise on the arrangement of bodies for treatment (Sp Coll MS Hunter 40 (T.1.8)) and the textbook published by Andreas Vesalius *De Humani Corporis Fabrica Librorum Epitome* (1543: Sp Coll Hunterian Ce.1.18), which set a new benchmark in anatomical illustration and is, without doubt, one of the great contributions to the medical sciences. The collection also covers the works

Other paintings from the John Banister set depict anatomical instruments and a scene showing vivisections. Archives & Special Collections, MS Hunter 364 (V.1.1). [H364_tablel.wf].

of Hunter's medical contemporaries, including fellow Scot, William Smellie, and the Swiss anatomist, Albrecht von Haller, whose eight-volume *Elementa Physiologiae Corporis Humani* (1766: Sp Coll Hunterian Y.4.1-8) was to become a landmark in medical history.

With the development of teaching hospitals within the city during the nineteenth century, the Glasgow medical school grew and attracted several important figures in the development of modern surgical techniques, including Joseph Lister and William Macewen. The latter's pioneering *Atlas of Head Sections* (1893: Store Maclehose f25) and *Growth of Bone* (1912: Store Maclehose 290) were both acclaimed by leading surgeons throughout the world. Combined with the work of John Macintyre on radiology (Store Maclehose 775), Thomas McCall Anderson on dermatology (Sp Coll RQ3019), John Glaister on medical jurisprudence, forensic medicine and public health (Store 25423-24),George Beatson on oncology (G16-f.26) and Ian Donald on ultrasound, particularly in obstetrics (Store 27543), these professors helped give Glasgow an international reputation for medicine. Today, it is one of the largest and most prestigious medical schools in Europe.

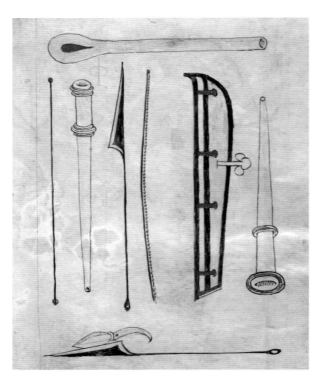

Illustration of surgical instruments, from John of Arderne, *Medical treatises*, c. 1475-1500. This heavily illustrated manuscript consists of several medical works by the renowned fourteenth-century surgeon John of Aderne, who is said to have learnt his skills during the Hundred Years War. A great believer in cleanliness, he was famous for his pioneering work in treating anal fistulas. Archives & Special Collections, MS Hunter 251 (U.4.9), fol. 43r [H251_0043rwf].

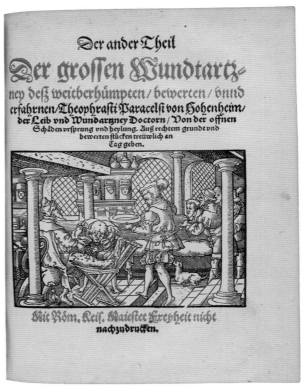

A man having mercury ointment applied to his legs for the treatment of syphilis. This procedure was done with a spatula to avoid the doctor coming into contact with the sores and the mercury. From Paracelus, *Erster Theil [-der dritte] der grossen Wundartzney die Frantzosen genannt*, Frankfurt: 1562. Archives & Special Collections, Ferguson Ap-d.51 [Ferguson_Ap_d_1].

More than 500 medical texts published before 1800 are recorded in the catalogue, ranging from a 1471 Venetian version of Nicholas of Salerno's famous medieval treatise on pharmacology and antidotes known as the *Antidotarium Nicolai* (Sp Coll Ferguson Am-z.41), through the sixteenth-century Parisian text by Antoine Chaumette *Enchiridion Chirurgicum* (Sp Coll Hunterian Z.8.21) to three works by the early English surgeon William Clowes (Sp Coll Hunterian Aw.3.28).

A recent Wellcome Trust project has seen the cataloguing of the Library's dispersed but significant holdings of early printed works on syphilis. This is one of the strongest collections in the United Kingdom and contains many extremely rare medical treatises (Sp Coll Hunterian Bx.3.38). In addition, it is a testament to the Library's holdings that Glasgow's participation in a further collaborative project, the UK Medical Heritage Library, has contributed more than 5,000 titles to the digitisation of about 15 million pages covering a very wide range of nineteenth-century texts relating to the history of medicine, which also includes sport and fitness, insurance, diet and nutrition, health spas, phrenology and hydrotherapy.

Other areas with unique national holdings reflect the University's teaching of dentistry since 1879 – *Le Chirurgien dentiste*, 1728 (JIML Case Medicine UD8 1728-F) and *Practical Observations on the Human Teeth*, 1782 (Sp Coll Bi2-f.16) – and veterinary science since 1862 – Manuel Diaz's 1500 text on diseases of horses (Sp Coll Hunterian By.3.1), a 1612 Paris edition of Nicolas Rigault's Latin treatise on

diseases affecting falcons (Sp Coll BC1-b.3) and a 1656 edition of Gervase Markham's collected works on farriery, first published from 1593 onwards (Sp Coll RB2907).

The Library's medical collection reflects both this multi-faceted history and the need to support

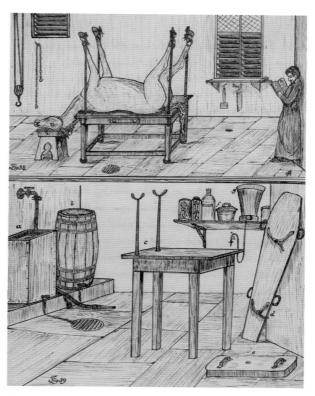

Illustration showing a horse during a procedure described in James Murphy's Anatomy note book, 1880s. The notebook contains three essays relating to the preservation of animal parts for anatomical purposes as well as shorter notes, press cuttings and excerpts from journals relating to both human and animal anatomy focusing on embalming, casting and dissection. James Murphy (1854-1919) was the first Professor of Anatomy at the Glasgow Veterinary College where he had been a student in 1877, before becoming an assistant to Dr H. S. Clark, anatomist at the Glasgow Royal Infirmary. Archives & Special Collections, accn3763 [accn3763].

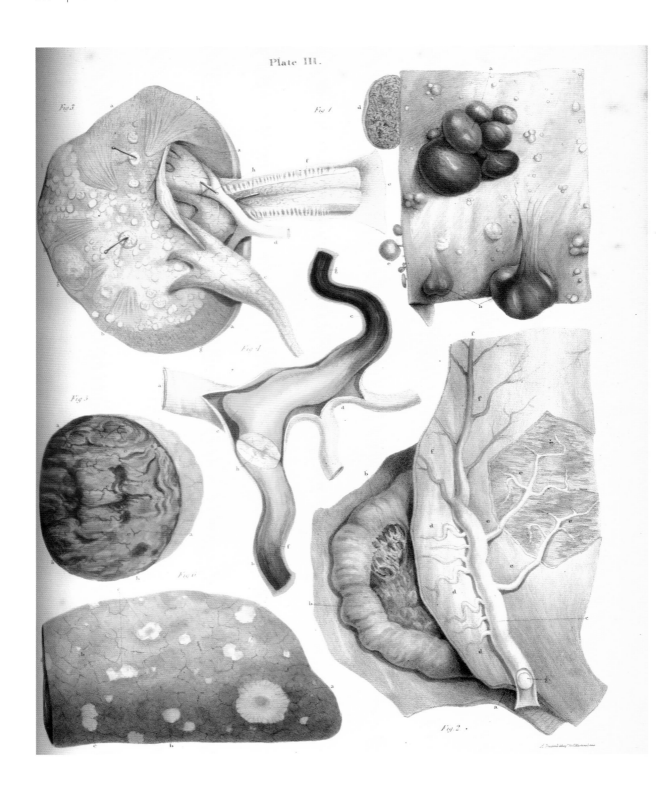

Plate III.

current teaching and research. Ranked as one of the world's top fifty universities for medicine and health-related subjects, the University today brings together expertise in clinical medicine and health care, with major research in the fields of cardiovascular disease and cancer, all well supported by its Library holdings.

John Moore

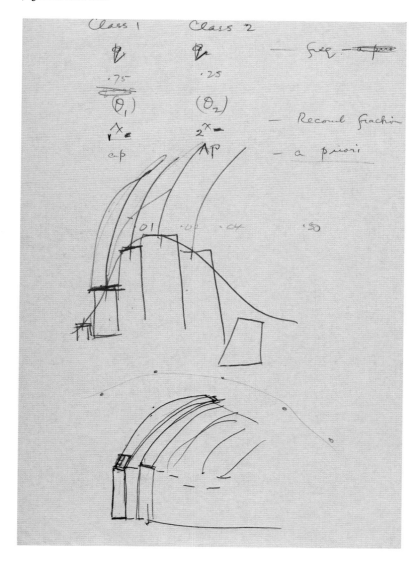

Facing page: Carcinoma, from Robert Carswell, *Pathological Anatomy: Illustrations of the Elementary Forms of Disease*, London, 1838. This richly illustrated folio volume consists of forty-four coloured lithograph plates with accompanying descriptions of various pathological conditions. The text and the drawings were undertaken by Sir Robert Carswell (1793-1857), who was both a distinguished practitioner of pathology and a skilled artist. Born in Paisley, Carswell studied medicine at the University of Glasgow. In 1828 at the age of thirty-five, he was nominated to become the first professor of pathological anatomy at the new University College, London. Archives & Special Collections, rf 110 [rf110_carcinoma_3wf].

A sketch by James Renwick illustrating the heterogeneity programme in development to link genetic data. James Renwick (1926-94) was a titular Professor of Genetics at the University of Glasgow from 1967-1968. From the early 1950s to the 1970s, he pioneered the use of genetic markers to map disease genes on human chromosomes, making a fundamental contribution to modern genetics, especially in the development of human gene mapping that paved the way for the Human Genome Project. Archives & Special Collections UGC155/3/8/1/1 [UGC155/3/8/1/1_0029].

Chapter 8

The Friends of
Glasgow University Library

Professor Gerrard Carruthers' discourse at a Friends Talk on 'The Songs of Robert Burns: A Glasgow Perspective' in 2016. Courtesy of Iain Wotherspoon.

Peter V. Davies
University of
Glasgow

Activities

The Friends of Glasgow University Library (FGUL) is a registered charity, open to all, that exists primarily to bring together people interested in the rich holdings and wide-ranging activities of the Library and those who wish to learn more about new topics in an enjoyable way. In particular the society aims to develop, support and promote the Library and Archive Services by funding the purchase and conservation of books, manuscripts, documents, photographs, sound recordings or other materials, as well as projects involving engagement with the wider community (e.g. by facilitating exhibitions, the publication of new books and by the hosting of school visits) and the usual requirements of academic staff and students at all levels.

We act as a channel for monetary gifts and bequests or for other donations such as books not already in stock, thereby helping to extend the Library's holdings, related resources – including those involving digitisation – and influence. Besides offering regular assistance in

Soprano and fiddler Alison McNeill, with her sister Fiona on guitar, performing at 'The Songs of Robert Burns: A Glasgow Perspective' in 2016. Courtesy of Iain Wotherspoon.

A group of prize winners in the *Scots Words and Place-Names* competition for schools in 2011. Courtesy of Iain Wotherspoon.

University Rector Charles Kennedy addressing the national prize-giving ceremony in 2011 of the *Scots Words and Place-Names* competition for schools. Courtesy of Iain Wotherspoon.

the acquisition and conservation or updating of print and electronic materials, we also sponsor Library exhibitions and accompanying catalogues plus online bibliographies devoted to particular strengths of the Library so as to enhance its local and international profile. Over the decades from 1977 our notelets and Christmas cards featuring illustrations from the Library's manuscripts and books have likewise contributed to this consciousness-raising exercise.

Every year we hold a series of well-attended events and talks given by guest speakers on a variety of subjects, generally with a Scottish if not specifically Glaswegian connection. Topics covered in the last few years have included, for example: the Euing Lute Book (2009); Robert Louis Stevenson and the theatre (2010); The Unknown Naomi Mitchison (2011); the digitisation of Thomas Annan's photographs of Glasgow from 1857 onwards (2011); non-invasive techniques of ink and pigment analysis as tools for dating or localizing medieval manuscripts (2012); Lord Kelvin's achievement today (2013); the pioneering research on isotopes done at Glasgow by 1921 Nobel Prize-winner Frederick Soddy (2013); magic in early modern Scotland (2013); Glasgow University and naval architecture (2014); the afterlives of medieval Scottish texts (2015); and the pioneering botanical work of Thomas Hopkirk (2016). As well as Library news, our biannual *Newsletter* (available in print and online at **www.friendsofgul.org**) offers short appetizing articles on other subjects, sometimes offering young researchers a platform for their first publications. Some events are also organised in conjunction with our younger sibling, The Friends of the Hunterian.

In addition to an annual Library Open Day held in the autumn and which is an opportunity to visit parts of the building that are usually off-limits and to award student prizes (e.g. for the 2013 'Blogathon' and SWAP, the 2011 national schools competition 'Scots Words and Place-names'), our diary also normally includes at least one excursion per year to a place of interest such as the Edinburgh Royal Observatory (2008), BBC Scotland and its library (2009), the Special

Collections Department of the University of St Andrews Library (2009), the Book and Paper Conservation Studio in the University of Dundee Library (2010), the Glasgow Museums Resource Centre housing the R. L. Scott Collection of Arms and Armour and associated books and manuscripts (2011), the Sir Duncan Rice Library at Aberdeen University (2013), and the Glasgow School of Art (2015). These outings always include a guided tour, sometimes accompanied by a lecture.

Membership of the Friends is open to all on payment of an annual subscription, which since 2002 has remained unchanged at £15.00 a year to encourage membership. To find us online within the University and Library website simply Google 'FGUL' or write to our postal address: The Secretary, Friends of Glasgow University Library, University of Glasgow Library, Hillhead Street, Glasgow, G12 8QE.

History of FGUL

Throughout its long history the University of Glasgow Library has benefited from the contribution of friends and donors who have had its welfare – and that of its staff and users – at heart. Eventually, under the benevolent tutelage of the progressive Librarian, Robert Ogilvie MacKenna, in the course of 1975 at the suggestion of the dynamic Deputy Librarian, Peter Hoare, plans were discussed on 18th December for the foundation of a society paralleling similar bodies created at Aberdeen and Edinburgh universities in 1962 and whose goal would be to support the work and content of the Library more systematically while also stimulating the pleasurable interest of its members.

With Peter Hoare as Secretary, an organizing FGUL Committee met in January 1976 under the chairmanship of David M. Walker (1920-2014), the eminent first Professor of Jurisprudence (from 1954) and Regius Professor of Law (1958 to 1990), and comprising half a dozen stalwart supporters from across the University (three of whom have contributed to this volume). David Walker was Convenor of the University's Library Committee and Chairman of the Friends for many years.

In accordance with the schedule of events devised for each term of the academic year, an inaugural meeting of members soon followed, attracting a sizeable audience as reported in the *Glasgow University Gazette*, n° 79, while the number of enthusiastic ordinary members, lured partly by the invitingly low initial annual subscription of £2, rapidly grew to over 200 in a few months. From its inception the society regularly produced a newsletter that had graduated from stencilled typescript to print and reached ten issues by June 1978, by which point Peter Hoare had recently left Glasgow to assume his appointment as Librarian at the University of Nottingham, to be followed as FGUL Secretary by Stephen Rawles from 1978, Nigel Thorp from 1981 and Tim Hobbs from 1990. Professor Walker was succeeded as Chairman of the society by the distinguished naturalist and writer Dr Jack Gibson, founder of the Scottish Natural History Library. Both became Honorary Presidents of the Friends.

Membership fees and donations soon provided funds of over £700 that were immediately put to good use in subsidizing book purchases starting with Elizabeth Diggle's *Journal of a Tour from London to the Highlands of Scotland,*

19th April-7th August 1788 (MS Gen 738), advertised by a Los Angeles dealer for US$250, and followed by a steady stream of other acquisitions, wholly or partly funded by the society.

Early book donations included a collection of Gaelic songs, presented by Seumas MacNeill, facsimiles of works printed by William Caxton for the Caxton Quincentenary, bestowed by Mrs Jessie Duncan of Aberdeen, and a three-volume set of *The Laws of the United States of America* (1796), given by a Glasgow solicitor, Harry Flowers.

Onwards and Upwards

By the 1980s the Friends were well established, giving support to subject areas across the Library as well as to specific interests such as the historic dictionary collection, the Alexander Stone Lecture in Bibliophily (nowadays superseded by the Library blog and the Special Collections archive of virtual exhibitions), and modern limited editions such as Kenneth White's *Methodos* (Nantes: Pré Nian, 1988), a sequence of five original haiku in French and English with five original silk screens by Bracaval (N° 30 of sixty numbered copies). Purchases wholly or partly funded by FGUL this century, during the convenorships of Margaret Paxton (2000-2003), in succession to Professor Graham Caie, and Helen Cargill Thompson (2003-2011), include: 2,000 plays from the Golden Age of Spanish theatre (2002); notebooks on alchemy (2006); and six mezzotint plates by various artists after Jan van Rymsdyck and Thomas Burgess (2007). Helen also oversaw the administration of the important MacKenna and Wyley bequests, together with the resulting introduction of discretionary investment management, and the

FGUL contribution to the permanent display cabinet featuring items from Special Collections on Level 12. The donation left by former Librarian Robert Ogilvie MacKenna specifically for the training of Library staff perfectly matches his lifelong concern for colleagues and has provided welcome funding for this purpose over the years since 2005. Undoubtedly, the most important purchase partly funded by FGUL, in the sum of £20,000, during Helen's convenorship was a collection of 450 letters and other material (papers, ephemera and photographs) relating to the great Glasgow-based scientist and inventor Lord Kelvin (1924-1907) and his brother James Thomson, bought in 2007-2008. This acquisition, which amplifies the Library's earlier holdings of Kelviniana and the permanent display of apparatus in the Kelvin Building, inspired an extremely stimulating talk in 2013.

The Wyley Bequest

In 2008 FGUL received a very substantial bequest from Mrs Agnes May Wyley, one of our former members, whose generosity has enabled us to fund far more Library purchases and projects than was previously possible. In this we have been considerably aided by the sound steerage of our financial advisor through the choppy waters of the post-2007 economic downturn. Thus in 2015, for example, besides making our largest ever donation, of £94,000, to the Library for state-of-the-art equipment in the redevelopment of the Level 2 Exhibition Space and Conservation Studio, the Friends contributed £15,000 (which included a generous gift from an anonymous donor) to the highly successful exhibition in the Hunterian Art Gallery of the Library's fifteenth-century printed books, *Ingenious Impressions*. Since 1977 the society has contributed to special

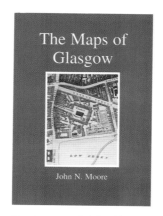

Front cover of John N. Moore's book, *The Maps of Glasgow*, published in 1996.

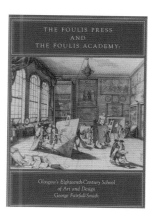

Front cover of George Fairfull-Smith's book *The Foulis Press and the Foulis Academy*, published in 2001.

Box set cover of *Comic Invention* by Laurence Grove and Peter Black, with Gareth K. Vile and Sha Nazir, published in 2016.

In 2011 we received from the estate of the highly esteemed Scots makar, Professor Edwin Morgan, a bequest which the society contributed to the ongoing project to digitise his scrapbooks.

In 2012 the late Joan (Lady) Williams, former Convenor of FGUL (1991-97), donated to the Library via the society two rare landmark studies to commemorate the work of her husband Sir Alwyn Williams (1921-2004), the eminent geologist, palaeontologist and former Principal and Vice-Chancellor of the University: Giovanni Michelotti's *Description des fossiles des terrains miocènes de l'Italie septentrionale* (1847) and the collected *Monographies d'échinodermes vivans et fossiles* (1838-42) by Louis Agassiz and others.

The society also helps fund the publication of new books, notably including: in 1996 *The Maps of Glasgow: A History and Cartobibliography to 1865*, by John Moore; in 2001 *The Foulis Press and The Foulis Academy: Glasgow's Eighteenth Century School of Art and Design*, by George Fairfull-Smith; *Comic Invention*, by Laurence Grove and Peter Black, published in 2016; and of course this new book *The University of Glasgow Library: Friendly Shelves*.

exhibitions, and continues this support including in 2016 *Comic Invention*, which centres on Glasgow's claim to have produced the first such publication (see Chapter 6); while we continue to support the conservation and rebinding of manuscripts, we increasingly donate to major digitisation projects including eighteenth-century maps, 400 significant Great War documents in the University Archives, items in the University sound archives, the New Lanark Visitors Book, the Turkey Red Pattern Book, and 250 selected larger designs of the Stoddard Templeton collection. Digitisation, of course, not only permits electronic publishing and remote access but also aids the preservation of rare manuscripts, incunabula, papers and photographs by reducing users' need to handle the material.

While the Wyley legacy has permitted the FGUL Committee, under the presidency of Graeme Smith, Chairman since 2011, to provide increased financial support to the Library, we continue to welcome donations and legacies.

Afterword

Susan Ashworth
University Library

As demonstrated in this fascinating book, the University of Glasgow Library is a constant work in progress, responsive to significant technological and social change: whether that is the move from manuscript to print, from print to electronic, or from silent study to group and social spaces, the Library has ensured that it remains at the heart of the University.

The Library building is being constantly redeveloped in response to growing student demand for space and to changing styles of learning. We are very lucky at Glasgow in having students who are critical friends of the Library and who work in partnership with us to develop space and services. The latest redevelopment will deliver more group study and social space, as we know that students today want to be together with friends, drink coffee, and use mobile devices while they study. This evolution will continue as the campus expands into the recently acquired Western Infirmary site and the University embarks on a hugely ambitious building programme. The new Learning and Teaching Hub will be the first major new building of this development. This complex will have lecture theatres, seminar rooms and a variety of study spaces, and we are heavily involved in promoting service models, ensuring that the Library's culture of student-owned space is taken forward into new spaces on campus.

The Library is one of the oldest and largest university libraries in Europe and holds collections of international significance to support learning, teaching and research. These collections are also managed as important assets belonging to the cultural heritage of Glasgow, Scotland and the world. The new Library redevelopment has a public exhibition space where Library staff can offer events showcasing our wide-ranging collections and giving the public the opportunity to come into the Library. There is enhanced space for conservation, to ensure that our collections are preserved for future generations, and for digitisation, so that users from all over the world are able to discover the extraordinary range of collections held in the Library. We are very grateful to the Friends of the Library for their financial support for the development of these spaces.

The Library service encompasses much more than the main building on Hillhead Street. It includes Archives Services; there are branch libraries at the Vet School, Dental School, as well as in Social Sciences and Chemistry; and the off-site Library Research Annexe is a repository for some of the Library's historic collections. The University is also developing its estate on the Garscube campus and we are looking forward to working with the Garscube Learning and Social Space which will deliver a fifty-seat flexible study/café space linked directly to the James Herriot Library.

A theme throughout this book is the evolving nature of scholarly communications and the Library's role in providing access to the scholarly record. The late twentieth and twenty-first centuries have seen the seismic shift from print to electronic content and with that shift a questioning of traditional models of scholarly communication, particularly the role of the journal. A significant continuing development is the move towards greater openness in the processes of research and scholarly communication. I hope that in future years free access to publications, research data and educational resources, which currently often sit behind paywalls, will be the norm. However, at the moment the scholarly communications landscape is evolving and confusing for staff. The Library is central to the University's engagement with open access, delivering support for researchers to understand its requirements for the national Research Excellence Frameworks, used to assess the quality of research outcomes, and to help them comply with research funder policies on ensuring open access. As well as the gateway to knowledge the Library is also the custodian of the University's scholarly record, and we will continue to work together with other university services and academic colleges to deliver the necessary infrastructure and support for managing and curating the outputs of the University, whether they are theses, publications, research data, corporate documents or born-digital materials. The University's institutional repository service, Enlighten, is the publicly available platform for hosting Glasgow's research outputs – there are repositories for publications, theses and research data. The material in these repositories has been downloaded millions of times, helping to ensure that research at the University of Glasgow achieves as wide a reach as possible.

None of our activities would, of course, be possible without dedicated, professional and customer-focused staff, who deliver excellent services and who are continually thinking about how to improve the Library. I am honoured to be the latest University Librarian, and as the book makes clear I am in very distinguished company. However, it is the achievement of all Library staff that the University of Glasgow Library remains central to the University, to the student experience, to the academic community and to the wider world.

List of Librarians across the Centuries

The post of librarian established by the Thomas Hutcheson endowment of 1641 applied until the late eighteenth century. Librarians were normally nominated in turn by the Town (T) or the College (C) and some librarians were nominated successively by both parties. All librarians from 1905 also held the title of Keeper of the Hunterian Books and Manuscripts and from 1998 Director of Library Services.

1641-45   **Andrew Snype**, MA (T) (later minister of the Scots Kirk in Holland, 1649-1686)

1646-47   **James Huchesoune** MA (T)

1647-52?   **Patrick Young**, MA (T, C?) (appointed Regent in 1651)

1652? – 55? **John Ross?** (C?)

1655   **Robert Hoggisyard** (T) (elected at an inquorate meeting but not admitted)

1655-58   **Robert Baillie**, Jnr, MA (T) (Regent, son of the namesake Professor of Divinity, elected in place of Hoggisyard. Died in office 1658)

1658-61   **John Bell** (T)

1661-67   **James Bell** (T)

1667-69   **William Wright**, MA (C) (appointed Regent in 1669)

1669-71   **David Oliphant**, MA (C)

1671-73   **George Pollok**, MA (T) (thought to have become minister in Ayrshire)

1673-78   **John Hamilton** (T, C)

1679-87   **James Young** (T, C, T) (appointed Regent in 1682, later Professor of Humanity, 1683-1687)

1687-91   **John Young** (C) (having previously been deputy for his brother)

1692-93   **David Ewing** (C) (later minister in Glasgow)

1694-97   **John Simson**, MA Edin (T) (appointed Quaestor in 1694; minister at Traquair from 1705 and later Professor of Divinity, 1708-1740)

1697-1703 **Robert Wodrow**, MA (T) (appointed Quaestor in 1698 and later minister and church historian)

1703-07   **Alexander Dunlop** (T, C) (son of William Dunlop, Principal; appointed Quaestor and Professor of Greek in 1704)

1707-10   **Matthew Crawford** (C) (having been Dunlop's deputy since 1704; later Professor of Ecclesiastical History in the University of Edinburgh, 1720)

1710-11   **William Dunlop** (C) (son of William Dunlop, Principal; later Professor of Divinity and Church History in the University of Edinburgh, 1714)

1711-16   **John Aird** (T, C) (possibly related to John Aird, Provost at the time of the Treaty of Union)

1716-19   **Alexander Carmichael**, MA (C) (probably the eldest of the four sons of Gershom Carmichael, Regent and later Professor of Moral Philosophy, 1727-1729, who served as College-nominated librarians until Glasgow burgesses opposed the quasi-monopoly)

1719-23   **Alexander Anderson** MA (T)

1723-24   **John Carmichael** MA (C) (died in post after just six months)

1724-25   **Alexander Carmichael** (C)

1725-27   **Frederick Carmichael** MA (C) (became minister in Inveresk, and later Professor of Divinity in Marischal College, Aberdeen, 1747)

1727-31   **Alexander Clerk** or Clark MA (T) (later minister in Neilston)

1731-35   **Alexander Carmichael** (C, T) (Ejected 1736)

1736   **William Craig** MA (T) (later minister in Glasgow; a retrospective 1736 appointment, replacing Carmichael)

1736-39   **Gershom Carmichael**, Jnr, MA (T)

1739-43   **Alexander Dunlop** (C) (grandson of William Dunlop, Principal; later Professor of Oriental Languages)

1743-46   **James Moor**, MA, LLD (T) (later Professor of Greek, 1746-1774)

1747-50   **William Patoun**, MA (C) (son of Rev Robert Patoun, Moderator of the General Assembly of the Church of Scotland, 1750)

1750-55   **James Wodrow**, MA, DD (C, T) (later minister in Ayrshire; son of church historian Rev Robert Wodrow)

1755-57   **Andrew Melville** (C) (having been deputy to Wodrow since 1753; died 1757)

1757-59   **James Muirhead**, MA, later Morehead (C) (later minister in Hamilton)

1759-63   **Thomas Clark**, MA (T) (later minister in Eaglesham)

1763-67   **William Craig**, MA, LLD (C) (later Rector, 1801-1803, after he had become Lord Craig, Judge of Court of Session, 1792)

1767-72   **John Finnie**, MA (T, C) (later minister in Glasgow; tutor and factor to the Orr family of Stobcross; and his name given to their new village of Finnieston on the Clyde; died 1772)

1772-73   **Henry Stevenson** MA (C) (later minister in Blantyre)

1773-74   **James Jack** MA (C) (resigned 1774)

1774-94   **Archibald Arthur**, MA (C, T, C) (appointed Librarian for life in 1784; later University Chaplain and Professor of Moral Philosophy, 1796-1797; and died 1797)

1794-95   **William McTurk**, MA, DD (later Clerk of Senate, University Chaplain, 1806-1810, and Professor of Ecclesiastical History, 1809)

1795-1823   **Lockhart Muirhead**, MA, LLD (later Professor of Natural History, 1807, and first Keeper of the Hunterian Museum; died 1823)

1823-27   **William Fleming**, (having been assistant librarian since 1818; later University Chaplain, 1821-1826, Professor of Oriental Languages, 1831, and Professor of Moral Philosophy, 1839-1866)

1827-45   **William Park**, MA, DD (having been sub-librarian since 1826; minister at Airth 1845-1889)

1845-63   **Nathaniel Jones** (Registrar of General Council, 1858; died 1863)

1863-67   **Robert Scott**, MA, FSA.

1867-78   **Robert Brady Spears** (having previously been assistant librarian)

1866-1901   **William Purdie Dickson**, Curator of the Library (Professor of Biblical Criticism, 1863; Professor of Divinity, 1873 to 1895; died 1901). Included here, given the importance of his role as Curator of the Library overseeing the work of librarians.

1878-1905   **James Lymburn** (having been assistant librarian since 1867)

1905-16   **James Lachlan Galbraith**, Librarian, and first to add the title Keeper of the Hunterian Books and Manuscripts.

1916-25   Librarianship vacant. Mungo Ferguson, MA, sub-librarian, 1908-1923: died 1924; **Wilson Steel**, acting librarian 1924-1925, then sub-librarian.

1925-51   **William Ross Cunningham**, MA, LLD.

1951-78   **Robert Ogilvie MacKenna**, MA, ALA.

1979-98   **Henry Joseph Heaney**, MA, BLitt, FLA.

1998-2001   **Andrew Wale**, BA, ALA.

2001-06   **Christine Anne Bailey**, MA, Dip, Lib. ALA

2006-15   **Helen Durndell**, MA, Dip Lib.

2015-   **Susan Ashworth**, MA (Glasgow), MA Lib (Sheffield)

Contributors and Acknowledgements

The publishers wish to record with gratitude the support of all involved in the research, writing and production of the book, and in particular the following, noted here with their interests and affiliations:

Dr Peter V. Davies is an Honorary Research Fellow attached to the School of Modern Languages and Cultures at the University of Glasgow, where he was previously a Senior Lecturer in French with a particular interest in French dialectology and medieval French and Occitan language and literature.

Professor Laurence Grove, Director of the University of Glasgow Stirling Maxwell Centre, is also a member of the University's School of Modern Languages and Cultures, where his research activities focus upon word/image interaction from the early days of printing onwards ranging from the emblem book (and related material) in the pre-industrial period to the *bande dessinée* today. His recent projects include the *Comic Invention* exhibition.

Peter Hoare, general editor of the three-volume *Cambridge History of Libraries in Britain and Ireland* (2006) and former Librarian at the University of Nottingham, was Deputy Librarian at the University of Glasgow Library from 1972 to 1978. He is Honorary President of the Library and Information History Group (LIHG) within the Chartered Institute of Library and Information Professionals (CILIP).

Professor Andrew Hook, Emeritus Bradley Professor of English Literature at the University of Glasgow, is an authority on American literature and on Scotland's cultural links with America. Scotland's only centre for American Studies was named in his honour at the University in 1997.

Professor John Hume is Honorary Professor at the Universities of Glasgow and St. Andrews, having also lectured on Economic and Industrial History at the University of Strathclyde for many years. A former Chief Inspector of Historic Buildings in Scotland, he was until 2015 Chairman of the Royal Commission on the Ancient and Historic Monuments of Scotland (RCAHMS).

John Moore is currently Collections Manager at the University of Glasgow Library and an authority on Scottish cartography.

Miles Kerr-Peterson is a final-year PhD student preparing a University of Glasgow thesis on George Keith (c. 1553-1623), 4th Earl Marischal and founder of Marischal College in Aberdeen, and studying the impact of the Reformation and Union of the Crowns on the Scottish nobility.

Dr Stephen Rawles is an Honorary Senior Research Fellow at the University of Glasgow Humanities Advanced Technology and Information Institute (HATII), having previously been a Principal Assistant Librarian at the University. He has particular interests in Renaissance and Early Modern print culture and typography, especially in France.

Dr Steven J. Reid is a Lecturer in History within the School of Humanities at the University of Glasgow and specialises in the intellectual, political and religious history of Scotland between c. 1450 and c. 1650. The Reformation, education and Scottish Latinity are among his particular areas of interest.

Lesley Richmond is the University Archivist and Deputy Director of the University of Glasgow Library as well as Honorary Senior Research Fellow at the University's Humanities Advanced Technology and Information Institute (HATII).

Graeme Smith is a Chartered Accountant whose career has centred mainly on the building of New Towns and on urban renewal. As a researcher and author his interests include economic development, business history, shipping, shipbuilding, architecture and theatres.

Professor Nigel Thorp was Deputy Keeper of Special Collections at the University of Glasgow Library, and subsequently Director of the University's erstwhile Centre for Whistler Studies, set up to edit the Whistler correspondence, donated by the artist's sister-in-law. He curated the exhibition of the Library's medieval and Renaissance illuminated manuscripts, *The Glory of the Page*, which toured North America in the 1980s.

For the emeritus Librarian **Helen Durndell** and current Librarian **Susan Ashworth**, please see *Librarians this Century* in Chapter 5, New Horizons.

For the writing of Chapter 7, Unique and Distinctive Collections, thanks go to the staff of the Library for their respective contributions as follows:

Julie Gardham (Senior Librarian, Head of Special Collections), **Morag Greig** (Arts College Librarian), **Honor Hania** (Former College Librarian, Arts and Social Sciences Library Support Team), **Sarah Hepworth** (Deputy Head of Special Collections), **John Moore** (Collections Manager), **Dr Kay Munro** (College of Social Sciences Librarian), **Clare Paterson** (Senior Archivist & College Librarian), and **Moira Rankin** (Senior Archivist & Head of Archives).

Most illustrations have been kindly supplied by the **University's Photographic Unit**, and on the few occasions when an external source of illustration has been identified permission has been generously given by lenders for its use, as noted beside such images.

Expert assistance has been given by **Robert MacLean**, Assistant Librarian in the Library's Special Collections Department. Supportive information has also come from **Barbara McLean**, Glasgow City Archivist at the Mitchell Library, and from **Dr Anne Cameron** of the University of Strathclyde Archives. Staff of the Search Room of the University of Glasgow Archives in Thurso Street have likewise been most helpful.

For the book's physical production the publishers are pleased to record the artistry and professionalism provided by **Bell & Bain**, of Glasgow, whose printing pedigree is unbroken since 1831, and by **Shirley Lochhead**, Interpretive Designer, The Whisky Bond, Glasgow, assisted in indexing by **Neil Wells**.

Bibliography

Abbreviations:

CHL: *The Cambridge History of Libraries in Britain and Ireland*, Cambridge: Cambridge University Press, 2006 (3 vols).

DNB: *Oxford Dictionary of National Biography*, ed. Henry C. G. Matthew and Brian Harrison, Oxford: Oxford University Press, 2004- (online edition: updated annually).

GPL: *Glasgow Public Libraries 1874-1966*, Glasgow: Glasgow Corporation Public Libraries, 1966.

GUAS: Glasgow University Archive Services.

JIML: The James Ireland Memorial Library

Sp Coll: the Special Collections department of the University Library.

* * * * *

Anderson, Peter John (ed.), *Fasti Academiae Mariscallanae Aberdonendis: Selections from the Records of the Marischal College and University MDXCIII-MDCCCLX*, Aberdeen: Printed for the New Spalding Club, 1889-1898 (3 vols).

Anderson, Peter John (ed.), *Officers and Graduates of University and King's College Aberdeen MVD* [sic] *-MDCCCX*, Aberdeen: New Spalding Club, 1893.

Anderson, Robert, Michael Lynch & Nicolas Phillipson, *The University of Edinburgh: An illustrated History*, Edinburgh: Edinburgh University Press, 2003.

Anon., *The University of Glasgow through Five Centuries*, [Glasgow]: Published by the University of Glasgow in commemoration of the Fifth Centenary, 1951.

Arnold, Harry J. P., *William Henry Fox Talbot: Pioneer of Photography and Man of Science*, London: Hutchinson, 1977.

Brown, Alfred Lawson, and Michael Moss, *The University of Glasgow: 1451-1996*, Edinburgh: Edinburgh University Press, [1996], revised edition 2001.

Budd, Adam, 'Thomas Hollis, his Library of Liberty, and his London bookseller'. (Paper read to the Bibliographical Society, London, and the Society of Antiquaries, Burlington House, Piccadilly, on 17th November, 2015.)

Bunch, Antonia J., *Hospital and Medical Libraries in Scotland, an Historical and Sociological Study*, Glasgow: Scottish Library Association, 1975.

Cant, Ronald G., *The University of St Andrews: A Short History*, [1946]; 4th edition, Dundee: Strathmartine Trust, 2002.

Chambers, Robert, *Lives of Illustrious and Distinguished Scotsmen from the earliest period to the present time, arranged in alphabetical order and forming a complete Scottish biographic dictionary: embellished with splendid and authentic portraits*, Edinburgh: Blackie and Son, [1832-35], new edition 1841 (4 vols: see the entry 'Moor, James, LL.D.', in vol. IV, 25-26).

Carey, Frances, 'The Apocalyptic Imagination: Between Tradition and Modernity', in *The Apocalypse and the Shape of Things to Come*, ed. Frances Carey, Toronto: University of Toronto Press, 1999, 270-319.

Coutts, James, *A Short Account of the University of Glasgow, prepared in connection with the celebration of the ninth jubilee in June* 1901, Glasgow: James MacLehose & Sons, 1901.

Coutts, James, *A History of the University of Glasgow from its foundation in 1451 to 1909*, Glasgow: James MacLehose & sons, 1909.

Dibdin, Thomas F., *A Bibliographical, Antiquarian and Picturesque Tour in the Northern Counties of England and in Scotland*, London: Printed for the author by C. Richards, 1838 (3 vols).

Dickson, William P., *The Glasgow University Library: Notes on Its History, Arrangements, and Aims, with Notice of the Euing Collection of Bibles*, by James Lymburn, Librarian, Glasgow: MacLehose, 1888.

Dickson, William P., *The Glasgow University Library: A Plea for the Increase of its Resources*, Glasgow: James MacLehose, 1889.

Dickson, William P., 'Report by the Library Committee', Glasgow, 1890 [GUAS, MS Gen. 1750/2/2/2].

Dickson, William P., *Statement by the Curator as to the Bearings of a Proposal to grant 'free access' to Selected Students*, [Glasgow: MacLehose, 1899].

Dunlop, Annie I. (ed.), *Acta Facultatis Artium Universitatis Sanctiandree*, 1413-1588, Edinburgh: Oliver & Boyd, 1964.

Durkan, John, 'The Early History of Glasgow University Library: 1475–1710', *The Bibliotheck*, 8, nos. 4-6 (1977), 102-26.

Durkan, John, and James Kirk, *The University of Glasgow 1451-1577*, Glasgow: University of Glasgow Press, 1977.

Emerson, Roger L., *An Enlightened Duke: The Life of Archibald Campbell (1682-1761), Earl of Ilay, 3rd Duke of Argyll*, Kilkerran: Humming Earth, 2013.

Emerson, Roger L., *Neglected Scots, Eighteenth-Century Glaswegians and Women*, Edinburgh: Humming Earth, 2015.

Finlayson, Charles P., *Clement Litill and his Library: The Origins of Edinburgh University Library*, Edinburgh: Printed for Edinburgh Bibliographical Society and the Friends of Edinburgh University Library, 1980.

Finlayson, Charles P., and Simpson, S. M, 'The History of the Library 1580-1710', in *Edinburgh University Library 1580-1980*, ed. Jean R. Guild and Alexander Law, Edinburgh: Edinburgh University Library, 1982, 43-54.

Fox, Peter, *Trinity College Library Dublin: A History*, Cambridge: Cambridge University Press, 2014.

Fox Talbot, William Henry, *The Pencil of Nature: anniversary facsimile edition* by Larry J. Schaaf, New York: Hans P. Kraus, Jr. Inc., 1989.

Fraser, Andrew G., *The Building of Old College: Adam, Playfair and the University of Edinburgh*, Edinburgh: Edinburgh University Press, 1989.

Ganoczy, Alexandre, *La Bibliothèque de l'Académie de Calvin: le catalogue de 1572 et ses enseignements*, Geneva: Droz, 1969.

Galbraith, James Lachlan, *The Curator of Glasgow University Library*, Glasgow: MacLehose, 1909.

Gardham, Julie, *Ingenious Impressions: Fifteenth-Century Printed Books from the University of Glasgow Library*, London: Scala Arts & Heritage Publishers, 2015.

Gaskell, Philip, *Trinity College Library: the first 150 years*, Cambridge: Cambridge University Press, 1980.

Gaskell, Philip, *A Bibliography of the Foulis Press*, [London: Rupert Hart-Davis, 1964], 2nd edition, Winchester: St. Paul's Bibliographies, 1986.

Grove, Laurence F., 'Reading Scève's *Délie*: The Case of the Emblematic Ivy', *Emblematica*, 6.1 (1992), 1-15.

Grove, Laurence F., 'A Note on the Emblematic Woman who Gave Birth to Rabbits', in '*Le Livre demeure*': *Studies in Book History in Honour of Alison Saunders*, ed. Alison Adams and Philip Ford, Geneva: Droz, 2011, 147-56.

Grove, Laurence F., *Comics in French: The European Bande Dessinée in Context*, New York and Oxford: Berghahn Books, [2010], new edition 2013.

Grove, Laurence F., and Peter Black, *Comic Invention*, Glasgow: BHP Comics, 2016.

Haynes, Nick, *Building Knowledge: an Architectural History of the University of Glasgow*, Edinburgh and Glasgow: Historic Scotland, 2013.

Heaney, Henry J., 'Glasgow University Library' [1997 typescript lecture], in *International Dictionary of Library Histories*, ed. David H. Stam, Chicago & London: Fitzroy Dearborn, 2001 (2 vols), Vol. I, 339-41.

Higgitt, John (ed.), *Scottish Libraries: with an introductory essay by John Durkan*, London: British Library in association with the British Academy, 2006.

Hoare, Peter, 'The Librarians of Glasgow University over 350 Years: 1641–1991', *Library Review* (Bradford), 40 (1991), 27-43.

Hume Brown, Peter, *Early Travellers in Scotland*, Edinburgh: Douglas, 1891 (reprinted Edinburgh: J. Thin, 1973).

Innes, Cosmo, and Joseph Robertson (ed.), *Munimenta Alme Universitatis Glasguensis: Records of the University of Glasgow from its Foundation until 1727*, Glasgow: Maitland Club, 1854 (4 vols).

James, Stuart (ed.), 'Papers in honour of Robert Ogilvie MacKenna', in *Library Review* (Bradford), 40, nos. 2/3 (1991).

Kirk, James, 'Clement Little's Edinburgh', in *Edinburgh University Library 1580-1980: A Collection of Historical Essays*, ed. Jean R. Guild and Alexander Law, Edinburgh: Edinburgh University Library, 1982, 1-42.

Kurtz, Leonard P., *The Dance of Death and the Macabre Spirit in European Literature*, New York, 1934 (reprinted Geneva: Slatkine, 1975).

McDermid, Jane, 'Women and Education', in *Women's History: Britain, 1850-1945 – An Introduction*, ed. June Purvis, London: Routledge, [1995] 2008, 91-110.

MacKenna, Robert Ogilvie, 'Glasgow: University of Glasgow Library', in *Encyclopedia of Library and Information Science*, edited by Allen Kent and Harold Lancour with William Z. Nasri, New York: Dekker, 1968-1998 (61 vols), vol. 10 (1973), 19-26.

McLaren, Colin A., *Rare and Fair: A Visitor's History of Aberdeen University Library*, Aberdeen: Aberdeen University Library, 1995.

Mackie, John D., *The University of Glasgow, 1451-1951: A Short History*, Glasgow: Jackson, 1954.

Mason, Thomas, *Public and Private Libraries of Glasgow*, [Glasgow]: T. D. Morison, 1885.

Miller, Christine M., 'The Effect of the Loss of Copyright Privilege on Glasgow University Library, 1790-1858', *Library History*, 7 (1985), 45-57.

Morgan, Alexander, ed., *University of Edinburgh Charters, Statutes, and Acts of the Town Council and the Senatus, 1583-1858*, London and Edinburgh: Oliver & Boyd, 1937.

Moss, Michael, J. Forbes Munro and Richard H. Trainor, *University, City and State: the University of Glasgow since 1870*, Edinburgh: Edinburgh University Press, 2000.

Nairn, Audrey, 'A 1731 copyright list from Glasgow University Archives', *The Bibliotheck*, 2 (1959), 30-32.

Pickard, James Roy, *A History of King's College Library, Aberdeen: Until 1860*, Aberdeen: The Author, 1987 (3 vols).

Reddick, Allen, 'Introduction', to William H. Bond, *'From the Great Desire of Promoting Learning': Thomas Hollis's Gifts to the Harvard College Library*, Cambridge, MA: Harvard University Press, 2010, 1-31. (Originally published in 2008 in the *Harvard Library Bulletin*, 19, nos. 1-2).

Reid, Steven J., *Humanism and Calvinism: Andrew Melville and the Universities of Scotland, 1560-1625*, Farnham: Ashgate, 2011.

Reid, Steven J., *The Parish of Govan and the Principals of the University of Glasgow, 1577-1621*, Glasgow: Society of Friends of Govan Old, 2012.

Roger, Elizabeth M., 'Henry J. Heaney: Bibliography and Chronology', *Library Review*, 47, nos. 5-6 (1998), 317-19.

Royan, Nicola, 'Boece, Hector (c. 1465 – 1536)', in *The Oxford Dictionary of National Biography*, Oxford: Oxford University Press, 2004. Online edition, October 2008.

Salmond, James B., and George H. Bushnell, *Henderson's Benefaction: A Tercentenary Acknowledgement of the University's Debt to Alexander Henderson*, St Andrews: W.C. Henderson & Son, Ltd., St Andrews University Press, 1942.

Smethurst, Michael, 'Henry Heaney: An Appreciation', *Library Review*, 47, nos. 5-6 (1998), 256-61.

Stevenson, David, *King's College, Aberdeen, 1560-1641: From Protestant Reformation to Covenanting Revolution*, Aberdeen: Aberdeen University Press, 1990.

Thorp, Nigel (ed.), *The Hunterian Psalter: University of Glasgow, MS Hunter 229, with two introductory essays*, Oxford: Oxford Microform Publications for Glasgow University Library, 1983.

Thorp, Nigel, *The Glory of the Page: Medieval and Renaissance Illuminated Manuscripts from Glasgow University Library*, London: Harvey Miller, 1987.

Weaver, Mike, *Henry Fox Talbot: Selected Texts and Bibliography*, Oxford: Clio, 1992.

Wiegand, Carl F., *Totentanz 1914-1918*, Zurich: Orell Füssli, n.d. [1919].

Further reading:

Butt, John, *John Anderson's Legacy: the University of Strathclyde and its Antecedents*, East Linton: Tuckwell, 1996.

Corporation of Glasgow, *Memorabilia of the City of Glasgow: Selected from the Minute Books of the Burgh, MDLXXXVIII-MDCCL*, [Glasgow: James MacLehose, 1865] reprinted by Reink Books, 2015.

Fairfull-Smith, George, *The Foulis Press and The Foulis Academy: Glasgow's eighteenth-century school of art and design*, Glasgow: The Glasgow Art Index in association with the Friends of Glasgow University Library, 2001.

Hamilton, Ian R. (ed.), *The Five-Hundred Year Book: to commemorate the fifth centenary of the University of Glasgow, 1451-1951*, Glasgow: Students' Fifth Centenary Committee, 1951.

McLaughlan, Robert, *Gifted Personalities and Treasures of the University of Glasgow*, Edinburgh and London: Mainstream Publishing, 1990.

Muir, James, *John Anderson, Pioneer of Technical Education and the College he Founded*, ed. James M. Macaulay, Glasgow: John Smith, 1950.

The University of Glasgow Story (see especially the Site Map and the section 'University People').
www.universitystory.gla.ac.uk

The white pelican
from John Audubon's
Birds of America,
London, 1827-38
(4 vols). Hunterian
Cd.1.1-4 [Hunter
Cd.1.1-4 plate 87].

Index

References to illustrations are indicated by italic type. University Librarians are distinguished by an asterisk (*)

Acton, Archibald, 112
Adamson, Robert, 200, *200*
Allan, David, 66, *67*
Anderson, John, 65, 68, 69
Annan, Thomas, 10, *71*, 200–1, *201*
architects
    William Adam, 64, 65
    George Gilbert Scott, 90, *209*
    Hughes & Waugh, 113
    William Nimmo & Partners, 142, 143–4, 145
    Walter Underwood & Partners, 120, 127
    The Holmes Partnership, 120
    William Whitfield & Partners, 116, 119–20, 122
Arthur, Archibald*, 40, 41 n. 1 &, 41 n., 9, 50, 54, 61, 66, 73, 86, 94, 271
Ashworth, Susan*, 147, 268, 271
Aublet, Jean Baptiste, 253

Bailey, Christine*, 147, 271
Baillie, Robert Jr.*, 31, 270
Baillie, Robert Sr., 14, 25, 28, 29, 31, 43, 45
Baird, John Logie, *206*, 208
Baldwin, Jack, 146
Balloch, Robert, 87
Banks, Joseph, 243
Barthes, Roland, 165
Beaton, James, 18, 20, 206–7
Bell, John*, 270
Bell, Patrick, 28
Bellahouston Trust, 79–80, 99
Black, Joseph, 48–9, *48*
Blackburn, Peter, 20
Blacklock, Isabella, 94
Blake, William, 182, *190*
Boswell, James, 67, 68
Bourne, Samuel, 200
Bower, Frederick Orpen, 74, 250, 253
Boyd, Alexander, 22
Boyd, James, Archbishop of Glasgow, 20, 41
Boyd, John, 28
Boyd, Robert, 23

Boyd, William, 4th Earl of Kilmarnock, 68
Boyd, Zachary, 27, *27*
Bradley, Andrew C., 13, 87
Brand (later Brand-Hollis), Thomas, 53, 56
Brandis, Lucas, *182*
Brereton, Sir William, 24
British Museum, 80, 88, 105, 110
Brogan, Sir Denis, 118
Brown, John, 18
Browne, Sir Thomas, 115
Bruce, William Spiers, *248*
Brydges, James, 1st Duke of Chandos, 61
Buchanan, George, 19, *19*, 41, 79, 185
buildings
    Adam Smith Library (Social Sciences), 105, 134, 145
    Chemistry Branch Library, 110, 145
    College
    High Street, 13, *16*, 24–5, *72*, 75
    New Library (Adam 1744), *51*, *60*, 61–4, *62–3*, 71, 88, 92
    Divinity Hall, 74, 85
    Gilmorehill (1870), *84*, 89–90, 90–3, 96, 99–103, 104
    James Herriot Library (Veterinary Medicine), 114, *132*, 134, 145
    James Ireland Memorial Library (Dentistry), *132*, 145
    Library Research Annexe, 141, 268
    The Library (1968), *111*, *114*, 116–23, *118*, 122–3, *126*, 127–30, *132*, *135*, *138*, 139–40, *140–1*, 142–6, *143–4*, *146–7*
    Round Reading Room (1936), *108*, 109–10, 113, 145
Bunch, Duncan, 18
Burns, Robert, 182, *189*
Burrell Collection, 13, 149
Byrd, William, *187*

Caird, Edward, 93, *94*
Caird, John, 93
Calvin, Jean, 22
Campbell, Archibald, 3rd Duke of Argyll, 50
Campbell, David, 208
Campbell, Jessie, 93
Campbell, Neil, 61
Campbell, Thomas, 88
Carmichael, Alexander*, 57, 58, 60–1, 270
Carmichael, Gershom*, 58, 60, 270
Carnegie, Andrew, 10, 13
Carnegie Medal, 230

Carnegie Trust, 99, 112
Caxton, William, 174, *181*
Certeau, Michel de, 160
Charles I, King of Scotland, 27
Charles VIII, King of France, *194*
Checkland, Sydney, 210
Coats, James, *217*
Colbert, Jean-Baptiste, *194*
Collections and Donors, 73–80
   gifts and bequests, 18, 21–3, 27, 28–30, 41, 43, 52–4,
     79–80, 106–7, 113–14, 118
    Alexander Robertson, 80
    Bissett, 232–3, *234*
    Blau, 185
    Botany, 250–5
    Bower, 250, 253
    Broady, 185
    Central and East European Studies, 232–5
    Children's Literature, 228–31
    Cullen Papers, 174, 257
    D. S. Robertson manuscripts, 101
    Dougan, 10, *16*, *60*, *77*, 113, 163, 200, *201*, 264
    Douglas Papers, 73, 159
    Eadie, 184, *191*
    Early Photographic, 200–5
     see also Dougan; Hill & Adamson Collections
    Edwin Morgan Papers, 170, 174, *179*, 196
    Edwin Morgan Scrapbooks, 163–5, *164*, 166, 167 n.
    Euing, 77, 79, 87, 96, 112–13, 126–7, 129, 171, 179,
     186, *187*, 196, 234–5, 264
    Farmer, 185
    Ferguson, 179
    Gemmell, 101–4, 150
    Hamilton, 79, 87, 185
    Hepburn, 185, *222*
    Hill & Adamson, 136, 163, 200, *200*
    House of Fraser Archive, 213, *220–1*
    Hunterian, *14*, *20*, *29*, 71, 73–4, 78, 79, 92, 94, 100,
     110, 117, 128, 131, *148*, 149, 151–5, *152*, *153*, *154*,
     159–60, *159*, 165–6, *168*, 236, 245, 251, 253, 254,
     257, 259, 270, 271
    Incunabula, 73, 77, 80, 118, 146, 174, *181*, *191*, 267
    James Paterson, 201
    Jane Duncan, 174
    Jebb, 185
    Jessie Marion King, 201
    John Hiden Baltic Research Archive, 234
    Kelvin, 80, 101, *see also* Thomson

    Left Book Club, 185, 232–3, *234*
    McGrigor books and pamphlets, 245
    Maps, *25*, *72*, 129, 133, 137, 174, *182*, 185, *232*, *233*,
     236–41, 245
    Mearns, 184
    Medicine, 256–61
    Monro, 115
    Murray, 100, 106–7, 150, 184–5, *192*
    Novels, 83, 182, 228
    Old Library, 73, 94, 181
    Papyrus fragments, 171
    R. D. Laing, 174
    Rare Books, 182
    Scarfe-La Trobe, 185, *193*
    Scottish Business Archive, 210–27
    Scottish Poetry, 185, *189*
    Scottish Theatre Archive, 128, 134, 196–9, *197*, *198*
    Simson, 52, 87, 186
    Smith, 76
    Special Collections, 148–67, 170–95
    Spencer, 185–6, *241*
    Stillie, 79
    Stirling Maxwell, 115, 131, 149–50, 155–7, 155–9, 158,
     165–6, 167, 179–81, *188*
    Stoddard-Templeton Design Archive, 213, *217–18*
    Syphilis, 259
    Thomson family papers, 174
    Tischendorf, 184, 245
    Travel, Topography and Exploration, 242–9
    Trinity College Library, 122, 184, *191*, 208
    University Archives, 206–9
    Veitch, 80, 185
    Walker-Arnott, 76, 87, 250
    Whistler Archive, 113–14, 122–3, 128–9, 174, *178*, 201
    Wylie, 185
Commelin, Jan, 253
Cook, James, 239, 243, 245
Copyright Act acquisitions and compensation, 44, 45 n.16,
   49–50, 73, 75, 79–81
Coubrough, Archibald, 10
Craig, William*, 61, 271
Crichton College, Dumfries, 136
Cromwell, Oliver, Lord Protector, 25, 27
Cullen, William, 48, *48*, 174
Cumin, Patrick, 54, *65*
Cumming, Alice, 95
Cunningham, William Ross*, 106, 110, 112, 271
Curtis, William, 250, *251*

Dalrymple, James, 25, *26*
Daniell, William, *81, 242*
Darien Scheme, 185–6
Darwin, Charles, 200
Davidson, Archibald, 54
Davidson, John, 18–19
Davies, Peter V., 13, 263, 272
Derby, Smith-Stanley, Edward, 14th Earl, 82–3
Desnitsky, Semyon, 47, 234
Dewar, Margaret, 95, *95*
Dibdin, Thomas, 73–4
Dickson, William Purdie*, 9, 74–6, 77, *77*, 79–80, 82, 86, 96, 99, 271
Diderot, Denis, 181, *189*
Dinwiddie, Robert, 53
Douglas, David, *251*
Douglas, James, 73, 159
Drennan, William, 55
Duncan, Jane, 174
Duncan, Jessie, 266
Dunlop, William, 35
Duns Scotus, John, 185, *194*
Durndell, Helen*, 139, *143*, 147, 271

Eadie, John, *191*
Eck, Frederick, 79
Elder, Isabella, 93
Elliot, Mr, 80
Elphinstone, William, 16
Elzevier, 43
Erben, Karel Jaromir, 235
Euing, William, 77, *77*

Fall, James, 207
Farmer, Henry George, 185
Ferguson, John, 179
Ferguson, Mungo*, 100, 271
Fleming, William*, 86, 88, 95–6, 271
Flinders, Matthew, 249
Follett Committee, 133–4
Foulis Academy of the Fine Arts, 66, *67*, 68, 267
Foulis, Robert and Andrew, 66–8, *66*
Fraser, Sir William Kerr, 130
French Revolution, 18, 54, 55
Friends of Glasgow University Library, 127, 129, 137, 262–7
Fuchs, Leonhart, 254

Galbraith, James Lachlan*, 94, 100, 271
Galloway, Janet, 94
Gass, Patrick, 245
Gibson, Jack, 265
Gilchrist, Marion, 95, *95*
Gillespie, Patrick, 26
Glaister, John Sr and Jr, 109
Glasgow
    Aye Write! Festival, 13
    Botanic Gardens, 250
    Caledonian University, 13
    Cathedral and *libraria*, 13, 15–16, *20*, 24, 26, 65
    City of Glasgow College, 13
    civic authorities, 12–13, 24, 30–1
    civic benefaction, 21–2, 27, 29
    Film Festival, 13
    International Exhibition, *98, 102–3*
    libraries
        Athenaeum, 10
        Baillie's, 11
        Council Chambers, 10–13
        Glasgow Public Library, 10, 87
        Institution of Engineers and Shipbuilders, 10
        John Smith's Lending, 10
        Mitchell, 11–12, 77, 92, 105, 127
        Royal Faculty of Procurators, 10
        School of Art, 13, 124
        Stirling's, 11, 69
        Strathclyde Andersonian, 10
        Trinity College, 122
        Whittaker Library, Royal Conservatoire, 10
    maps of, *25*, 237
    trade and industry, 9–10
Glasgow Herald, 87, 89–90, 115, 123
Gmelin, Johann Georg, 253
Gould, John, *246*
Graham, Margaret, 28
Gray, Alasdair, 128, 174
Gray, Asa, 252
Grew, Nehemiah, 253
Grove, Laurence, 149, 267

Hajek, Igor, 235
Haller, Albrecht von, 253
Hamilton,Sir William, 79, 87, 185
Hay, Andrew, 19
Heaney, Henry*, 79–80, 125–7, 130, 131, 134, 136, 271

Heath, William, 160
Henderson, Alexander, 27
Hepburn, Charles A., 185, *229*
Hetherington, Hector, 109
Hill, David Octavius, 200
Hoare, Peter, 265, 272
Hobbs, Tim, 265
Hogarth, William, 159–60
Hoggisyard, Robert*, 31, 270
Hollis, Thomas, 53–4
Hook, Andrew, 47, 272
Hooker, Joseph Dalton, 250
Hooker, William Jackson, 250
Hopkirk, Thomas, *192*, 250
Howieson, John, 22
Hume, John, 105, 137, 272
Hunter, William, *70*, 71, 73–4, *74*, 128, 152, 165–6, 257
Hunterian Art Gallery, 74, *111*, 119, 122, 125, 146, 266
Hunterian Museum, 74, *76*, *83*, 89, 92, 94, 122
Hunterian Psalter, *148*, 151–2, *152*, 153, *168*, 170, *170*
Hutcheson, Francis, 48, *48*, *55*, *56*
Hutcheson, James*, 31, 270
Hutcheson, Thomas*, 30, 60, 270

James VI, King of Scotland, 21, 23, 185, 256
Jameson, Mark, 20
Jebb, Richard Claverhouse, 185
Jeffray, James, 54, 73
Jenson, Nicholas, *181*
Johnson, Samuel, 181
Jones, Nathaniel*, 96, 271
Jungmann, Josef, 235

Kelvin, William Thomson, Lord, 80, 101, 264, 266
Kennedy, Charles, Lord Rector, *264*
Ker, William, 87
Kerr, Graham, 101
Kerr-Peterson, Miles, 24, 272

Laing, John, Bishop of Glasgow, 18
Law, James, Archbishop of Glasgow, 22, 41, 43, *44*
Librarian (post of), 30–2, 60–1, 94–7, 109, 124, 125–7
    list of post holders, 270–1
library *see* University of Glasgow Library
Liddell, Duncan, 21

Lightfoot, John, 253
Lindley, John, 253
Linnaeus, Carl, 250
Liverpool, 11, 87
Livingstone, David, 118, 245
Low, Bet, 174
Lymburn, James*, 87, 96, 271
Lyness, Dorothea, 95

MacAlister, Sir Donald, 104
MacArthur, Dugald, 110, 124
MacCunn, Hamish, 185
MacFarlan, Duncan, 83, 90
McGrigor, Alexander, 90
MacKenna, Robert Ogilvy*, 110, 112–13, 118, 125, 131, 265, 266, 271
MacLehose & Co. (printers), 81, 106
Maconochie, Allan, 73
Macpherson, Robert, 200
McTurk, William*, 94, 271
Mair, John, 9, 16
Manchester, 11, 87
Manpower Services Commission, 123, 125, 127
Manutius, Aldus, *184*
Marshall, John, 250
Mary I, Queen of Scotland, 19
Mason, Thomas, 12, 77, 87
Mattioli, Pietro, 252
Maubray, John, 159
Mearns, James, 184
Melville, Andrew, 9, 19, *19*, 20, 22
Melville, Frances, 94
Michelotti, Giovanni, 267
Millar, Andrew, 53
Monro, Thomas K., 115
Moor, James*, 67–8, *68*, 271
Moore, John, 272
Morgan, Edwin, 163–5, *164*, 166, 167, 170, 174, *179*, 196, 267
Muirhead, Lockhart*, 94, 271
Murray, David, 100, 106, 184–5

Nichol, John, 93

Ockham, William of, 185
Olearius, Adam, 245
Orr, John, 52–3

Palestine Exploration Fund, 239, 245
Paoli, Pasquale, 67
Park, William*, 96, 271
Parkinson, Sydney, 242–3
Paterson, James, 201
Paxton, Margaret, 266
Philip, Rosalind Birnie, *178*
Pickard, Fanny, 200
Plumier, Charles, 254
Potter, Sir John, 11
Public Libraries Acts, 11

Queen Margaret College, 93–4, 95

Rankine, William J. M., 10
Ratdolt, Erhard, *183*
Rawles, Stephen, 34, 265, 272
Reformation, 9, 16, 18–19, 52, 93
Reid, David Wilson, 206
Reid, Steven J, 15, 272
Reid, Thomas, 48, *49*
Richmond, Lesley, *143*, 169, 272
Robbins Report, 13, 119
Robertson, J. Monteath, 112
Robertson, Rev. Alexander, 80
Royal Commissions (1831 and 1852), 80, 89
Royal Geographical Society, 249
Ruddiman, Thomas, 66

St. Andre, Nathaniel, 159
St Andrew's College, 136
Sanders, Robert, *193*
Scève, Maurice, 156–7
Schaaf, Larry, 136
Scott, Robert*, 96, 271
Scottish Higher Education Digital Library, 141
Scottish Higher Education Funding Council, 134
Scottish Universities Commission, 82, 92
Shakespeare, William, 179, *195*, 196
Sibthorp, John, 253

Simson, John*, 61, 270
Simson, Robert, 52, 186
Sinclair, Louis, 232
Smith, Adam, 48, *48*, *189*, *209*
Smith, Graeme, 13, 267, 273
Smith, John of Crutherland, 76
Smith, John Sr., 10, 68
Snell, John, 27–8, 37, 45
Snype, Andrew*, 31, 270
Sowerby, James, 253
Spang, William, 28
Spears, Robert*, 92–3, *93*, 96, 271
Special Readers, 85, 110–11
Spencer, John James, 185–6, *241*
Steel, Wilson*, 105, 114–15, 271
Stewart, William, 17
Steyner, Heinrich, *188*
Stillie, Thomas, 79
Stirling, John, 42, 52
Stirling Maxwell, Sir John, 115, 130
Stirling Maxwell, Sir William, 149, 165–6, *188*
Stirling, Walter, 11, 69
Stitt, John, 105
Story, Robert Herbert, 96
Strang, John, 24, 26
Struthers, William, 22, 41
Stuart, John, 3rd Earl of Bute, *50*
Sulman, Thomas, 237
Sweert, Emanuel, 254

Talbot, William Henry Fox, 150, 162–3, 200
Tallis, Thomas, *187*
Thompson, Helen Cargill, 266
Thomson, James (Kelvin's brother), 266
Thorp, Nigel, 73, 99, 129, 130, 273
Thunberg, Carl, 250–1
Tischendorf, Constantin von, 184
Toft, Mary, 159–60
Treaty of Union (1707), 10, 49, 270
Tretyakov, Ivan, 47, *56*, 100

UK Research Reserve, 141
University of Glasgow, 9–10, *17*, 26–7, *29*, 47–9, 90–4, 206, *209*
　foundation, 9, 15–23
　Learning and Teaching Hub, 268

University of Glasgow Library
  buildings *see* buildings
  catalogues
    digital, 121, 125, 127–9, 134, 136, 141
    manual, 34–45, 57, 64–6, 67, 74, 77, 79, 86–7, 96, 100, 105, 116
  class and departmental libraries, 69–70, 83, 86, 105, 107–10, 112, 114, 116, 121, 127–8, 133
  classification systems, 35–7, 86, 115–16, 123
  collections *see* Collections and Donors
  conservation and digitisation, 144–6
  digital services and media, 136, 139–46
  fees and finance, 28, 29, 50, 56–7, 79–84, 85–6, 99–100, 104, 112–16, 120–1, 123, 130, 132, 134, 141, 144–5
  laws of the Library (from 1643), 32–5, 58–9, 70, 81, 83, 88
  space and services today, 144–6
  staffing, 96, 106, 109, 113, 116, 117, 118, 123, 129–30, 133–4, 141, 145
  stock, 50, 73–4, 81, 99, 106, 121, 134, 140
  stores, 122, 127, 136
  student access and reading rooms, 28, 57, 82, 83–5, 86–90, 87–8, 92, 93, 96, 100, *108*, 109–10, 113, 115, 127, 129, 131, 145
  student life, 28, 89–90, 90
  theses, 25, *26*, 110, 121, 141, 269
  women's education, 93–5

Van Veen, Otto, 158–9
Veitch, John, 185

Wale, Andrew*, 134, 136–7, 147, 271
Walker, David, 265
Walker-Arnott, George, 76, 87, 250
Weir, Duncan Harkness, 73
Whistler, James McNeill, 114, 122–3, 128–9, 174, *178*, 201
Whymper, Edward, 239
Wilberforce, William, 54
Williams,(Lady) Joan, 267
Williamson, Bessie, 211, *214*
Wilson, Patrick, 32, 54, 85
Wodrow, Robert*, 32, 270
Wolfson Foundation, 131
World Wars I & II, 104–5, 110–12
Wyley, Agnes May, 266
Wylie, Robert, 160

Young, James*, 32, 270
Young, John*, 74, 270
Young, Patrick*, 31, 270